ML
457
.D65
1974

Donington, Robert.
    A performer's guide to Baroque music.   New York,
C. Scribner's Sons [1974, c1973]

    320 p. music. 26 cm. $20.00

    Bibliography : p. 301-306.

    1. Music—Performance. 2. Style, Musical. 3. Music—History and
criticism—17th century. 4. Music—History and criticism—18th century.   I. Title.

ML457.D65 1974   780'.9032   72-3659
ISBN 0-684-13155-2   MARC
                                    12/8/78
Library of Congress   74 [4]   MN

A Performer's Guide
to Baroque Music

by the same author

THE INTERPRETATION OF EARLY MUSIC
WAGNER'S 'RING' AND ITS SYMBOLS
STRING PLAYING IN BAROQUE MUSIC

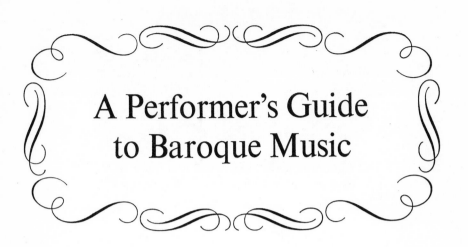

A Performer's Guide
to Baroque Music

ROBERT DONINGTON

CHARLES SCRIBNER'S SONS
New York

A – 9.72 (I)

Printed in Great Britain
Library of Congress Catalog Card Number 72–3659
SBN 684–13155–2 (cloth)

Contents

5

CONTENTS

CONTENTS

7

CONTENTS

CONTENTS

PART FOUR: THE EXPRESSION

CONTENTS

PART ONE

THE BAROQUE ATTITUDE

CHAPTER ONE

Composer and Performer

1. WHY A BOOK ON PERFORMING BAROQUE MUSIC?

(a) This book is meant for those who are concerned, as performers, editors, teachers and listeners, in our great revival of baroque music.

So neglected was most baroque music by previous generations that we have inherited no *original* tradition of how it used to be performed. We have, of course, our own good musicianship; and that is something which has not essentially changed on the way down. But there are many missing parts of the interpretation which can only be pieced together again by a scholarly investigation of the surviving evidence. That calls for good musicianship, too, and cannot be done without it; yet we are coming to realize that the matter is not altogether simple, and can best be approached from two sides at once.

This book is designed to be of practical assistance, on both lines of approach. It is designed to help on the active partnership, which although comparatively novel has already well proved its value, between the practical musicologist and the practising musician.

(b) No musicologist can be right all the time, and the partnership has to be based on mutual give and take, and that in turn on mutual respect.

An example of what has probably been a musicological mistake is teaching a somewhat dry and ruthless style of string playing for baroque music, although the reaction against an unsuitable romantic style was right enough. Unmusical results cannot be correct results.

(c) It is the argument of this book that results which are musicianly enough, and correct enough, to satisfy our general needs *can be got within the ordinary conditions of modern performance.*

This book, therefore, is not only for those fortunate enough to be able to reconstruct early performing conditions with some thoroughness and accuracy. It is also for those who will be taking baroque music more or less in their stride. For example, they may for the most part be using ordinary modern instruments, in their ordinary modern state. But they

13

may nonetheless be open-minded enough, as the present fashion is, to want to get as much right as can be got right under these ordinary modern conditions. And that is undoubtedly a very great deal.

How crucial a difference this up-to-date attitude towards early music is capable of producing may be quite surprising for those who have not yet made the experiment. But in what, then, does this experiment consist?

(d) Briefly, the experiment consists in meeting the expectations of the baroque composers, not only where these are more or less what we should imagine from our own good musicianship today, but also where they are considerably different from what we might otherwise imagine.

This book provides information necessary for that purpose, together with suggestions for applying it in a musicianly manner. Some of my own most recent researches are incorporated here, especially on the practical difficulties of getting baroque accidentals right, and also on the fascinating challenge of *bel canto* voice-production. I and other musicologists have been keenly engaged, too, on the baroque use of ornaments, and on those adventurous modifications of rhythm which a performer who knows the style may enjoy introducing, as part of his wide liberty to take, in the spirit of those times, a discretionary hand with what a baroque composer wrote down in his notation.

All this and much else will be found explained here, with the support of enough quotations from the contemporary evidence to make matters clear. But for those readers who want a more extensive survey of the baroque scene, and a very careful consideration of all those controversies among the scholars which so inevitably and on the whole so fruitfully arise in any field as rapidly and excitingly developing as the performance of baroque music, I should like to draw attention to my longer book, *The Interpretation of Early Music* (new version) (London, 1973).

Though they obviously share some basic material in common, that longer book and this shorter book are quite distinct, for reasons which will be found fully set out in the introductory chapters of the longer book. Both are, at the moment of writing (1973) equally up to date, since the longer book was completely reworked and greatly expanded for its new version, containing as it now does some 45,000 words of additional matter as well as intensive revisions to its previous text. But other issues come off better here; and there is intended to be a complementary relationship between these two contributions which I have now made towards a more informed and understanding performance of baroque and certain other early music.

14

2. ENCOURAGING INDIVIDUALITY IN THE PERFORMER

(a) We may notice at once that what baroque composers such as Bach or Handel, Couperin or Purcell, Vivaldi or Monteverdi expected from their performers was farther from what the great romantics such as Beethoven or Brahms, Verdi or Wagner, Mahler or Richard Strauss expected, and nearer to what Boulez or John Cage or their younger successors expect today.

(b) This difference shows as much as anywhere in the attitude towards the written text.

It was not by any means a baroque attitude to be conscientiously faithful to a carefully notated text. The baroque ideal, like one modern ideal, was to depend upon the individuality of the performer to fill out the implications of a sketchily notated text. The baroque performer, like the modern performer under similar circumstances, was required not so much to be conscientious as to be spontaneous.

Whoever took on the performance, whether he were the composer or not, took on responsibility not only for virtually the whole of the expression, but even for many of the notes, as for example in the free ornamentation of slow movements or da capo repeats, and in the realization of figured bass.

It is because baroque composers did not spell it all out in notation, and because we have no unbroken tradition of how it used to be bodied out in performance, that we have to dig some of it out again now with the tools of modern scholarship.

(c) That has nothing to do with being rigid or pedantic. On the contrary, rigid interpretations are particularly out of place in baroque music.

In any music, one performance may, for example, bring out more of the latent brilliance, while another performance may bring out more of the latent expressiveness; and if it really is latent, and not artificially worked up, this variability resulting from the performer's individuality is all to the good.

In baroque music, however, the performer's individuality has particularly wide scope, with all the opportunities and difficulties which result from that.

(d) Nevertheless this wide scope has its limitations. There are always outer boundaries to a style. Even if we are not interested in getting a good historical match, we shall certainly be interested in getting a good artistic match. This means, in practice, avoiding a clash of styles between the music and its performance.

How are we, as performers, to avoid this clash of styles? One answer is that we cannot absolutely avoid it. There is going to be a certain

15

amount of inadvertent modernization, do what we may, simply from the fact that we are living in the twentieth century. The disadvantage of this inadvertent modernization is that we are probably diluting the full original strength of the music without knowing it. On the other hand, we can reduce the amount of such inadvertent modernization by acting on the relevant information in so far as we are able to have access to it. That seems in every way a good idea.

But there can also, of course, be deliberate modernization, and modernization which, if not exactly deliberate, is at least deliberately tolerated. This is by no means invariably or inevitably undesirable; far from it. And in any ordinary circumstances, it is certainly going to happen in some degree. But if it is going to happen in desirable rather than in undesirable ways, then there is all the more necessity for us to know, so far as possible, just what we are doing and to what.

In course of providing information for that purpose, this book has for its guiding principle a recommendation which may be summarized as follows. Keep it flexible; but keep it within the boundaries of the style.

3. KEEPING IN STYLE

(a) There is probably quite general consent now to the principle of keeping in style. Where some understandable opposition still arises is to the idea of learning style out of scholarly research, as opposed to innate musicianship. In actual practice, however, both are required, and the skill lies in combining them satisfactorily.

A practical musicologist who is himself a competent performer, preferably seasoned in the ordinary rough and tumble of professional concert life, will waste no time and provoke no irritation by vague and tactless propaganda. He should be able to put his finger right away on the crucial points as they come up in actual rehearsal. Tempos and dynamics; phrasing and articulation; bow-strokes and tone-qualities: these are matters which a practising musician can appreciate, and try out immediately. When he finds the musicologist talking his own language and getting good results, his initial indifference or hostility may quickly melt away. That can be a wonderful experience, and I have had it often.

(b) Any technical or musicianly incompetence, on the other hand, is bad recommendation for the principle of authenticity. An authentic performance can only be as good as its performers. And as we know now, lack of competence was, and is, no part of baroque style.

4. BEING FAITHFUL TO HISTORY

(a) A good artistic match often coincides with a good historical match. But not, for example, when we play part-time and not very competently

16

on historical wind instruments whose difficulties could be mastered (they were) only by very competent baroque professionals playing on them full-time. We have players who master them again today.

(b) Provided that this difference is fairly pointed out, it can be both informative and enjoyable to put our students on to baroque instruments in class, or for lecture recitals, or for collegium concerts.

For more public concerts, professional standards are really as much part of authenticity as is keeping within the style. We must make sure of that.

5. AIMING AT SUBSTANTIAL AUTHENTICITY

(a) How authentic, then, can we hope to get?

We cannot, unfortunately, check up against any contemporary sound-recordings. Our surviving evidence is not of this directly audible kind. Instead, it ranges from perfunctory, out-of-date little baroque textbooks all the way to masterly treatises by the great teachers and innovators, with a certain amount of subsidiary evidence of other kinds.

Yet even when our surviving baroque evidence is less reliable and consistent and directly informative than we should wish, even when it is less exactly focused on the exact date and place required, even when it neglects as too obvious for mention matters not now in the least obvious to us, it is still all that we have, and very much nearer to the scene of action than we are ourselves.

By comparing enough contemporary statements, and not relying too much on any one of them, we are finding it quite possible to build up a substantially convincing picture of baroque performance.

Of course there are gaps remaining, and of course there are uncertainties. Hence our many controversies of detail, within our less publicized, but more important, general areas of agreement. Whenever did experts altogether admit to agreeing?

(b) Any ideal of *absolute* authenticity can only be illusory, and perhaps harmful in so far as it has encouraged a rather puritanical and quite unauthentic underplaying of baroque music (and indeed, of Haydn and Mozart) in some modern performances.

(c) But *substantial* authenticity is a realistic aim, capable of bringing improvements such as have already transformed our modern experience of baroque music. For we are of this modern age; and much has changed which could not be changed back even if we so desired. But not our deeper human nature, and not the essential musicianship so intimately bound up with our human nature. These do not change.

The start of good baroque performance is knowing that there were ordinary human beings under those concealing wigs and crinolines, that deceptive etiquette and courtly protocol. Obviously there is discipline in great baroque music; but it is the discipline of strong

17

feeling, strongly ordered. Cold formality and cautious reticence have no place in a good baroque performing style.

We can hope to share in the deeper feelings which give to baroque music its modern relevance, provided that we approach it with good musicianship and the necessary information.

CHAPTER TWO

Feeling in Baroque Music

1. STRONG FEELING APPROPRIATE IN BAROQUE MUSIC

(a) It is of the greatest importance to know that strong feeling and strong playing are often appropriate in baroque music.

(b) It may therefore be helpful to consider the following brief passages, out of so much that was written to the same effect within and around the baroque period.

2. EVIDENCE OF STRONG FEELING IN BAROQUE MUSIC

(a) In general, strong feeling was as much involved then as it is now in the practice and enjoyment of music.

(1) Baldesar (Baldassare) Castiglione, *Il libro del Cortegiano*, Venice, 1528, ed. B. Maier, Turin, 1955, pp. 147–8:

'Music . . . so full of art, ready, intense, inspired and of such varied melodies, that the spirits of the hearers are all moved and fired . . . [or] by a quiet way and full of flexible smoothness makes souls tender and pierces them, implanting sweetly in them a delightful passion.'

(2) Richard Hooker, *Lawes*, V. London, 1597, Everyman ed., p. 146:

'An admirable faculty which music hath to express and represent to the mind, more inwardly than any other sensible mean, the very standing, rising and falling, the very steps and inflections every way, the turns and varieties of all passions whereunto the mind is subject.'

(3) Charles Butler, *Principles of Musik*, London, 1636, p. 91:

[The composer is] 'transported as it were with some Musical fury; so that himself scarce knoweth what he doth, nor can presently give a reason for his doing.'

(4) Thomas Mace, *Musick's Monument*, London, 1676, p. 19:

'*Sensibly, Fervently* and *Zealously Captivated*, and drawn into *Divine*

Raptures, and *Contemplations*, by those *Unexpressible, Rhetorical Uncontroulable Persuasions*, and *Instructions* of *Musicks Divine Language* . . . *Quietness, Joy*, and *Peace; Absolute Tranquility*, and *Unexpressible Satisfaction*.'

(5) François Couperin, *L'Art de toucher le Clavecin*, Paris, 1716, ed. of 1717, preface:

'I declare in all good faith that I am more pleased with what moves me than with what astonishes me.'

(6) Francesco Geminiani, *Treatise of Good Taste*, London, 1749, p. 4:

[The performer will be inspired] 'if he chuses a Work of Genius, if he makes himself thoroughly acquainted with all its Beauties; and if while his Imagination is warm and glowing he pours the same exalted Spirit into his own Performance.'

(7) F. W. Marpurg, *Der critische Musicus an der Spree*, Berlin, 2 Sept. 1749:

'All musical expression has an affect or emotion for its foundation . . . to interpret rightly every composition which is put in front of him a musician needs the utmost sensibility and the most felicitous powers of intuition.'

(8) Joachim Quantz, *Essay*, Berlin, 1752, XVIII, 28:

'The composer and he who performs the music must alike have a feeling soul, and one capable of being moved.'

(9) C. P. E. Bach, *Essay*, Berlin, 1753, III, 13:

'A musician cannot move others unless he too is moved. He has to feel in himself all the feelings he hopes to raise in his hearers, for it is the showing of his own emotion which calls up a similar emotion in the hearer.'

3. VARIETIES OF FEELING IN BAROQUE MUSIC

(a) But there are, of course, many different expressions of musical feeling. Some are unsuitable to any baroque music; others are suitable only in the proper contexts.

(b) National differences of temperament were recognized, especially between the two leading styles of baroque music: the Italian and the French.

(10) Marin Mersenne, *Harmonie universelle*, Paris, 1636–7, II, vi, 356.

'The Italians represent as much as they can the passions and the feelings of the soul and spirit . . . our Frenchmen are content to caress the ear.'

20

(11) Georg Muffat, *Florilegium*, I, Augsburg, 1695, preface:

[The French have] 'natural melody, with an easy, and smooth tune, quite devoid of superfluous, extravagant variations, and too frequent and harsh leaps.'

(12) François Raguenet, *Comparison between the French and Italian Musick*, Paris, 1702, tr. ? J. E. Galliard, London, 1709, ed. O. Strunk, *Musical Quarterly*, XXXII, 3, pp. 415ff.:

[The French] 'touch the violin much finer and with a greater nicety than they do in Italy' [where the violinist] 'is seized with an unavoidable agony; he tortures the violin; he racks his body; he is no longer master of himself, but is agitated like one possessed with an irresistible motion.' [translator's footnote:] 'I never met with any man that suffered his passions to hurry him away so much whilst he was playing on the violin as the famous Arcangelo Corelli, whose eyes will sometimes turn as red as fire; his countenance will be distorted, his eyeballs roll as in an agony, and he gives in so much to what he is doing that he doth not look like the same man.'

(13) Joachim Quantz, *Essay*, Berlin, 1752, X, 19:

'Italian music is less restrained than any other; but the French is almost too much so, whence it comes about perhaps that in French music the new always seems like the old. Nevertheless the French method of playing is not at all to be despised, above all an apprentice should be recommended to mix the propriety and the clarity of the French with the chiaroscuro of the Italian instrumentalists. [XVIII, 53:] Other nations are ruled in their taste by these two.'

(c) Regardless of nationality, the function of the music affects its interpretation.

(14) Pier Francesco Tosi, *Opinioni de' cantori antichi, e moderni*, Bologna, 1723, tr. J. E. Galliard as *Observations on the Florid Song*, London, 1742, p. 92:

[There are three distinct styles of performance]: 'for the theatre . . . lively and various; for the chamber, delicate and finish'd; and for the Church, moving and grave.'

(15) Johann David Heinichen, *General-Bass*, Dresden, 1728, Introd., p. 24:

[Nevertheless] 'how wonderfully it pleases the ear, when, in an exquisite piece of church music or other composition, we hear how a master musician has tried from time to time, by his *galant* idioms and the closeness of his expression to the verbal text, to move the feelings of his hearers and thus to achieve successfully the true aim of music.'

[Note:] 'Whence practical modern musicians are rightly inclined to depart from the unseasoned character of a too antique church style.' [N.B.: this is true among others of J. S. Bach, whose recitatives and arias, in his cantatas and Passions, are in the modern, *galant*, and indeed operatic style of his day.]

(16) Joachim Quantz, *Essay*, Berlin, 1752, XVII, vii, 12:

'Church music requires a grander and more serious air than theatre music, and this last allows more liberty.'

(d) Finally, there are simple human differences of mood and temperament.

(17) Roger North, British Museum MS. Add. 32536 (c. 1690), f. 14:

'Some affect one kind, and will not hear another, and few allow any to be good that jumps not with their caprice.'

(18) Joachim Quantz, *Essay*, Berlin, 1752, XI, 9:

'Almost every musician has a different expression from that of others. It is not always the different teaching that they have received which causes this variety; the difference of temperament and character also contributes.' [XVII, 8:] 'Some like what is majestic and lively, and others what is tender and gay. The diversity of taste depends on the diversity of temperaments . . . [and finally] one is not always in the same mood.'

4. ADDING BAROQUE STYLES TO ONE'S RESOURCES

(a) One is not always in the same mood. One's interpretation of the music does not always have to be the same. Personality; individuality; temperament: there was room for all these at the time, and there is room for them now.

(b) But at the time, a musician good or bad could not help being at least basically within the boundaries of baroque style. What other style was there in which he could be?

We have to work at it deliberately if we want to keep within the boundaries of baroque style.

CHAPTER THREE

The Text and the Performer

1. THREE AREAS OF HIDDEN DIFFERENCE

(a) The first problem of baroque interpretation is to know that there is a problem of baroque interpretation. Here are three kinds of difference which are commonly overlooked:

(i) Differences of *notation*. Baroque notation, besides having some unknown signs, is misleading to us wherever it has a meaning which is perfectly obvious to us, and a meaning which was perfectly obvious to them, but they are not the same meaning.

Examples include some of the notated signs for ornaments; dots of articulation; dots of rhythm; tempo-words, time-signatures, note-values.

(ii) Differences of *convention*. Without even a misleading indication, it may have been obvious to them in many places, where it is not in any way obvious to us, that something further is needed beyond what the notation shows.

Examples include the more or less improvised addition of fresh ornamental figuration to the da capo repeats of arias, or to many slow movements of which the notation gives only the bare structural notes; unnotated trills at cadences and appoggiaturas in recitatives; cadenzas; spontaneous alterations of the notated rhythms.

(iii) Differences of *texture*. There are tacit assumptions which are not capable of being indicated in any notation, and which we from our upbringing may naturally take one way, whereas they just as naturally took them another way.

Examples include qualities of tone; manners of attack and articulation; colourings and techniques on various instruments including the voice.

(b) In baroque notation, there is no longer so much that *looks* unfamiliar to us as there is in renaissance notation and still more in medieval notation. But there is much which *is* unfamiliar to us, without appearing to be.

Getting beneath this deceptive appearance of familiarity can be a revelation to the beginner in the field of baroque interpretation.

2. BACK TO THE ORIGINAL TEXT?

(a) If we look at a Bach autograph, or a facsimile reproduction of it (which may be nearly as good for this purpose), we can compare the business-like simplicity of his powerful but supple handwriting with the heavily edited pages of some of the modern editions we are accustomed to using.

So much that is in our modern editions was not in Bach's own manuscripts or early prints; and so much that was there may look rather different from our expectations.

(b) It is an instructive experience to read straight off a facsimile. That, and no more than that, is what a baroque musician had on his stand in front of him.

The notes themselves may be somewhat incomplete; the expression is hardly conveyed at all. We have much to learn before we can produce as fully worked-out a performance as they undoubtedly did, when reading off the uncommunicative document which this facsimile of the original manuscript or early print will seem to us.

(c) Is a modern Urtext edition (German prefix *Ur*, 'original') really possible? Is it, for example, the composer's first thoughts, as set down in his first autograph if we are so lucky as to find this preserved? Or is it his later thoughts, if we have a later autograph version? Is it in his autograph at all, which may be quite careless and uncorrected, always supposing that any autograph exists? Or in a subsequent fair copy which may or may not be more careful and better corrected, by himself or someone near to him?

Or again, is it not in any of the surviving manuscripts at all (if there are any), but in an early printed edition, especially when the composer can be known or surmised to have corrected the proofs? If we have both an autograph in the composer's hand and an early print known to have been corrected, and very possibly revised, by the composer, which of these is then the Urtext?

Of the many manuscripts used or authorized for use by the composer of the *Messiah* on different occasions or for different singers, which is Handel's 'original text', and how much does it matter, since they all apparently had his sanction? And how much does it matter if similar satisfactory adaptations are used which did not have his sanction?

Unless there is only one good early copy surviving, there have already had to be editorial decisions in selecting the material for an Urtext edition, and the personality of the editor has already had to intervene between the composer and ourselves. And rightly so.

24

(d) In any case, is it strictly possible to print an original text in modernized notation?

Every time a modern editor alters the graphic outline of a clef, a note or a rest for the sake of intelligibility or readability; every time he rearranges the stems of notes, or the beams of groups of notes, for the sake of clarity or consistency; every time he transcribes an obsolete sign for an ornament into a current sign hopefully equivalent; every time he guesses where a vague slur or underlay was meant to come; every time he changes an accidental to accord in the best of his belief with our modern convention of governing the force of accidentals by the bar-line (a convention which did not then exist), or replaces a cancelling sharp or flat by a natural (which was not then by any means the standard usage); every time he completes a defective (but then normal) key-signature and removes (hopefully with accuracy) the no longer required accidentals from the text; every time he translates an obsolete time-signature into what he supposes to be its modern counterpart (an exceptionally hazardous operation in view of their transitional and inconsistent condition in the baroque period); every time he departs in matters small or large, as he has continually to depart, from the literal appearance of his original, he is making an editorial decision, and often one of some musical substance and not only of presentation.

(e) It is an editor's business to make decisions. From start to finish, these decisions are more difficult and responsible than a musician without experience of skilled editing could imagine possible. Musicians owe more than they commonly recognize to the musicologists who make them the editions they use every day.

(f) But, of course, the more editing, the less Urtext; and in fact, though it remains an instructive experience to perform from an Urtext edition, it is usually much more helpful to play from a good performing edition. Or make your own, for which you need considerable know-how.

3. EDITIONS SCHOLARLY AND UNSCHOLARLY

(a) Apart from more or less *unscholarly* editions, we may distinguish:

(i) *Scholar's* editions. These may carry a heavy but invaluable load of information about the original sources and their variant readings; they normally give little or no practical assistance to the performer.

(ii) *Performing* editions. These may be based either on new scholarship or on existing scholar's editions. They should give a precise reference to the source or sources used. Their function is to provide a practical text, without comment, but with adequate assistance to the performer.

(iii) *Combined-purpose* editions. These combine the most essential information for the scholar with the most helpful assistance to the performer. They can be difficult to design successfully; but they are being developed increasingly for publishing early music in an informative and accessible, but not misleading form.

(b) Without going so far as to make the page difficult to read, a modern edition can generally distinguish what is editorial from what is original by typographical methods duly explained in the preface. This gives the performer his choice, and is very desirable except in (ii), which should just settle for the best text and print it.

(c) It is generally wise to prefer an edition which shows a clean page.

A page which looks black with expression marks has certainly been made so by modern editing. No original baroque source carries more than a very few expression marks at the most. The baroque habit was few expression marks, but plenty of expression.

(d) It follows that we, too, having got our nice clean page, must work out plenty of expression; for no music, new or old, can sound well in a perpetual andante mezzo-forte.

4. BE YOUR OWN EDITOR

(a) An edition, good or bad, is only one man's working solution. It is never final; it can always be changed. It was not J. S. Bach who put in all those expression marks which appear to be so firmly rooted in the printed page. It was some modern editor, as the following incident may illustrate.

I was rehearsing, with new students, the last movement of J. S. Bach's C major trio sonata (attributed in the eighteenth century both to Bach and to Goldberg, but the arguments recently advanced for Goldberg are less convincing than the overall greatness in the style of Bach).

The big opening entry of the first violin is quickly taken up by the second violin playing the same entry, on the same bass and harmonies; and both should be given the same strong playing and strong continuo support, in the spirit of *concertante* rivalry implied by the music. But on this occasion the second violin crept in very meekly; and even when I said 'second violin come in forte' I got no better than a grudging mezzo-piano. When I said 'much louder than that' I was told in no uncertain terms, 'oh, but it is marked piano!'

And so it is, as I quickly discovered, in the modern edition they were using. But not by J. S. Bach, who put no dynamic markings anywhere in this work. Once this was explained, they were happy to cross out that ridiculous piano; but they had quite taken it for granted that since it was printed, it was Bach's and unavoidable.

(b) A baroque performer would not have regarded such a marking as unavoidable even on the assumption that it was Bach's. Baroque markings, including Bach's, are infrequent, inconsistent and unreliable:

26

hints to the performer rather than commands. The real shaping up was fully enough done; but it was done in rehearsal and performance, rather than on paper.

(c) Though a modern performing version is only a provisional version, and not sacrosanct, it should nevertheless be published ready for use as it stands. Most modern performers will need it so.

This is generally taken to mean complete with a realization of the figured bass; to which should perhaps now be added a realization of the free ornamentation in essential passages. Also any more or less obligatory trills and appoggiaturas, and perhaps some hints for optional ornaments at desirable places. Also adequate suggestions for accidentals; and a broad scheme of dynamic markings, and of tempos and rallentandos. These can all be put forward as provisional, and (in combined-purpose editions) distinguished typographically from the source material.

More advanced performers can use such editorial assistance either as a working sample for their own editing, or as a starting point for their own modifications.

(d) To check the text of some modern performing edition with photocopies of original sources (or with a reliable modern scholar's edition) and then to modify its editorial assistance for the sake of getting a more personal interpretation (if only by changing a few of the dynamic markings, or taking out a few of the slurs, or putting in a few missing but desirable ornaments, or improving the continuo realization here and there) is an excellent start towards the truly baroque position, which can be summed up: be your own editor.

CHAPTER FOUR

Style and the Performer

1. RELYING LESS ON THE TEXT AND MORE ON THE STYLE

(a) To put ourselves into the baroque position, we have to focus our attention less on the notated text, and more on the implied style.

(b) Baroque manuscripts and early prints vary in their accuracy as well as in their elegance. They may be remarkably free from mistakes, or remarkably full of them. But they share in common a certain casual indifference to the smaller details of rhythm, ornaments, figuration and much else besides. In such matters, they are so endlessly and unnecessarily inconsistent that there can have been no incentive felt, we must conclude, to make them otherwise.

Since performers in any case regarded the details as falling within their own responsibility to decide, composers and copyists apparently spared themselves the pains of notating them with exactness.

(c) We in our turn have therefore to take up these details into our own responsibility, relying on our sense of style to get them reasonably authentic.

2. A PREFERENCE FOR SPONTANEITY

(a) The baroque musicians had at their disposal virtually the same standard musical notation as ourselves.

(b) It was therefore by preference and not by necessity that they left their text more open and its interpretation more flexible. They had evidently a preference for spontaneity.

Where we tend to trust as much as possible to the notation, they tended to trust as much as possible to the performer. Where we try to be definitive, they were content to be suggestive. Where we are inclined to put the text before the interpretation, they were inclined to put the interpretation before the text. (But our avant-garde position is nearer to theirs.)

(c) Certainly the baroque critics complained loudly about egregious singers and vain virtuosi who abused their liberties. But though it was asked that these liberties should be better exercised, it was not asked that they should not be exercised; and we read high praises as well as loud complaints of contemporary performances in these respects.

Certainly it is interesting to find Couperin demanding (but on his own statement, not getting) a closer adherence to his own written (but not altogether unambiguous) signs for ornaments (see Ch. XVI, Sect. 1(b) (iv), below).

Still more is it interesting that J. S. Bach made a habit of writing out (very much in the florid, galant and most modern style of his day) freely ornamental figuration for his own slow movements, rather than outlining them in the ordinary baroque way as skeletons for improvisation. He was generally (in spite of Scheibe's criticism, for which see Ch. XV, Sect. 5, below) regarded at the time as well within his rights, but nevertheless as setting an example which should not be widely followed. It was not.

Neither Couperin nor Bach departed from the casual baroque attitude towards notation in any more general way.

(d) Our own younger generation, with its aleatory music, should be thoroughly appreciative of the baroque preference for spontaneity.

But it is important to bring it out at the start of a student's training that the only realistic approach to the problem is the baroque approach, and that this means the flexible approach.

So many difficulties for which definitive solutions cannot be found, and should not be found, cease to be difficulties when we stop looking for definitive solutions, and simply try to keep, as the baroque musicians would naturally have kept, within the appropriate boundaries of style.

(e) It was an elderly though very great conductor who at a recent rehearsal, when his soloist put in an unwritten but strongly implied long appoggiatura, called out formidably: 'play what is written!' To play what is written in baroque music is so often the very way not to play what is implied by what is written. It is no service to a composer being scrupulously faithful to a written text which is not scrupulously notated, but deliberately left open to the performer's initiative.

We have to enter into the spirit of the thing, and use our own initiative.

3. NOTES LEFT TO THE PERFORMER

(a) We shall find that even for the notes, the implications of baroque music are flexible.

(b) One example is figured bass, left to the performer to realize in whatever manner of accompaniment he decides.

(c) A second example is free ornamentation, left to the performer to elaborate over melodic structures which may be no more than outlines; and specific ornaments, some of which may, or must, be added, signs or no signs, where the context requires.

(d) A third example is accidentals, still partly left to the performer in early baroque music, and to some extent a problem even in later baroque music.

4. EXPRESSION LEFT TO THE PERFORMER

(a) We shall find that for the expression, the implications of baroque music are not merely flexible. They are left wide open to the performer.

(b) Many details which we now class with the notes were then classed with expression. This is particularly the case with numerous and quite substantial details of the rhythm, as we shall see when examining inequality, variable dotting and the like.

(c) Expression in our narrower sense was notated only to a very small extent. An ample variety of expression marks was already in use; but so sparsely that we must give up any attempt to establish a scheme of expression as intended by the composer. That is for the performer, which is to say for us; and it needs doing very thoroughly.

5. COMPOSER AND PERFORMER

(a) Composer and performer were frequently the same person in virtuoso baroque music, and therefore in a position to blend composition and improvisation in the readiest manner.

Thus Handel played the slow movements of his organ concertos from a few sketchy fragments of notation, differently each time, and leaving us to do the same as best we can. Mozart, Beethoven, Chopin and others likewise varied the figuration, especially of their slow movements, at each performance, merely finalizing the best of it for publication.

(b) But a baroque performer was expected to set his stamp on the music in much the same way even if he were not the composer. It may not have been his music; but it was emphatically his evening.

6. SUBSTANCE NOT SEMBLANCE

(a) We may think, then, of J. S. Bach, who had no hesitation in making the most imaginative alterations in his own music, when using it again, nor in other men's music, as when he adapted Vivaldi's fine originals to his own still finer transcriptions. Handel had the same attitude.

Or we may consider Michel de Saint-Lambert (*Traité*, Paris, 1707, Ch. VI, p. 71) suggesting that 'you can sometimes change the chords' from those written, 'when you judge that others will suit better'; or C. P. E. Bach (*Essay*, Berlin, 1753, Foreword) advising the accompanist 'to perform with judgement, often departing from the written text'.

(b) Our fashionable modern reverence for the written text can indeed be a virtue in the proper context. But it was no part of the baroque attitude; and we must not let it mislead us into missing the implied substance of baroque music through too stubborn an adherence to its notated semblance.

7. ASKING THE RIGHT QUESTIONS

(a) It is not necessarily the best question to ask: what exactly did the composer *notate* in his written text?

A text deliberately left incomplete is not meant to be exactly established. It is meant to be imaginatively realized.

(b) It is not necessarily the best question even to ask: what exactly did the composer *intend* by his written text?

Options deliberately left open by the composer cannot be tied down to any exact intention. The intention was that they should remain performer's options.

(c) But it may well be the best and most realistic question to ask: what broadly might a good baroque performer have *made* of the written text?

Somewhere within that broad but not unlimited range of possibilities a good modern performer can find an authentic answer which is not definitive, but individual. It is authentic because it lies within the boundaries of the style.

31

CHAPTER FIVE

Performing Spontaneously

1. IN BAROQUE MUSIC THE PERFORMER IS KING

(a) No musician need feel afraid that his imagination is going to be hampered by knowing about the style of baroque interpretation. On the contrary, the interpretation of a baroque text offers more performers' options than the interpretation of a text from a hundred years later.

(b) It is true that a skilled modern editor may tactfully suggest some approximation to an interpretation. But it is not satisfactory to tie down the interpretation in too much detail. The editor's suggestions are better treated as a point of departure than as a point of arrival.

(c) In baroque music, the performer is king. It is baroque spontaneity that we are trying to recapture.

2. RECAPTURING A BAROQUE SPONTANEITY

(a) Baroque music cannot be performed well simply out of textbook instructions. No music can. That is the merest beginning towards a sense of style. We can get the notes right, and still be wrong in the proportioning and the balancing of the notes.

(b) Trills, for example, may all begin correctly with their upper notes, but with these upper notes not prolonged enough or stressed enough to take their proper prominence or to give that strong (unwritten) discord on the beat which is the purpose of starting them with their upper notes.

Or appoggiaturas may be correctly inserted, in all the proper places, but likewise in too brief and gentlemanly a manner to make their proper effect as powerful and expressive dissonances, resolving more gently on to the main (written) note.

There are many other situations in which it is not the correctness of the notes which counts for most, but the naturalness of their nuancing. It is this nuancing, deeply felt and finely moulded, which has to carry conviction with the performers, and through them with the listeners.

(c) It is always a mistake in rehearsal to press a point of style against the convictions of the musicians concerned.

If they can take it into their own musicianship after a trial run or two, they will soon forget that they ever had to have it pointed out to them. If not, the musicologist may have misunderstood something in the evidence, or not absorbed it properly into his own musicianship, or just not found how to make a practical matter of it with those particular musicians in that particular rehearsal, with those instruments and that amount of time at their disposal.

Rehearsal is a co-operative enterprise. A good musicologist is generally learning just about as fast as he is teaching. Every rehearsal is different, but no rehearsal can be a good rehearsal unless those who are taking part in it can feel themselves as a working team. We are not rehearsing to dig up an antique past. We are rehearsing to get a performance in the immediate future. Usually the very immediate future.

(d) Can modern musicians absorb baroque interpretation so thoroughly into their systems that it comes out spontaneously? In my experience, yes; but only after a certain amount of specialized training.

3. EDITOR AND PERFORMER

(a) We may sum up as follows the difference between the baroque relationship of composer, editor and performer, and our conventional modern relationship.

(b) We have to realize that the baroque training was long and thorough, including as it did a solid grounding in composition as well as in performing skill. Editing was a less necessary function then.

It was their grounding in composition which enabled baroque performers to develop their remarkable capacity for more or less improvising free ornamentation and figured-bass accompaniments; for adjusting their own accidentals, where necessary, as they went along; and for taking the expression habitually into their own hands.

(c) A number of modern performers have shown how possible it is to overcome the barrier of the centuries, and to improvise more or less at sight a really inspired ornamentation or accompaniment with no greater preparation beforehand than an equally gifted baroque performer would have required: that is to say, little or none.

A larger number of modern performers have shown themselves able to do these things with sufficient ability.

(d) It is usual for editors to supply a working realization of the figured-bass accompaniment. Perhaps it should become usual for editors to supply a working realization of any free ornamentation which is urgently required. This is already beginning to be done. Gifted performers can always ignore the editorial suggestions; but others may need them.

Editors normally assume responsibility, though not always quite adequately, for the accidentals.

33

Such editorial services are still necessary for most modern performers.

(e) We do not want to go back to numerous or anachronistic expression marks, which tend to over-determine the expression. But a few printed expression marks, well chosen and well placed to suggest a broad working scheme, are extremely desirable in performing or combined-purpose editions.

(f) It saves valuable rehearsal time if the parts are privately marked up beforehand: preferably with a pencil to allow for later changes of mind. The smaller nuances should hardly ever be marked; but the main tempo changes and rallentandos, some brief phrasing marks, slurrings or bowings, occasional articulation marks, enough louds and softs to outline the broad contrasts, sometimes crescendos and diminuendos, together with any obligatory and perhaps a selection of optional ornaments: these are the sort of detail which should be in the parts, either ahead of the rehearsals or at an early stage. They are necessary for a fully achieved performance; and either the editor or the performers will have to be responsible for them.

Here, too, the secret is for all those concerned to regard themselves as members of a working team.

PART TWO

THE BAROQUE SOUND

CHAPTER SIX

Sound and Sense

1. MATCHING THE SOUND TO THE MUSIC

(a) Perhaps the most elusive of our practical problems in baroque interpretation, and perhaps the most crucial for the entire effect, is the actual sound in which the music is to be produced.

(b) Who can describe a sound in music? We can hardly say more than that there seems to have been a preference for clear and incisive timbres rather than for thick and heavy timbres.

This impression is confirmed by the acoustic features of instruments surviving in original condition from the baroque period. It is still more strongly confirmed by the musical consequences.

The surest way, for example, to make Handel dull is to perform his music in what used to be thought the Handelian manner, and sometimes still is: weighty; pompous; relying more on force than subtlety.

Merely reducing the size of the choir and the orchestra brings immediate relief. Introducing plenty of oboes and bassoons sharpens up the colouring wonderfully; for doubling with winds, especially reeds, was common baroque practice, and sometimes we come, for instance, upon *senza oboi*, without oboes, or *senza fagotti*, without bassoons, in scores where their previous presence has in no other way been indicated. Add to this the sharp, transparent string tone which seems proper to baroque music, and the Handelian scoring begins to glow and sparkle.

2. TRANSPARENCY AND INCISIVENESS

(a) We shall mainly seek:
   (i) a *transparent* sonority;
   (ii) an *incisive* articulation.

(b) The techniques for producing these qualities of transparency and incisiveness overlap. Their musical effects are complementary, and add up to a vitality which is impressive without being pretentious.

Transparency and incisiveness are basic attributes of the baroque sound.

3. THE CHOICE OF INSTRUMENTS AND THE USE OF INSTRUMENTS
(a) We can consider:
    (i) the *choice* of instruments;
    (ii) the *use* of instruments once chosen.

(b) Thus, for example, choosing a harpsichord, rather than a piano, introduces a change in sonority and articulation alike; and so does choosing a well-designed, well-constructed and well-fitted harpsichord, rather than one which is either too harsh or too feeble in its acoustic and mechanical properties.

But with the best harpsichord (and there are many good variants), if the harpsichordist has the touch and the technique, he will draw out every resource of sonority which that harpsichord possesses, and every idiom of articulation which completes the true character of harpsichord playing. But if he does not, the weakness of the sonority and the dry misuse of the harpsichord's natural articulateness will undo the value of using the right instrument.

(19) Joachim Quantz, *Essay*, Berlin, 1752, XVII, vi, 18:

'Experience confirms that if two players of unequal abilities play on the same harpsichord, the tone will be far better in the case of the better player. There can be no reason for this except the difference in their touch.'

(c) Again, we may have a choice between a cello and a gamba. If it is a matter of continuo work, either is authentic, though certain places and times favoured one rather than the other; either is good if well handled, though each is different. In solo work of an idiomatic quality, the differences are more significant, and a substitution of one for the other may bring about an obvious lessening of musical effectiveness.

There is an acoustic difference: the table of the cello is thicker, vibrating less freely but more massively; its strings are thicker and tighter to correspond. The gamba is more lightly constructed and more lightly strung, with the opposite effect. The cello yields more amplitude, but the gamba, when well played, rings out with its own sharp colouring to the very back of the hall.

There is also a technical difference: the bowing lends itself to a more weighty articulation on the cello, and to a crisper articulation on the gamba. This difference in technique works in with the difference in acoustics; and the combined result is two instruments with much in common, but with quite distinctive characters.

Yet, once more, the gamba does not ring out to the back of the hall of its own accord; it is the gambist who has to get the strings vibrating so firmly yet freely that the wave-form, though of lesser amplitude, is pure enough to carry far, like a good singer's voice-production. The cellist, on the other hand, can lighten his sonority and crispen his articulation to accompany small forces with as much delicacy as a gamba, provided that he knows what he should be aiming at.

(d) Though the choice of an instrument is important, the manner of using the instrument once chosen is still more important. It is not the instrument but the imagination which knows what to do.

CHAPTER SEVEN

The Choice of Instruments

1. INSTRUMENTS LARGELY A PERFORMER'S CHOICE

(a) We have to distinguish between the scanty indications for instruments which may be shown in the notation, and the rich and musicianly effects which may have to be worked out for the actual performance.

(b) Title pages or prefaces of baroque editions, where they specify instruments at all, often specify a considerable range of alternatives. This enabled more copies to be sold; but the performer was supposed to confine himself to what is suitable.

(20) François Couperin, *Troisième livre de pièces*, Paris, 1722, preface:

'These pieces, indeed, are suitable for two flutes or oboes, as well as for two violins, two viols, and other instruments of equal pitch; it being understood that those who perform them adapt them to the range of theirs.'

(c) Whatever is suitable, is acceptable; but this does not make an idiomatic violin sonata any the less idiomatic, nor does it obliterate the subtle and valuable distinction between a transverse flute and a recorder; nor does it make an oboe sound like either; nor does it make a bassoon sound like a cello or a gamba. Such agreeable distinctions are among the incidental delights of music; and they enjoyed them in the baroque period just as much as we do ourselves.

(d) Where the music is highly idiomatic for a particular instrument, the especial qualities of that instrument are essential and not incidental to the effect. Thus the unaccompanied violin music of J. S. Bach requires the violin, and nothing else will do.

Where the music is well composed for a particular instrument, but is not highly idiomatic for that instrument, an effect which is different but not less good may be produced on another instrument; and this was a very common baroque occurrence. We have simply to ask ourselves: is this instrument, or is it not, capable of giving us a full experience of the music?

(e) We are not, therefore, confined to the suggestions (if any) made by titles or prefaces, nor necessarily to baroque instruments. I have performed some baroque trio sonatas, very successfully, using a pair of clarinets (not common baroque instruments); though in other sonatas, they would not be so successful. In American schools and colleges, clarinets are much more plentiful than violins; and I see no reason, either theoretical or practical, to deprive these young clarinetists of some enjoyable share in amateur baroque performances.

2. THE BAROQUE ORCHESTRA MORE COLOURFUL THAN STANDARDIZED
(a) Orchestras throughout the baroque period remained more colourful than standardized. Only the central body of strings remained fairly constant; and this might vary in the number and distribution of the parts.

Wind colourings tended to be applied to entire passages or movements, rather than to brief phrases or parts of phrases. They also tended to be applied in lines rather than in masses. To change the colouring of an orchestral line will certainly alter its effect, but the distinction may be more incidental than essential. That is why a modern substitution, though never negligible, may be acceptable.

(b) This is an opposite situation to the romantic orchestra, where the resources are standardized though subject to extensions and modifications; but where the instrumental colouring tends to be applied in smaller patches and mosaic patterns. To a much greater extent, the music is the colouring, and the colouring is the music. Substitutions are less likely to be acceptable.

(c) About forty instrumentalists is probably as near as we can come to an average size for a baroque orchestra.

Many small German principalities, Italian dukedoms, princes of the church in any European country and suchlike lordly residences would afford, if they could, a musical establishment on this scale, or approaching it, together with a chorus of some twenty singers, and perhaps soloists in addition.

Smaller establishments existed in much greater quantity, including those of all but the most sumptuous churches. Quantz (*Essay*, Berlin, 1752, XVII, i, 16) lists as barely adequate four violins, one viola, one cello, one bass; his preferred list in this passage is twelve violins, three violas, four cellos, two basses, four flutes, four oboes, three bassoons, and when required, two horns. (One or two harpsichords are also assumed in his lists; and one theorbo.) These estimates are on the small side.

For gala performances and festival occasions, the singers and instrumentalists together might run into the hundreds: i.e. massed choirs and orchestras, assembled regardless of either financial or artistic economy. Orchestras of fifty or sixty were by no means rare, though never standard.

Opera houses also averaged around forty instrumentalists.

There were 'forty instruments . . . of all sorts' at a Venetian opera performance reported in April, 1679, by the *Mercure galant*. Thirty-two are visible in a painting (Turin, Museo Civico) of the new Teatro Regio at Turin, probably 26 December, 1740. The Teatro Comunale in Bologna, completed in 1757, had an orchestra pit 'capable [of holding] approximately 69 instrumentalists' (description printed Bologna, 1763). Other pictorial evidence shows 40 (Versailles, 1674, twice); 44 (Dresden, 1719); 57 or 58 (Versailles, 1745). The *Lettres historiques* of [Nicolas Boindin], Paris, 1719, pp. 112ff., list as members of the Opéra 16 solo and 33 choral singers, 27 dancers, and 43 instrumentalists. F. W. Marpurg (*Historisch-kritische Beyträge*), Berlin, 1754, etc., lists many musical establishments, including that of the Paris Opéra, which he gives (1754) as 20 solo and 38 choral singers, 9 solo and 32 chorus dancers, and 48 instrumentalists.

(d) It must be appreciated that mere size tells only half the story about baroque orchestral sonority. The transparency and incisiveness of the string playing counts for at least as much as the numbers of string instruments. The clarino brilliance of baroque trumpets and (rather later and in lesser degree) horns; the relatively small volume even of late baroque flute tone; the relative pungency even of late baroque reed tone; the row of bassoons doubling on the bass line: these are all important factors of balance and colouring.

Though there is plenty of baroque precedent for a wide variety in the size and composition of the orchestra, and though the size of the auditorium should greatly influence the decision, it is on the whole desirable to keep somewhere around the average size of forty, with a higher proportion of woodwind (particularly reeds) than became the classical custom of the post-baroque period.

Such an orchestra of about forty, when trained to a baroque transparency of sonority and incisiveness of articulation, should serve most baroque purposes extremely well. Thirty or even twenty may still serve. But two violins to a part is not a good sound nor sufficient for ordinary baroque weight and sonority.

3. THE ORCHESTRAL CONTINUO

(a) The necessary role of the harpsichord (or harpsichords) in a baroque orchestra must be clearly understood.

Even in an orchestra of forty, playing with baroque transparency and incisiveness, and even with a fine concert harpsichord and a fine continuo harpsichordist, it will not usually be possible, without electrical amplification (not for this use recommended), to hear that harpsichord distinctly in the tuttis. No attempt should be made to give it melodic or rhythmic independence in the tuttis, but merely to keep a smooth, uncomplicated part going. It will, nevertheless, be heard as brightening the sonority and giving the articulation a cutting edge.

(20a) C. P. E. Bach, *Essay,* Berlin, II, 1762, Introd., 7:

'Thus one can perform no piece well without accompaniment from a keyboard instrument. Even in the most powerful pieces of music, [even] in operas, even under the open sky, where one would certainly think not to hear the least thing from the harpsichord, one misses it when it is not there.'

(b) In the seventeenth century, continuo instruments of various plucked families might be very numerous. Even in the eighteenth century, a mere harpsichord and cello is not always enough. In French opera from Lully on, a concertino section, including keyboard and other plucked strings and several treble and bass melodic instruments, alternated with a full orchestra of strings and wind.

In large ensembles of the eighteenth century, it was a standard plan to have two harpsichords: one, supported by melodic bass instruments as required (commonly a double bass as well as a cello), for accompanying solo passages in opera, and the concertino sections in concertos; the other, supported by further bass instruments, to accompany chiefly the tuttis. One or more lutes might still be included as further continuo. The first harpsichordist often shared the conducting with the first violinist, unless, as in the Paris opera, there was a regular conductor in addition.

4. CONDUCTING

(a) Regular conducting, with stick, staff, roll of music paper or the arm alone, was quite common from the sixteenth century at latest, as several pictures confirm, and a delightful description of an instrumental ensemble of nuns at S. Vito in Ferrara, conducted by their leader with a stick (Ercole Bottrigari, *Il Desiderio,* Venice, 1594, ed. Carol MacClintock, [n.p.] 1962, pp. 56–60). André Maugars (*Response* . . . [Paris, ? 1640]) described one master conductor who 'beat the main time in the first choir' and two subordinate conductors each of whom 'did nothing but cast his eyes on this original time' and pass it to the two other choirs. Roger North (Hereford Cathedral Library, MS R. II. xlii, f. 36v., in *Roger North on Music,* ed. John Wilson, London, 1959, p. 106, and footnote) recommended subdividing down to eighth notes if required, and thought there was 'nothing like a roll of paper in the hand of an artist; without noise and above board'.

(b) It is not possible to get a really good ensemble, in anything larger than a chamber group, by trying to wave an encouraging hand in the intervals of supplying a continuo accompaniment at the harpsichord, with energetic motions of the head to keep things going meanwhile. To dispense with a conductor in baroque fashion necessitates sharing the direction with the first violinist; and this division of responsibilities carries, and always did carry, problems of its own.

It is possible to keep a chamber orchestra well together from the first violin, if he stands and leads more conspicuously than a quartet leader; he can also beat time at crucial moments with his bow, though it is still better if this can be avoided.

Nevertheless, in most modern circumstances, and always when more than a chamber orchestra has to be controlled, the presence of a traditional conductor, using our traditional stick-technique and our traditional gestures of the left hand, is likely to get much more successful results from most modern performers, in much less time; and it is therefore usually to be recommended.

5. PITCH AND TEMPERAMENT

(a) The belief in a prevailing baroque pitch about a semitone below A440 has not stood up to careful examination (especially by Arthur Mendel, 'Pitch in the 16th and Early 17th Centuries', *Musical Quarterly*, 1948, Jan., pp. 28–45, April, pp. 199–221, July, pp. 336–57, October, pp. 575–93; 'On the Pitches in Use in Bach's Time', *Musical Quarterly*, 1955, July, pp. 332–54, October, pp. 466–80). There was no prevailing pitch in the baroque period. We gain nothing in authenticity, and lose much in convenience, by departing from our present international standard at A440, except for special reasons in particular instances.

(b) Transposition was frequent in the baroque period, and may be used to secure the best tessitura, provided that keys giving the brightness of many open strings on violins, viols, lutes etc. are not changed for keys giving the darkness of few or no open strings, or impossible difficulties on early wind instruments if these are used, and so forth.

(c) Temperament affects keyboard instruments and the harp. Meantone is very worthwhile if it does not run into too many practical difficulties; but it is not necessary, even for solos and chamber music, and is scarcely appreciable in the orchestra. Equal temperament has advantages which usually outweigh its slight and familiar impurity, except perhaps on the organ, where this is so much more conspicuous.

Other instruments (viols and lutes included) in any case keep a sort of flexibly just intonation, whatever may be the temperament of a keyboard accompaniment.

6. THE EFFECTIVENESS OF AUTHENTIC SONORITIES

(a) Other things being equal, authenticity in the choice of instruments, as in other matters, pays good dividends. But not when bought at too much cost in lowered standards of technique.

(b) We have no reason to believe that modern instruments are superior to baroque instruments in general. Some (such as woodwind) are superior in some respects, others (such as violins) are not, and in some the balance of gain and loss is about equal, in others not.

Moreover, we have always to ask: superior for what? The piano is undoubtedly superior for nineteenth-century keyboard music, but not for baroque keyboard music, especially as a continuo instrument. The cello has obviously the superiority over the gamba in string quartets, but not in trio sonatas, where each gives equal and different beauties; still less in a chamber work like Couperin's *La Sultane*, where the two low parts, closely scored, sound thick on cellos but radiant on gambas. Music so well conceived in terms of certain instrumental sonorities must always suffer from a change of instruments.

(c) Nor have we reason to believe that modern technique is superior to baroque technique in general.

Many baroque instruments required and got a technique since lost, and only being recovered with some difficulty and uncertainty. High trumpet and horn parts for long, valveless instruments of narrow bore are a case in point; and here there is no wholly satisfactory modern substitute. However, modern high trumpets and horns can do the work reasonably well; moreover, some players have now recovered the old techniques, on the old instruments, extremely well.

In singing, we are bound to admit that the great baroque parts in opera and cantata demand a lost virtuosity and resourcefulness of voice production which we are so far only recovering by slow degrees.

Improvised ornamentation and the improvised realization of figured bass accompaniments are further techniques which we are having to work quite hard to catch up with again.

(d) The sonority of most baroque instruments, in their original baroque condition, is extremely beautiful and extremely well suited to the situations in which they were employed. They have special colourings of tone which are a delight in themselves. Their capabilities are equal to the demands made upon them, when they are handled with some approach to the high skill and mastery which the best, but only the best, of the baroque performers evidently brought to them, as contemporary comparisons describe. These descriptions are confirmed by the difficulty often encountered in the parts themselves, especially in solos. But such difficulty is by no means insuperable.

It is, therefore, a very reasonable ambition to get hold of old or reproduced examples, to re-learn their technique with determination, and to use them in place of modern substitutions so far as the practical considerations (including the acoustics of the hall) permit. Nevertheless, it is only realistic to recognize that practical considerations (and especially financial considerations) must still limit the extent to which we can use baroque instruments, in their original baroque condition.

7. HOW FAR COMPROMISE IS DESIRABLE

(a) Instruments like the harpsichord and the recorder, though not professionally available everywhere, are now relatively common; others like the lute and the viol are growing almost as common among amateur enthusiasts, and not uncommon among reliable professionals.

(b) When only rather unproficient performers are available, they should not as a rule be used in public, welcome though they may be in private gatherings. The effectiveness of an authentic instrumentation cannot altogether be judged or enjoyed, we must always remember, until the performance is of the same professional excellence as would be expected on modern instruments.

(c) Likewise, when authentic instruments only of poor construction or in poor condition are available, they should not be used in public merely for the sake of appearances.

The proper restoration of old harpsichords, for example, and the proper construction, scaling and stringing of new harpsichords, are matters now better understood; and similar advances have been made with many other instruments. Yet thoroughly unsatisfactory examples are frequently encountered; and there comes a point beyond which they will not really do their job. Here, too, we have to remember that only fine instruments in fine condition allow a fair judgement and a full enjoyment.

(d) When fine performers using fine instruments of authentic character are available, are we nowadays unanimous in preferring them? By no means. There are still plenty of fine modern musicians who do not want the fine early instruments on any conditions; and while this is now a somewhat old-fashioned taste, it is a perfectly legitimate one.

We have sometimes to remind ourselves that this is not a moral issue. Artistic compatibility is the only issue which really concerns us as practising musicians. This is itself a matter of degree; but it is certainly not ruled out by using modern instruments.

CHAPTER EIGHT

The Use of Instruments

1. USE OF INSTRUMENTS AS IMPORTANT AS CHOICE

(a) There is a minimum level of authenticity in our choice of instruments which is the lowest that most of us will now want to tolerate.

(b) A good example of this is the size and constitution of the orchestra. An orchestra of baroque proportions for baroque music is becoming a minimum requirement. But how far does this take us?

(c) By reducing the orchestra to baroque proportions we are certainly removing the grossest incompatibility between sound and sense. But this in itself may only leave uncovered, and much more audible than before, all those incompatibilities of sonority and articulation which are not gross, but subtle.

(d) If there are misphrasings or insufficient phrasings, if there is ruthlessness in the rhythm, hardness in the feeling, or insensitiveness in the tone, if there is that overall rigidity which used to pass for good baroque style though it certainly is not, then this shows up all the more mechanically when it is no longer swept along by the brute force and resonance of a big symphonic orchestra.

2. GOOD BAROQUE MUSIC NEVER MECHANICAL

(a) A mechanical conception of baroque music is a misconception of baroque music. See 4 below.

(b) There are, for example, many brilliant baroque allegros, some of the best of them by Vivaldi, of which the energy is so perpetual as to be almost obsessive. They obviously require a considerable momentum in performance.

But if this momentum sounds like the unrelenting momentum of a machine, then the brilliance becomes a mechanical brilliance, and the energy becomes in the end more wearisome than exhilarating.

Nothing can make Vivaldi altogether dull; but he can be made much duller than he ought to be. The surface excitement begins to pall: one concerto begins to seem very like another; and we end with the very amusing .but not entirely justifiable libel that Vivaldi wrote not four hundred concertos, but one concerto four hundred times.

(c) There really is, of course, a strong and genuine element of orderliness and symmetry in most baroque music; and in the clear outlines and sequential regularity of a Vivaldi concerto, this orderliness and symmetry are particularly conspicuous.

Yet there is also an element of romantic passion in the controlled and obsessive energy of Vivaldi, and even in the disciplined and classic serenity of Corelli, so that we found Galliard telling us, at quotation (12) above, that he 'had never met with any man that suffered his passions to hurry him away so much whilst he was playing on the violin as the famous Arcangelo Corelli'. That implies some romantic flexibility.

An even worse enemy of baroque music than the romantic orchestra, or than the romantic legacy, is the anti-romantic fallacy.

3. ELECTRONIC BACH

(a) The perennial tendency to mechanize baroque music reaches a logical extreme in recordings using electronically synthesized sounds in place of musical instruments.

'We have tried to make our performances musically expressive, electronically idiomatic, and spiritually and musicologically faithful to Bach–conditions probably not totally reconcilable', writes Benjamin Folkman on the record sleeve of 'Switched-on Bach' (Columbia Stereo MS 7194, Lib. of Congress catalog card number R 68–3516). And indeed, they really are not reconcilable.

It is the old question of incompatibility between the sound and the sense.

(b) We disturb the texture of a composition at our own risk. 'No combination of live instruments could achieve the clarity of texture of this recording', claims Mr. Folkman. 'At last, every note and line can be heard'.

This is true. Every background counterpoint is brought startlingly into the foreground. There is no background any longer. There is therefore no depth.

Where everything is spot-lit, everything accosts us with the tireless insistence which is at once the strength and the temptation of machinery: themes and counterthemes; rhythms and harmonies; novel electronic colourings and simulated instrumental colourings alike, with impartial ingenuity.

(c) None of this ingenuity lies within the implications of baroque music. It is not bad; it is simply misplaced. Its place and its value lie in creating actual electronic music.

48

4. FLEXIBILITY NECESSARY TO BAROQUE PERFORMANCE

(a) What the genuine element of orderliness and symmetry in baroque music requires of us is not rigidity in performance, but proportionableness.

No factor is more important than the ability to keep a steady tempo. But there is a way of keeping a steady tempo which is nevertheless not unyielding. We can yield to each passing nuance as the music itself implies it, while holding the underlying tempo with the utmost sureness. That will not feel unsteady; it will simply feel natural.

Nothing that grows out of the music itself will feel unnatural. Only when expression is imposed from the outside, merely for expression's sake, will it feel forced, or artificial, or arbitrary, or overdone. And in baroque music, there is the paramount necessity for keeping an unfailing sense of line. Anything artificial or too self-conscious may interfere with that.

There is a proportionable balance about genuine expressiveness which does not contradict, but complements, genuine orderliness and symmetry. The audience will not notice that the performance is rhythmically flexible. The audience will simply experience it as relaxed and spacious.

(b) For example, baroque music is full of cadences. It is no use riding rough-shod across these cadences. The more perfunctory they sound, the more they will obtrude.

So soon as the harmony becomes momentarily cadential, we need to yield ever so slightly in acknowledgement. The rhythm must stretch just enough for the music to sound at ease, and no more.

Where there is a more decisive cadence, the stretching will need to amount to an appreciable though not necessarily an obvious rallentando, begun as soon as the harmony begins to feel unmistakably cadential.

In many baroque allegros, there comes a return to the opening material. If this is run straight into, it goes for very little. If it is prepared by a broadening in the bar or two before, and then placed a little more deliberately than strict time would allow, it makes its full effect, probably without anyone in the audience noticing just how or why. And all this can be done within the basic continuity of the line, provided that the performer has a fine sense of shaping and proportion.

(c) The pick-up after a stretching or a broadening, and still more after a rallentando, will almost invariably gain from just the right amount of deliberate unpunctuality. Even the start of a new phrase usually wants to be a little poised and placed, which means that it is delayed by a hair's-breadth of stolen time. The start of a repeat or of an ensuing new section may need quite a substantial space of stolen time before the right moment has really come.

(d) Sequences in baroque music need particularly sensitive handling. These, too, are very numerous; these too become paradoxically more obtrusive and more irksome in proportion as they are made to sound perfunctory.

If all that we are given is an unbroken chain of sequential units, their repetitiveness is bound to seem mechanical and therefore monotonous. If each unit is perceptibly separated and lovingly shaped, it can take its place as one component of an interesting pattern.

The interest is in the phrasing; and the phrasing needs a far more substantial and audible separation between each phrase than many performers realize. It is not enough to have the phrasing beautifully clear and logical in one's own mind. It needs to be heard by the audience; and this cannot be achieved without a very perceptible break in the sound, which if necessary should be enlarged by a fraction, however minute, of stolen time. This, too, does not disturb the overall sense of line, but enhances it, provided that it is done with good judgement and a real feeling for the shapes of phrases and the proper places for dividing them.

5. MENTAL IMAGE AND ACOUSTIC LIMITS

(a) All these necessary baroque qualities of transparent sonority and incisive articulation, of flexible rhythm and clear phrasing, of shaping and of continuity, are brought more nearly within reach by using as authentic an instrumentation as the circumstances encourage.

Nevertheless, by far the most influential factor is the mental image in the head of the performer.

(b) When, for example, a virtuoso violinist or cellist conveys a sense of undue strain in Bach's unaccompanied suites by too massive a sonority and too heavy an articulation, this is not from any unsuitability in his noble instrument. It is not even from the increase of tension produced in changing it from its original baroque fittings, though this is not a negligible factor. It is first and foremost because the virtuoso is applying a mental conception which, powerful and impressive as it may be, does not really lie within the baroque boundaries of style, and is not really matched to the implications of the music.

This leads to difficulties which largely disappear when the lighter sonority and crisper articulation native to the music are mentally conceived. Such virtuoso music never becomes easy; but the sense of strain on performer and listener alike can be avoided by a more relaxed and baroque conception.

The instruments are the same. The use of them is different.

(c) There remain acoustic factors which cannot be avoided by conceiving a more baroque mental image.

For example, violins have always had thicker wood and tenser strings than viols. Their construction, acoustics and technique all tend towards a more massive sonority and a more assertive articulation. The qualities of the two families largely overlap; but no mental conception can make violins sound satisfactory in the close, low scoring and tight counterpoint of a big fantasy from early seventeenth-century England, in five or six densely written parts, all admirably instrumented for the lucid viols.

On the other hand, many of the more open fantasies for viols in three or four parts, especially if their scoring lies higher, can be made to sound well on violins, provided that the mental conception is appropriate and insightful.

Similar considerations of good judgement and suitability have very commonly to be weighed in baroque music of different kinds. If it sounds right, it is right; but it will not by any means always sound right merely because of a general similarity of timbre and tessitura.

6. A PRACTICABLE BAROQUE ORCHESTRA

(a) It is not yet practicable to use even a close approximation to an authentic baroque orchestra, except under somewhat rare circumstances.

(b) For even an approximate reconstruction of a baroque orchestra, we have some formidable problems to overcome, though it has now been proved beyond a doubt that it can be done successfully (including the intonation), and that the effect can be wonderful.

All members of the violin family have to be reconstructed with their original fittings, and bowed with the slightly outcurved bows most common in the baroque period. The change in both sonority and articulation can be wonderful.

All woodwind must reproduce the bores, the materials, the mainly keyless holes and the different embouchures or reeds common in that period. Brass must be mainly valveless; trumpets or horns must be long baroque instruments designed for high clarino playing, not short modern instruments designed for low or moderate harmonics. Again the change is startling and can be very beautiful.

(c) In the growing circumstances in which it is technically and financially practicable to carry through such a reconstruction, it is of fascinating value and interest.

(d) An orchestra of modern instruments, even when suitably reduced to baroque proportions, is not going to sound very like a baroque orchestra in timbre and colouring. But it can be got to sound transparent and incisive enough to produce somewhat different, but excellent results.

51

(e) The most crucial department to get right is, as experience confirms over and over again, the strings. If the strings are giving their tone the right kind of transparency, and their bowing the right kind of incisiveness, all other problems of sonority and articulation can usually be handled. If the string tone is too opaque or too luscious, or if the bowing is too massive or too smooth, that problem must be handled first. And it cannot be handled merely by putting hard sounds in place of luscious sounds.

Suggest playing more into the string, using less bow (further from the heel), and a slower bow-stroke, a little nearer to the bridge; and a rather smaller and more relaxed vibrato. Especially using *less* bow (i.e. a less swift stroke). That is not the whole answer, of course; but the difference it makes may be quite surprising.

CHAPTER NINE

The Voice

1. THE DECLINE IN VOICE-PRODUCTION

(a) The voice remains, as always, one of the great instruments of music.

In one respect, but only one, the voice has undergone organic change: we no longer have castrato male sopranos and altos.

In all other respects, the voice as an instrument remains unchanged. But voice-production has changed, and we have a problem there.

(b) In comparison with fifty years ago, not very many modern singers are so trained as to be able to sing difficult operatic roles with sureness, accuracy and good intonation. In the hardest passages, we commonly hear, not the notes, but an approximation to the notes, more or less covered up by the orchestra. Even in the simplest passages, bad voice-placing and bad intonation, and even downright scooping, are fairly common, not only in theatres of the second rank, but in the great opera houses of the world.

(c) The contemporary descriptions of great nineteenth-century singers, backed by the scratchy but incontrovertible evidence of their primitive recordings, are sufficient to give us an accurate idea of *bel canto* in its last period of perfection.

The descriptions of great baroque singers are so remarkably similar to the nineteenth-century descriptions that we may believe these earlier periods of *bel canto* to have used essentially the same technique.

(d) It will therefore be my assumption here that we need to recover the normal technique of Italian *bel canto* as fully as possible in order to give the finest performances of Monteverdi, Carissimi, Purcell, Bach or Handel.

2. DESCRIPTIONS OF BAROQUE VOICE-PRODUCTION

(a) We may compare a few of the numerous descriptions of *bel canto* voice-production which begin about on the threshold of the baroque period, and continue through that period with increasing clearness and

53

frequency. None of them is ideally clear: but what we read seems remarkably consistent, so far as it can carry us.

(21) Baldesar Castiglione, *Il libro del Cortegiano*, Venice, 1528, ed. B. Maier, Turin, 1955, pp. 147–8:

'The singing of Bidon [Astigiano], which is so full of art, ready, intense, inspired and of such varied melodies . . . Our Marchetto Cara moves us no less by his singing, but with a sweeter harmony . . . full of flexible smoothness.'

(22) Giovanni Maffei, *Delle lettere*, Naples, 1562, pp. 5–81:

'It is necessary to explain many arts of nature, to know the finest ones (*bellissimi*), and above all how many things the voice is required to do, and to what power of the spirit the voice is brought . . . the motive power of the chest are [*sic*] the principal causes of the voice . . . a conscious thing required of the voice, reverberation of the air, must issue forth with violence (*furia*), which when one breathes naturally, does not happen . . .

'Some are found, bass, tenor and every other voice, singing with much facility; and ornamenting, and embellishing with the throat, make passages, now in the bass, now in the middle, and now in the treble, very fine (*bellissimi*) to hear . . . the passage-making (*passagiata*) voice . . . is no other than a sound produced by the minute and controlled reverberation of the air in the throat, with intent to please the ear . . .

'One should extend the tongue so that the tip reaches and touches the roots of the teeth below . . . one should hold the mouth open, and exactly, no more than it is held when one talks with friends . . . one should push the breath with the voice little by little, and be very careful that it does not come out through the nose, or through the palate, for one and the other would be a very great fault . . . One should frequent those who sing in the throat with much fluency, because listening to it leaves in the memory a certain image and conception, which implants no small aid . . .

'The pupil, counselled by [i.e. listening, literally, to] the Echo of his voice, and informed of his accents by [watching himself in] the mirror, and helped by continual exercise, and likewise by listening to those who sing fluently, will acquire such a disposition that he will easily be able to apply passages [florid ornamental figuration] in every sort of madrigals or motets.'

(23) Alfonso Fontanelli, letter to Alfonso d'Este, Duke of Ferrara, dated Naples, 16 September 1594, preserved in Archivio di Stato, Modena, quoted by Anthony Newcomb, in 'Carlo Gesualdo and a Musical Correspondence of 1594', *Musical Quarterly*, LIV (Oct. 1968), p. 432:

'Don Antonio, who is the leading bass of Naples [and] who was form-erly in the service of Your Highness, has truly a fine voice (*bella voce*) and supports (*fonda*) [it] most sweetly; nor is his voice in the low [register] at all inferior to the high and to the middle, but all are very equal, which is a fine quality (*bella parte*).'

(24) Ercole Bottrigari, *Il Desiderio*, Venice, 1594, ed. of 1599, p. 40:

'Good voices, and fine (*belle*), and graceful manners of singing (*cantare*).' [*Bel canto* in so many words.]

(25) Claudio Monteverdi, letter to the Duke of Mantua, 9 June, 1610:

'A fine voice, strong and long; and singing in the chest, he reached all places very well.'

(26) Letter, writer unknown, from Milan, 29 August 1611, praising the prima donna Adriana Basile Baroni, quoted in Alessandro Ademollo, *La bell'Adriana ed altre virtuose*, Città di Castello, 1888, pp. 175–7:

'The sweet sighs, the discreet accents, the restrained embellishment, the felicitous carryings (*portate*), the daring descents, the high ascents' the interrupted passages, the driving on, the dying away of a note . . .,

(27) Vincenzo Giustiniani, *Discorso sopra la musica*, [1628], ed. A. Solerti, *Le origini del melodramma*, Turin, 1903, p. 108:

'To diminish and increase the voice loudly or softly, thinning or swelling, according as it comes opportunely, now with dragging, now dividing, with the accompaniment of a soft interrupted sigh, now drawing long passages, followed well, detached, now *gruppi* [trills], now by leaps, or with long *trilli* [single-note trills], now with short, and now with sweet passages and things softly sung . . . and with pronoun-cing the words distinctly in such a manner that one might hear even the last syllable of every word, which was not interrupted or suppressed by passages or other ornaments.

p. 121: 'And above all making the words well understood, applying to each syllable a note now soft, now loud, now slow, now fast, showing in the face and in gestures a sign of the idea of which one is singing, but with moderation and not excesses.'

(28) Ignazio Donati, *Il secondo libro de motetti a voce sola*, Venice, 1636, *Parte per sonare*, preface:

'One must try to have the boy practice solfeggio well with a strong and full voice . . . for the first times [the exercises] are not to be sung with much speed, but on repeating [them] always a little more, with more speed, to produce the habit of singing them all in one breath . . . so many times A, so many times E, and so many times O, with the voice and the breath equal from the first to the last note . . . the mouth half open so as not to lose so much breath . . . keep the head high, with the glance upward, try very hard not to raise the eyebrows, not to move the lips, and not to make an unseemly expression of the face; but see that it is possible to beat the throat with the Adam's apple [*nodo del Gargozzo*], since this is the true [manner].'

(29) Giano Nicio Eritreo (pseudonym of Giovanni Vittore Rossi), *Pinacotheca altera*, II, Cologne [actually Amsterdam], 1645, p. 217:

'Moving his voice gradually from the lowest to the highest sound, and the same from the highest to the lowest, passing it through various turnings with incredible fluency, [Loreto Vittori] showed that he could twist and bend it, like the softest wax, wherever he wished . . . [p. 218] swift and splendid, and capable of being made most apt to any alteration . . . high, low, swift, slow, great, slight . . . for each passion of the soul its own kind of voice.'

(30) Pier Francesco Tosi, *Opinioni de' cantori*, Bologna, 1723, p. 14:

'Unite [the head voice, called by Tosi *falsetto*] with the chest voice, so that they may not be distinguished one from the other, for if the union is not perfect, the voice will be of several [disunited] registers, and consequently it will lose its beauty (*bellezza*).

[p. 100:] 'The mellifluous study of the carrying of the voice (*Portamento di voce*)' [explained by J. F. Agricola in his German translation, entitled *Anleitung zur Singekunst*, Berlin, 1757, p. 220, thus: 'To carry the voice (*portar la voce*) means to draw one note to the other with continuous sustaining, increasing and decreasing in strength, without ceasing and breaking off.']

(31) Joachim Quantz, Autobiography (1754), in Marpurg, *Historisch-kritische Beyträge*, I, Berlin, 1755, pp. 231–2:

'[Paita's tenor voice] would not have been by nature so fine and even, if he himself, through art, had not known how to join the chest voice with the head voice.

[p. 235: Carestini] 'had a great dexterity in passages, which he, according to the good school of Bernacchi, like Farinelli, produced with the chest.'

(32) Jean-Philippe Rameau, *Code de Musique Pratique*, Paris, 1760, p. 17:

'One notices the degree of breath during which the sound has its greatest beauty, whether for power, or whether for colouring; one returns to it frequently, one tries to give this sound at the first impact of the breath, without forcing and without constriction . . .

'The breath must be so managed during the florid passages as not to

56

force them . . . yet to give more breath a few days later, to test if one can do so without forcing; then finally to augment and diminish it during the same florid passage . . .'

(33) Charles Burney, *Present State of Music in Germany*, London, 1773, II, p. 111:

'[Schmelling's] voice was sweetly toned, and she sang perfectly well in tune. She has an excellent shake [trill], a good expression, and facility of executing and articulating rapid and difficult divisions, that is astonishing . . .

[p. 174: Senesino] 'sang rapid *allegros* with great fire, and marked rapid divisions, from the chest, in an articulate and pleasing manner . . .

[p. 179: Orfino] 'articulated divisions . . . always from the breast [chest].

[p. 188: Faustina's] 'execution was articulate and brilliant. She had a fluent tongue for pronouncing words rapidly and distinctly, and a flexible throat for divisions, with so beautiful and quick a shake [trill], that she could put it in motion at short notice, just when she would. The passage might be smooth, or by leaps, or consist of iterations of the same tone, their execution was equally easy to her, as to any instrument whatsoever.'

(34) Giambattista Mancini, *Pensieri, e Riflessioni Pratiche sopra il Canto Figurato*, Vienna, 1774, p. 12:

'[Ferri] in a single breath ascended and descended two full octaves, continually trilling, and marking all the chromatic steps with so much accuracy, even without accompaniment, that if the Orchestra suddenly played that note on which he found himself, whether it be a flat, or whether it be a sharp, one felt at the same instant an accord so perfect as to surprise everyone.

'[p. 45:] There is no doubt that among so many difficulties that are met in the art of singing, the greatest is perhaps that of uniting well these two registers [of the chest, *petto*, and of the head, *testa*]: but yet it becomes not impossible to overcome it for him who will study earnestly to do it.

'[p. 52:] when the singer pushes his breath and forces violently the bellows of the voice . . . the intonation is then very uncertain, it robs brightness and agility from the voice . . .

'[p. 85:] When there is occasion to have to sing in some vast crowded Church, or Theatre, it happens very often that that Musician is mistaken about the extent [i.e. the carrying-power] of his own voice . . . and therefore to hear clearly a strong repercussion of his own voice in his own ear, he forces . . .

'He then who has once tested his voice, and has with repeated experience found it sufficient to make itself heard in any vast location, although sometimes it may seem to him weak, and feeble; he must not for this [reason] force it, but must accept that on the audience it is making its normal impression . . . forcing the voice is always one of the biggest mistakes that a singer can make.'

(b) There are several features recurring through these descriptions which may surprise modern singers and teachers of singing: particularly the repeated insistence on developing and exploiting the chest voice as fully as the head voice, besides uniting them into an unbroken compass throughout the registers.

But none of this would have surprised nineteenth-century singers and teachers of singing. On the contrary, their instructions read remarkably along the same lines; and their surviving recordings from the early twentieth century (for the most part made in old age, when their voices were impaired although their voice-production was not) appear to confirm their continued alliegance to the technical methods of the baroque period.

We may therefore turn to the evidence of these recordings for what they have to tell us about the last great period of Italian *bel canto* technique.

3. RECORDINGS OF BEL CANTO VOICE-PRODUCTION

(a) It is immeasurably fortunate for us that the last exponents of true Italian *bel canto* just overlapped with the first achievements of recorded sound.

It is obvious, indeed, that the most interesting and authentic of these late *bel canto* singers were past their prime when the opportunity of recording them first occurred. Nevertheless, it is one sign of true *bel canto* technique that while the beauty of the voice inevitably fades with old age, the purity and accuracy and finesse do not. The voice is not worn out, as it will long have been worn out if produced by any other method: it is merely tired, less well supported, not capable of so long a breath, and largely deprived of its youthful bloom.

We must not forget that we are hearing, with a few exceptions, voices wonderfully preserved at an age at which singers other than *bel canto* singers will have no voice left at all. It is the more remarkable that their vocal quality still glows so warmly, while their technical procedures are almost as clearly displayed as if they had been able to make recordings in their middle years.

Further, it is obvious that the engineering techniques by which the early recordings were made range from disastrous at the worst to moderately and sometimes surprisingly faithful at the best. At the worst, a few radiant but tantalising phrases emerge through a blast of surface noise. At the best, the accompaniment may still be rather a caricature, but the voice itself may emerge with startling clarity and uncanny beauty through a surface noise which is never slight, but which with a little good will can be ignored mentally. We must always allow, of course, for some substantial loss of colour in the recording of the voice itself.

Many old recordings have been re-recorded now for better hearing and easier accessibility; there are even regular broadcasts on some radio stations. We have much to learn from them.

(b) Almost the oldest and perhaps the most interesting of the singers thus recorded is the soprano Adelina Patti (1843–1919). She made a good recording of Lotti's 'Pur dicesti' in December, 1905, at the age of sixty-two (Gramophone and Typewriter Company, 03052), a very fine example of her art. Her famous trill is beautifully heard: it is narrower than a semitone; and there are other ornaments no less exquisite. But still more noteworthy are the astonishingly warm and sustained cantilena and the sharp and artistic declamation of the words, both very character-istic of the *bel canto* style at its best and purest. No less wonderful is her recording, at the same date, of 'Casta diva' from Bellini's *Norma* (G and T, 03082).

A fascinating comparison is the soprano Emma Albani (1847–1930) in her recording of 'Ombra mai fu' from Handel's *Serse*, made in 1904 at the age of fifty-seven (G and T, 53325). There is, rather surprisingly, no added cadenza; and the execution of the ornaments, not at all surprisingly, is far from correctly Handelian. But as a specimen of finely spun cantilena and unflagging vocal imagination, this is indeed a revelation to modern ears. A vibrato is never quite absent, but it is never very big, and it is varied from note to note, quite considerably, and with consummate artistry and control.

A little later comes the contralto Eugenia Mantelli (1860–1926), for example in 'Non più mesta' from Rossini's *La Cenerentola* (recorded U.S.A. 1904–5 on Dark Green Zonophone 12615); and the contralto Guerrina Fabbri (1866–1946), for example in the 'Rondò' from Rossini's *L'Italiana in Algeri* (recorded Milan, 1903, on G and T, 053007). Fabbri's tone is incredibly bright and open: the very opposite of the fruity contraltos of a later date. The chesting in her lower register is of re-markable darkness and power; the attack on her notes is sometimes terrific, but done quite without *coup de glotte*. She opens her throat with great suddenness; but without quite stopping the tone beforehand, so that the effect is not so much staccato as forcibly portato. It is as clean as it is sudden; but it is not at all explosive.

An outstanding *bel canto* tenor can be heard in the recording (Milan,

1903, on G and T, 52017) by Francesco Marconi (1853–1916) of 'Stanze' from Anton Rubinstein's *Nerone*; and another in the recording (Milan, 1904, on G and T, 052078) by Fernando de Lucia (1860–1925) of 'Ecco ridente' from Rossini's *Barbiere di Siviglia*, where the embellishments are exceedingly ornate and the agility at the full power of the voice is astounding, although the charm of voice-production is decidedly less.

The agility and lightness even of a *bel canto* bass can be heard in a recording such as that by Francesco Navarini (1855–1923) of 'La calunnia' from Rossini's *Barbiere* (Milan, 1906–7, on Fonotipia 74033). There is some exquisite descending glissando (done properly on steps of the scale, not as a slide); and incidently some quite striking parlando, used after the manner of the time for strictly comic purposes. It is not heard at all in this singer's other and more serious recordings, such as 'Vieni la mia vendetta' from Donizetti's *Lucrezia Borgia*, a wonderful example recorded at the same place and time (Fonotipia 62026).

For pure warmth, beauty and continuity of line in a baritone voice, an excellent example is the recording (made on Fonotechnica C5002 in 1920, at the age of sixty-four) of Tosti's *Ideale* by Mattia Battistini (1857–1928). Every word is clearly enunciated, and every enunciation is artistically exploited for its musical value. But there is no coup de glotte. There are no hard gaps in the sound, and no explosive attacks. Once more, there is a sort of portamento of the breath, often punctuating but never chopping up the phrases. The high baritone register is of astonishing power and brightness, yet without a hint of ranting or of tearing. There is, perhaps, just a foretaste of that extra-musical dramatization which afterwards went to inartistic extremes in the *verismo* style. But there is nothing inartistic here. It is cantilena as cantilena ought to be.

Throughout the whole of this culminating period of *bel canto*, the beneficent influence of the younger Garcia (1805–1906), Spanish by descent but Italian of the Italians by style and conviction, continued as it must have seemed unendingly, though in fact it led on to the beginning of the end. We have, amazingly, recordings by so old a Garcia pupil as the baritone Sir Charles Santley (1834–1922), knighted in old age for his singing: a remarkable occurrence indeed at that time. We can hear him in 'Non più andrai' from Mozart's *Figaro* on a recording made in 1903 at the age of sixty-nine (G and T, 052000); and by way of contrast, in Watson's all too popular ballad, *The Vicar of Bray* (recorded at the same time on G and T, 2–2863), as a reminder of how often high vocal artistry went with low musical taste in Victorian programmes.

A much younger Garcia pupil was the soprano Marie Tempest (1864–1942), well heard in her recording while still in her prime (1901, on Black G and T, 3233) of the 'Air des bijoux', from Gounod's *Faust*.

It is interesting to compare with this the soprano Mafalda Salvatini (1886–   ), a pupil of Jean de Reszke and Pauline Viardot-Garcia (daughter of the elder Garcia); for example, on her recording, also in her splendid prime, of Nardini's *La barchetta* (recorded *c.* 1920, Polydor 19231). It is impossible to imagine a more ecstatic flow of pure and unflawed cantilena; and equally impossible to imagine it without having heard it as it is done here and elsewhere among the numerous surviving recordings of that golden age.

For they are not, as is sometimes imagined, few and unsatisfactory. They are very numerous indeed; and on very many of them, the voice, at least, comes through in superlative quality. The accompaniment (being inevitable placed further from the acoustic horn which had to gather in the sound) does not; the scratching has mentally to be ignored, but only in the worst cases is this difficult to do. What we can learn and enjoy of the pure *bel canto* tradition from this available treasury of early recordings is incomparably worth the difficulty.

A little outside the pure Italian tradition, but still well within the *bel canto* style, come the two Polish-born brothers de Reszke, the tenor Jean (1850–1925), and the bass Eduard (1855–1917). Jean de Reszke can hardly be heard on two catastrophic cylinders from which the best that can be done has been well taped off by the former curator of the outstanding Historical Sound Recordings Collection at Yale University, Jerrold Moore, my valued guide in the present discussion. It is just possible to hear that Jean de Reszke takes the 'Forging Song' from Wagner's *Siegfried* in a vigorous but mellifluous cantilena without a trace of shouting (Mapleson Cylinder recorded – pre-electrically! – during the actual performance at the Metropolitan Opera House on 19 March, 1901). Eduard de Reszke can be quite well heard in 'Ernani infelice' from Verdi's *Ernani* (recorded 1903, on Columbia 1221). There is a deliberate pathos here which, though still entirely musical, points the way once more to the exaggerated and at times quite unmusical pathos of the subsequent *verismo* school.

4. THE DECLINE OF THE BEL CANTO STYLE

(a) The decline of *bel canto* came somewhat unexpectedly, and not from such external causes (though they exacerbated it) as World War I or II or the hectic influence of air travel (allowing too many engagements).

There were two prime causes: one for which Puccini can be blamed, and the other for which Wagner can be blamed, in both cases not altogether fairly, but not altogether unfairly either.

(i) Puccini was the greatest of the *verismo* opera composers. Yet the soprano Cesira Ferrani (1862–1943), whom Puccini must have liked (since she created several of his roles), was not a singer in the *verismo*

61

style, as can be heard on her recording (1903, on G and T, 53282) of 'Addio' from Puccini's *Bohème*. There is no *coup de glotte*, no undue stretching of the tempo for cheap effect, no dynamic excess, no interpolated screams, no sobbing or catching of the breath. The cantilena is full of vocal nuances; but they are vocal, and they are musical, not inserted into the music to serve supposedly (but not very genuinely) realistic purposes.

This is no longer quite to be said of one of the first unmistakable *verismo* singers, the soprano Emma Carelli (1877–1928), as can be heard in her recording of the same famous scene (recorded in 1904 on G and T, 053029). The fabulous tenor Enrico Caruso (1873–1921) completed both the debasement and the glorification of the *verismo* style, as can be heard, for example, on his recording of 'E lucevan le stelle' from Puccini's *Tosca* (recorded 1909 on Victor 87044), when compared with his own much less exaggerated, earlier recording of the same piece in 1902 (on G and T, 52349). His art, of course, was magnificent, in its own way; but it was not *bel canto*.

(ii) Wagner made increased demands on the stamina and cutting-power of his singers by his glorious use of the orchestra; but we must remember that he wanted, and eventually got at Bayreuth, an opera house with covered orchestra pit, which reduces the problem to a completely acceptable level. In any case, the only voice-production capable of cutting easily through a Wagnerian orchestra is a very forward but unforced technique, based essentially on *bel canto* principles, even when modifying them quite substantially.

This Wagner got, though we have not got much of it now, since most modern voice-production is covered rather than forward, and apt to be forced in the vain attempt to make up for that.

(b) The modification of *bel canto* technique which went the Wagnerian way, ironically enough, began with one of the most celebrated of the younger Garcia's pupils, the German-born soprano Mathilde Marchesi (born Graumann, 1821–1913). It is possible to see Marchesi and her school as the last summit of true *bel canto*; but it seems more exact to discern here the first small beginnings of the downward slope. Italian trained, and well trained, as Marchesi was, it is difficult to resist the conclusion that something in the native German tongue entered ineradicably into her habits of voice-production during the impressionable childhood years; and that this applies likewise to the numerous other great German singers (at least the northern Germans) of the generation she so signally influenced. It is something harshly or at least hardly consonantal, as opposed to the limpid though quite articulate consonants of Italian speech.

We can hear the hardness, together with an almost inhuman precision, virtuosity and exactness, in the most famous of all Marchesi pupils, the soprano Nellie Melba (1861–1931). It is positively icy in one of Melba's earlier recordings, such as that from Meyerbeer's *Les Huguenots* made in 1901, or the 'Melba Waltz' by Arditi recorded in 1910 (on Victor 88076): wild, heartless, stunning performances with nothing Italian about them except the consummate accuracy and the very bright and forward technique. Yet some unknown change took place in her personality later in life; and her farewell performance at Covent Garden in 1926, at the age of 69 (mainly unpublished recording, but available at Yale) is anything but heartless. It deeply moved those who heard it then; and it is moving on this excellent recording.

A far less dazzling but more endearing Marchesi pupil, the soprano Emma Eames (1865–1952) can be well heard in her recording (1911, on Victor 88010) of 'Vissi d'arte' from Puccini's *Tosca*. The soprano Blanche Marchesi (Mathilde's daughter, 1863–1940) can be heard in her recording (1937, on H.M.V. JG41) of 'Ah, methinks' from Handel's *Hercules*. This very late recording is nevertheless an excellent demonstration of the style. Nothing could be brighter than the Marchesi style; nothing could be cleaner. There is the cutting-power to come through any orchestra, though there is very little actual *coup de glotte*. But also there is very little true cantilena, and the phrases have some tendency to fall apart. And there is not so much as there had previously been in the way of purely vocal nuance and imagination. It is fine singing, but it is not *bel canto* singing quite in the old Garcia sense.

Other German singers of the finest quality carried the same modifications of the *bel canto* style to much further lengths, with or without a further dubious influence from the fashionable *verismo*. The soprano Lilli Lehmann (1848–1929), who was so favourite a singer of Wagner's, came too early to share in this ultimately very harmful tendency away from pure *bel canto*; but there is nevertheless something intrinsically Germanic, some inherent consonantalism from her native tongue, which makes her attack perceptibly other than Italian. There is also perceptibly less vocal imagination than an Italian of the *bel canto* tradition would have used. As a vocal singer, she is a little duller; as a dramatic singer, she does some pushings and stressings which look forward towards without actually being *verismo*. There is much *portamento*, rather more *coup de glotte* than would have then been done by an Italian, and a magnificent chesting on low notes which no Italian could have excelled. Her recording of 'Du bist der Lenz' from Wagner's *Walküre* (recorded 1907, on Odeon 50393) puts me most interestingly in mind of the soprano Frieda Leider (1888–   ), whom I so often and delightedly heard in Wagner, and to whom the not much less wonderful though vocally less varied successor was Kirsten Flagstad (1895–1962).

63

That is the line of descent; but not of *bel canto* in the strict sense intended here. Wonderful it certainly was, but not Italian. Lauritz Melchior (1890–   ) was the great Germanic (actually Danish) *Heldentenor* of that last great period, with immense power, ring and colourfulness, which some thought vulgar but most of us thought magnificent in his somewhat inaccurate way; but he was not much good in Italian opera.

Other singers who contributed to the rise of a distinctly Germanic or at least un-Italian school were the contralto Ernestine Schumann-Heink (1861–1936), still very Italianate in her chesting and her good *mezzo voce*, but very Germanic in her hard attack; and that wonderful Bohemian soprano, Emmy Destinn (1878–1930) a warmer singer, and less cold and steely, than any Marchesi pupil, but with considerable leanings towards *verismo* pathos. Schumann-Heink can be suitably heard in her recording (1929, on Victor 7177) of Arditi's Bolero, 'Leggero invisibile'; and Emmy Destinn in her recording (*c.* 1907, on Gramophone 2–43316) of 'Elsa's Dream' from Wagner's *Lohengrin*–a haunting performance of which it seems likely that Wagner would have much approved.

5. THE PROBABLE SIMILARITY OF ALL BEL CANTO TECHNIQUE
(a) It must be clearly understood that in this account of the last culmination and subsequent decline of Italian methods of *bel canto* voice-production, the aspect relevant to this present book is solely the traditional aspect before the modifications set in which at first altered and finally destroyed that traditional aspect.

It is not from Emmy Destinn, wonderful as she was, or even from Lilli Lehmann, that we can learn about the vocal methods which may stem from Faustina or Cuzzoni in the eighteenth century and even from Baroni or Archilei in the seventeenth. It is to be learnt, if at all, from Patti or Albani, from Fabbri or Mantelli, from De Lucia or Marconi, from Navarini or Battistini, at latest perhaps (but all the better recorded) from Salvatini, and in our own time, at the remotest sunset of the ancient glory, from Ebe Stignani. Theirs is the technique which seems consonant with the surviving instructions from the baroque period; theirs is the vocal art, at the same time intensely disciplined and radiantly flexible, which seems the nearest, within our still attainable experience, to the baroque descriptions.

(b) The immediate successor to the *bel canto* style was shaped in part by *verismo* excesses, attacking from within, and in part by a sort of Germanic hardness, attacking from without. Already by the end of the nineteenth century, the growing speed and certainty of international travel had encouraged a correspondingly international style of singing. A great singer would learn, because he could count upon being engaged for, a wide repertoire of different roles. The de Reszke brothers, themselves not quite Italianate, were prominent among the first singers thus to play the international circuit. The result represented a decline of *bel canto*, but not yet of singing. But that, too, was implicit; for other considerations than purely vocal beauty began to be in the ascendant.

At the present time, the *verismo* excesses are (fortunately) out of fashion; and the Germanic hardness has (unfortunately) been replaced by a tendency, far more destructive of good singing, to cover the sound. The hard singing was still good singing: it was forward, and therefore it was bright; it was unforced, and therefore it could ring and carry.

(c) There is no reason whatsoever to associate *verismo* excesses with baroque singing, impassioned and dramatic though we certainly know that to have been. Nor is it a hard ring nor a violent attack of which we seem to be reading in the baroque descriptions.

But it is a forward voice-production, and (very important) it is an articulate enunciation, such as can be heard on the recordings of Italian *bel canto* before the changes set in which gradually modified it out of existence, so that to recapture it now we must, if we really mean business, at least make the best use we can of these recordings. They are available in a number of important collections, such as those at Yale University (Historical Sound Recordings Collection), in the New York Public Library (Rodgers and Hammerstein Archives of Recorded Sound), in London at the British Institute of Recorded Sound, and elsewhere.

6. MAIN FEATURES OF BEL CANTO TECHNIQUE

(a) It must also be clearly understood that the lessons to be learnt, if they are indeed to be learnt, concern voice-production primarily, and interpretation secondarily and only in so far as it is inseparably bound up (as to some extent it is) with voice-production.

Certain features of *bel canto* voice-production do emerge with certainty, and link up with baroque instructions and descriptions almost as certainly.

(b) One unmistakably common feature is the exploitation of the registers.

If the chest voice is weaker than the head voice, or if the head voice is weaker than the chest voice, then that weakness must be remedied by hard and skilful practice (see quotations 22, 25, 31 and 33 above), until all parts of the compass are of equal strength (23).

When both registers are equally controlled and powerful, they must be joined impeccably. No instruction appears more insistently in baroque discussions, nor is better borne out in *bel canto* recordings, than the uniting of the registers (30, 31, 34).

But this does not mean our modern ideal of minimizing the differences between the registers, in the attempt to secure a similarity of tone over the entire compass of the voice. This can only be done by refraining from chesting the bottom, and by covering the top (which, among other grave disadvantages, makes clean articulation difficult and verbal clarity impossible).

On the contrary, the meaning as conveyed by baroque descriptions and heard on *bel canto* recordings is to cultivate a range of some few notes in the middle of the compass, where the chest voice can pass imperceptibly up into the head voice, and the head voice can pass imperceptibly down into the chest voice, without any abrupt change of register.

Chest sounds, moreover, can be brought up into head notes, and head sounds can be brought down into chest notes, for a better blend of power and brightness.

But the contrast between the registers, once reached, is exploited to the utmost. Even two consecutive notes an octave or more apart may be completely contrasted, the one a raw chest sound, the other a ringing head sound. Low passages are chested to the full, and high passages are headed to the full. It is this (especially the low chesting) which may seem rather startling to unaccustomed modern ears. But we hear it again and again on the *bel canto* recordings: we read about it in the baroque descriptions; and it comes to seem extraordinarily beautiful.

There is no *bel canto* without a proper equality, and a proper contrast, of chest and head.

(c) The placing of the voice in *bel canto* is as far forward as possible: i.e. right up in the mask.

This forward placing is, of course, varied for special effects. But it is the basically forward placing which gives that extraordinary combination of lightness with fulness so characteristic of *bel canto* technique.

There did not have to be coloratura sopranos then: all good sopranos were coloraturas. Mezzo-sopranos had the same agility, together with their transparent (because chested) bottoms; contraltos, instead of sounding lush and covered, were like lower mezzos. Tenor and basses shared in the agility, as their passage-work shows from Monteverdi on. It is particularly to be noticed how many baroque singers were praised (22, 31, 33) for taking their ornamental passages from the chest.

So forward a tone implies a certain fearlessness in the singer's personality. Only a singer who has come to terms with his own anxiety can dare to pour out sound as *bel canto* requires him to pour out sound. We today have not the nineteenth-century confidence, nor the baroque boldness, and it is hard for us to overcome our unconscious fear of emotion. But it can be done.

(d) Along with brightness and agility went the capacity for impeccable accuracy.

However rapid they are, and however difficult, the notes have to be there, not just vaguely, but precisely, and with precise intonation (33, 34). The more rapid and difficult the passage, the more accurate the placing and the breath-control required (22, 26, 28, 29, 30). Ornamental figuration was as much prized for its precision as for its invention, and for its flexibility as for its precision (21, 27). Variety was an admired quality (21).

(e) Through all difficulties, an unflagging cantilena must be able to be maintained. It must not fail for lack of support or of control. Without forcing and without faltering, the pure line of sound has always to flow on: never fluctuating unintentionally; never devoid of intentional inflection; but above all, just solidly and reliably there.

Once securely there, the cantilena can be phrased and articulated in all manner of nuance, both forceful and delicate. Legato and staccato can be brought within the line, and nothing is too smooth or too declamatory provided that the underlying balance and continuity is not disturbed. The shapely stream of sound can indeed be interrupted, but not disrupted.

It is for this reason that there is in true *bel canto* little place, and perhaps no proper place, for that explosive attack or termination which requires a *coup de glotte*: i.e. the abrupt and total stoppage of the flow of sound prior to its release, or subsequent to its completion. A stoppage not quite abrupt and not quite total gives a much more characteristic articulation.

Faltering and forcing are both negations of the *bel canto* style; but it is against forcing that we are more specifically warned (32, 34), no doubt because it is the more insidious temptation.

Even an accomplished singer, feeling overwhelmed by the orchestra, may force his voice in order to reassure himself, instead of relying on the purity of vibration to cut through and carry to the back of the hall, as nothing else can (34).

The pure and limpid sound, the perfectly moulded line, the avoidance of unintentional waxing or waning, the exquisite subtlety of phrasing and articulation, dynamic and rhythmic nuance: all this comes under what was called the *portamento*, the carrying of the voice (26, 27, 29, 30, 33, 34). It is of the very essence of the *bel canto* style. And of all these matters, so relevant to baroque music, the very first importance attaches to the ability to maintain the line; and the next importance to the ability, whilst still maintaining it, to mould it and divide it.

(f) In some sense (not very clear anatomically) the voice was felt to be produced in (rather than above or below) the throat (22, 33).

THE BAROQUE SOUND

Franklyn Kelsey, writing of 'Voice-training' in *Grove's Dictionary* (5th ed., London, 1954, IX, p. 65), quoted an 'old Italian singing-teacher in New York' as having said: 'You modern singers always seem to want to make your notes in your mouths. We old singers always made our notes in our throats, long before they came into our mouths!'

(g) There is general agreement that the breath should be unfailingly well supported from the diaphragm, and should in turn support the sound (23). This steady abdominal support is indispensable to good singing in general, and to *bel canto* in particular.

(h) A finely controlled vibrato is an integral element of *bel canto*. An uncontrolled vibrato is one of the worst faults into which a singer can fall, and once established, one of the hardest to eradicate. But a voice properly supported should be capable of the most steady and delicate control over what Praetorius (*Syntagma*, III, Wolfenbüttel, 1619, p. 231) already recommended (but in moderation) as a 'voice trembling and shaking (*zittern und bebende*)'.

Pulsation both of pitch and of intensity can occur in a good vibrato. The best singers appear to rely more on intensity fluctuation than on pitch fluctuation. The speed varies with the expression, but is never very fast or very slow. The width is not great at the most. The control is complete; and the effect is nearly always unobtrusive. But it is extremely beautiful.

Such unobtrusive yet beautiful vibrato belongs as much to baroque as to subsequent *bel canto*; a more obtrusive and occasional vibrato also occurred, but as a specific ornament, for which see Ch. XVI, Sect. 6 below.

(i) In *bel canto*, the enunciation of the words is inseparable from the production of the notes, both in their sonority (colouring) and in their articulation (declamation).

The baroque insistence (27, 33) on making the words intelligible is carried out in *bel canto* far better than is now customary. But there is also an astonishing singer's imagination in the play of sounds. Every verbal finesse is exploited: every suaveness or sharpness inherent in precisely enunciated consonants; every shading or brightness yielded by pure vowels at different pitches. Above all are the consonants to be made unfailingly distinct and articulate, even in the smoothest Italian cantilena (a necessity neglected by nearly every modern singer who is not Italian born and bred).

It is all incredibly subtle, and all immensely dramatic. The words are like a further dimension to the vocalization, and the combined effect is incomparably vital.

We can see very well, in the light of this, what Manfredini disliked (*Regole armoniche*, 2nd ed., Vienna, 1797, p. 55) in those singers who, while 'they have a beautiful voice (*bella voce*), nevertheless have not the style, the expression, or the power, and the spirit to move the feelings; they sing without zest, and without colouring; and they declaim (*recitano*) with so much indifference, that they seem like figures of plaster'.

There can be no proper *bel canto* without a full understanding and intelligent exploitation of the words.

(j) The story may not be literally true (there are others like it) that Porpora kept his famous pupil Caffarelli on a single page of vocal exercises for five years without allowing him (so the story runs) to sing anything else at all, but then dismissed him with the assurance that he was the greatest singer in Europe. The page survives (and can be seen reproduced by Marietta Amstad, 'Das berühmte Notenblatt des Porpora', *Musica*, XXIII, Sept-Oct. 1969, pp. 453–5, where she describes having been taught the same exercises by her own singing-teacher, a rare modern enthusiast for Italian voice-production). The surviving Porpora exercises, being mainly scale-wise without leaps or arpeggios, would not in fact suffice, and there must have been others. But the point of the story (that years of patient repetition and of careful correction of small faults, before they have time to grow big and ineradicable, go to the making of a *bel canto* singer) should not be lost on us.

7. THE NECESSITY FOR BEL CANTO

(a) Most musicians are aware that Handel expected great vocal feats in his Italianate cantatas and operas: but they may not be so well aware that Bach's cantatas and Passions are in the same basically operatic idiom and require the same technique of voice production; or that Purcell stood in the same close relationship to Lully and the French opera (as well as to such Italian masters of the voice as Carissimi); or that Monteverdi's or Cavalli's audiences might run into thousands, and were by no means the chamber-opera occasions which some of our more reticent revivals present.

Cavalieri seems to have thought that he was being reticent when in the preface to his *Rappresentatione di anima, et di corpo* (Rome, 1600), he asks through his spokesman Guidotti that the theatre, 'if it is to be proportionate to this recitation in music, should not be capable of holding more than a thousand people so as to avoid having to force the voice'. Doni's comment on this (in Chapter IX of his *Trattato della musica scenica* of about 1635) was that it would be all very well for 'a play of nuns, or of young students, and not for a drama performed with royal magnificence'. But to sing even to an audience of a thousand, in a performance including as Cavalieri's did much ballet and 'a large quantity of instruments (*gran quantità di stromenti*)', implies a big vocal technique, capable of filling a sizeable auditorium without forcing the voice. A baroque theatre might hold up to 5,000 or more.

(b) There was and is no place in any baroque music for an unsophisticated voice-production, lacking the power, the variety and the control of *bel canto* technique. Except as a rare and deliberate dramatic effect, there was and is no place for the so-called 'white voice', the notorious *voce bianca* so disapproved by all traditional teachers, so unsuitably recommended by those teachers today who believe that it is authentic at least for certain kinds of early music.

Both the choirs and the soloists for baroque vocal performances of the first quality, in church, chamber or theatre, were singers trained in the skilled resources of *bel canto*. Certainly they were capable, none better, of a chamber-music refinement (not at all the same as reticence). Certainly they drew a clear distinction between the styles appropriate to church, to chamber and to theatre. But in no circumstances was their interpretation deliberately unimpassioned or lacking in full dynamic contrast; and in no good professional circumstances was their singing acceptable without a highly developed voice-production and a highly resourceful vocal technique.

Bel canto is always impassioned, and generally declamatory. Even in chamber music, it is a dramatic style. It combines great subtlety and poise with great power and vibrancy. It is an art of contrasts and an art of effects. It appears to be the most highly developed art of singing which the West has known.

(c) The actual term *bel canto* literally means nothing more than 'fine singing'; and though perhaps not a standard term until the nineteenth century, it is approached very closely in the wording of such baroque passages as at (22), (23), (24) and (30) above.

For nineteenth-century singing, we can give the term a more explicit meaning; and it is only in this explicit meaning (i.e.) pre-Marchesi and pre-Caruso) that it appears to correspond with the descriptions from the baroque centuries.

(d) It used to be temperamental singers who expected to dominate the operatic scene; now it is temperamental conductors. But the margins of tempo, volume and nuance within which a great operatic role can be greatly sung are usually quite narrow. It may be much better for the conductor to indulge the singer a little than for the singer to feel either pressed or covered by the conductor. The singer must have considerable freedom both to set and to stretch the tempo for good vocal reasons.

Above all is this so if the singer is to restore the traditional liberties and refinements of the *bel canto* style.

(e) It is a further practical necessity that as many influential critics as possible should appraise knowledgeably such attempts as are now being made, not unsuccessfully, to re-establish *bel canto*, among the other prerequisites of better baroque performances.

A singer who may already have had to do battle with the conductor to be allowed the rightful ornaments (particularly appoggiaturas), and the necessary conditions of tempo and dynamics, needs knowledgeable critics to back up these progressive achievements. The critics, too, may have much to learn from our surviving recordings of the *bel canto* style.

8. THE REVIVAL OF THE COUNTERTENOR VOICE

(a) The countertenor voice appears to be nothing more mysterious than a predominantly head voice achieving its high tessitura by the perfectly normal method of employing a portion only of the vocal cords.

This is commonly called *falsetto*, but regrettably, since there is nothing false about it, and nothing abnormal. Indeed, the term *falsetto* was used by some baroque writers interchangeably with the term *testa*, head, as the opposite of *petto*, chest (compare 30 with 34 above).

When a countertenor needs to use the bottom of his normal compass, he must draw upon his chest voice in the ordinary way, to get sufficient power and colouring, or even to get the notes at all. In addition, he will probably possess a tenor or a baritone compass, and be capable of using this as an alternative tessitura. But being a specialist in the high tessitura, he will quite properly expect to stay within it, since that is what he has best cultivated.

(b) Male altos of normal constitution (i.e. not castratos) have remained a living species in the cathedral tradition, but became little regarded until the remarkable musicianship and vocal gifts of Alfred Deller brought new and timely attention to this (the so-called countertenor) voice, for which so many baroque parts were written. It is often possible to transfer these parts to female voices with excellent effect, but always with the loss of a particular character and charm well worth retaining if good countertenors can be engaged.

An extremely fine recording, by the male alto Alessandro Gabrieli, of Gounod's ridiculous *Ave Maria*, can be heard on Lyric 6603. Gabrieli's background, and that of this recording, are obscure; but his singing is pure countertenor, and of quite extraordinary power and beauty. Since he seems to lie well within the *bel canto* tradition, he may provide a valuable model, especially for the strength with which an outstanding example of this high male voice may evidently be endowed, given the *bel canto* training.

9. THE LOSS OF THE CASTRATO VOICE

(a) The loss of the male castrato voice, soprano or alto, is presumably (and hopefully) irreversible.

(b) The majority of the great heroic roles in baroque opera are soprano roles, or alto roles, composed in high tessitura for male castratos. One compromise solution is to drop them an octave, and to treat them as tenor roles or baritone roles. This is quite often done, in modern German revivals of Handel especially. But the musical results are seldom satisfactory and often disastrous. The whole texture of the score is upset by pushing what should be upper parts down into the middle of an orchestration never intended thus to cover them.

Earlier Italian opera has also castrato roles (e.g. Nero in Monteverdi's *Poppea*, whose part is in the soprano clef, but *not* Monteverdi's Orfeo, whose part is in the tenor clef). But here we can better accommodate a transposition to the lower octave (i.e. a tenor Nero) because we have to realize the accompaniment anyhow, and can do so suitably for the tenor tessitura (Nero's final duet with Poppea can be sung by a tenor mostly at written pitch).

(c) Another compromise is to retain the original tessitura of the castrato roles, but to give them to female voices. This can be really quite satisfactory from the musical point of view, and tolerably satisfactory from the dramatic point of view.

To have a female soprano or mezzo-soprano singing the part of a boy, or of a very young man, is not a difficult stage convention to accept. It does not, for example, disturb us at all in Strauss's *Rosenkavalier*, where the composer intended it and arranged for it with the greatest success. It does not actually displease us for the three boys in Mozart's *Magic Flute*, though good boy singers are better there. But the grown and warlike heroes of baroque opera do not accord quite so acceptably with palpable impersonation by female singers; and while we may still enjoy the performance (and much more so than with male singers at the wrong octave), we are inevitably not quite enjoying it, from the dramatic point of view, at its full original tension. Nevertheless, Handel himself often made this substitution.

(d) A less distracting compromise, dramatically, is to give the high tessitura to countertenors, i.e. to normal male altos, high or low, provided that we can engage singers of the requisite quality, strength–and altitude.

Castrato soprano parts may well soar beyond the reach of countertenors; but this may sometimes be met by a moderate transposition downwards, taking the orchestra down as well. The brightness will suffer somewhat, but not too greatly if the case is suitable. There is no objection in principle to reasonable transpositions in baroque opera; they were habitual at the time. Unmusical transpositions ought always to be avoided, and very great discretion is required.

Where reasonable transpositions allow a rather high dramatic

Heldentenor to take a rather low castrato part, we may count ourselves fortunate; but this will not generally occur.

(e) A radical solution, no compromise at all, is thoroughly to recompose the baroque opera with tenor or baritone roles in place of male soprano or alto roles. Gluck, for example, transformed his (Vienna) castrato Orfeo to his (Paris) tenor Orfeo partly by transposing the voice down a fourth and the orchestra up a fifth; partly by more or less considerable re-composing in the same keys as the original. We might well follow this example.

This would not have shocked any musician of the baroque period; and we have musicians who might be very capable of it today. But the difficulties both artistic and diplomatic would not be slight.

(f) And what about the original stage convention by which a heroic part was taken by a castrated man singing in a woman's tessitura?

Not every critic liked it in the baroque period; but on the whole, those were most hostile who were least musical. The vast majority of music-lovers, and all composers of serious Italian or Italianate opera, accepted it with the greatest equanimity. It could be and was ridiculed by some contemporary satirists at the time, as it is by some historians of our own time personally unacquainted with the object of their ridicule; but it could not have been taken so seriously over the centuries if it had been inherently ridiculous.

There have always been some critics who have regarded opera itself as ridiculous, on the irrelevant grounds that in real life, by which they mean outer life, no one sings his way through love-affairs, war-like adventures, intrigues and death-scenes in operatic fashion. The arts, however, are not concerned with outer life so much as with the inner experience, which they convey by stylization, so that one does not look for photographic realism in an El Greco nor for anatomical reliability in a Henry Moore.

The operatic convention uses the forms of outer life just so far as is needed to provide good dramatic imagery; but it makes, even in *verismo* opera (some would say most of all in *verismo* opera), a very poor show of being realistic drama. If we can accept the convention by which the hero sings (as a character not so much lifelike as larger than life), it requires very little more of us to accept the convention by which he sings (or used to sing) in a soprano voice.

We are fortunate, once more, in being able to hear recordings (made in Rome, 1904) by presumably the last of the long line of castrato singers, Alessandro Moreschi (1858–1922). We can hear him in Gounod's *Ave Maria* (G and T, 54777); we can hear him in Tosti's *Preghiera* (G and T, 54776) (1902–3). To do so is a very remarkable experience.

Contrary to our modern expectation, there is nothing feminine, still less anything effeminate, in this voice of massive weight and silky power. It is far more male and far more mature-sounding than any boy soprano. It outsoars any countertenor, both in range and in dynamic force. Just as one reads in the baroque descriptions, there is the strength of a powerful man, in the tessitura of a woman.

Moreschi's artistry is a little less interesting than his technique, and he does not seem to have been an outstanding example of his kind. But he answers our main question for us very effectively: he sounds, in spite of his tessitura, like a man; and he would have no inherent tendency to appear ridiculous in a hero's role.

If Moreschi at least carried the vocal weight to be dramatically and musically impressive, what impression might we not have got of Farinelli?

There is and there can be no real substitute for the castrato voice: it is just something which we shall have to do without. We shall, of course, want to stage Handel operas and others such as effectively as possible, which probably means giving most of the castrato parts to female singers. It cannot be altogether satisfactory, but it can be done very successfully, though a Gluck-like re-composing might be better still. We should certainly not wish to miss the experience of this magnificent variety of opera.

10. BEL CANTO AND THE BAROQUE CHOIR

(a) The voice-training of baroque choral singers, though not carried so far, was in the same *bel canto* technique as that of soloists. The best professional choirs were highly trained, both in voice-production, and in the use of traditional embellishments. We have almost as much to recover of their bright colouring and open attack as we have in solo singing. The same forward placing of the voice holds the secret of success.

(b) Modern choirs, however splendidly drilled and rehearsed, are inclined (i) towards either too white or too covered a tone, and (ii) towards too smooth an attack, to do full justice to the impassioned masterpieces either of renaissance or of baroque choral music.

'Devotion and passion' is what Thomas Morley (*A Plaine and Easie Introduction to Practicall Musicke*, London, 1597, p. 179) required of 'church men', who 'ought to studie how to vowell and sing clean'. The ringing sonority and the declamatory articulation of *bel canto* are the proper means to such passion and such cleanness.

We can hear just such a transparent ring and glowing clarity on early recordings by the Sistine choir at the Vatican (*Cappella Sistina*), for example in Mozart's *Ave Verum*, directed by Alessandro Moreschi (the castrato mentioned above), recorded in Rome (1902–3, on G and

T, 54767). Not only is this a most moving performance of a most moving piece; it is, to modern ears, something of a revelation in choral sound. The voice-production is about as forward as it can get, short of an Oriental and positively nasal technique. It fairly resounds with 'devotion and passion': it is as clean as a whistle; yet it is warm and vibrant into the bargain.

There is, indeed, a beautiful vibrato, as there has to be for all normal *bel canto* tone. But it is, as usual in *bel canto*, a vibrato rather of intensity than of pitch: a pulsation rather than a fluctuation. Therefore it does not interfere with the clearness and accuracy of the harmony. The more polyphonic the music, the less the width of the vibrato which is compatible with clarity; but a tone without vibrato is a tone without vitality, and is altogether contrary to *bel canto* principles whether in baroque polyphony or any other context.

(c) The usual *bel canto* exploitation of the words is just as necessary in choral as in solo music. The vowels are to be exploited for their variety of colouring; the consonants (above all) for their variety of declamation and their cutting edge.

English-speaking singers, with the impure vowel sounds of their native language, have great difficulty with the pure vowels of other languages: especially of Italian, where not even the shortest vowel is swallowed, slurred over or debased in colouring.

Nor is English a language of very precise and distinctive consonants, as Italian is for all its smoothness. The Germans have an opposite difficulty, since their native consonants are gutteral and explosive beyond the acceptable requirements of *bel canto*. French is a delightfully pure and incisive language, though the rather nasal quality native to its vowels makes for another kind of difficulty in different languages.

Pure vowels and incisive consonants are essential to good enunciation in the *bel canto* style. It is especially important to give the consonants a good cutting edge in choral music, where the words are in still more danger than elsewhere of getting swallowed up. One of the rewards of proper *bel canto* technique is that the words become so very much easier to hear; and that in turn makes the music more meaningful and more enjoyable.

(d) The average number for a baroque choir may be around thirty to forty singers.

Much smaller numbers were common, especially in the private chapels of secular or ecclesiastical dignitaries.

The famous memorandum from J. S. Bach at Leipzig in 1730 (see J. A. Philipp Spitta, *J. S. Bach*, Leipzig, 1873–80, Engl. transl. repr. New York and London, 1951), asks for twelve, or eight as a minimum, but calls sixteen 'much better'. Marpurg's lists (*Historisch-kritische Beyträge*,

Berlin, 1754, etc.) show 8 singers at the Prussian Court at Berlin, 1754; but 22 at Dresden in 1756. There are 7 at Gotha, 1754; only 5 in the Bishop's chapel at Breslau, 1754; but a strength of 10 soloists (2 short at the time) and 44 choristers in the Archbishop's music at Salzburg, 1756. The Paris Opéra in 1754 had 20 soloists and a chorus of 38; and the Concerts Spirituels at Paris in 1755 had 8 soloists and a chorus of 38.

Other sources convey a similarly wide range of numbers. For festival occasions, very large choirs indeed might be assembled. For normal occasions, we may aim at 8 to 12 as the least, about 30 to 40 as the average, and about 50 as the most singers compatible with the characteristically baroque delicacy and poise; not forgetting, however, that verve and impetus are also characteristic of the baroque scene.

Indeed, eight is really too few, having, in four-part music at two to a part, that same disadvantage (of being neither soloists nor a choir) which results from two violins to an orchestral part (neither string quartet nor string orchestra). The choruses in J. S. Bach's Passions and his B minor Mass, for example, are big music needing a certain weight and power, by no means ponderous, but not in chamber-music style either. As usual, robustness is one necessary ingredient for all the stronger sorts of baroque music.

CHAPTER TEN

Strings

1. ADAPTING TECHNIQUE TO STYLE

(a) Our problem with the voice, we have seen, is to get back enough of the right technique, and to build up the best possible style on that.

Our problem with the strings is to use our existing technique (which is very good) in the best way to suit the style.

(b) Before turning to technique and style, however, we must consider the changes made in the fittings and accessories of the violin family since the baroque period.

2. CHANGES IN FITTINGS

(a) Recent scientific investigations have given us a clearer understanding of the complex mechanical and acoustic factors involved in the materials and structure of string instruments, though they are not likely to improve upon the intuitive judgement and the empirical excellence of shapes and thicknesses which put the best of the baroque violin-makers into a class of their own.

(b) But whereas the body has not been improved, its internal and external fittings have been substantially altered. In brief: the bass-bar is longer and heavier; the angle of the neck is steeper; the bridge is a little higher and more sharply arched than the baroque average (but there were wide variations there); the strings are not plain gut but either steel or covered, and more massive so that they are tighter for a given pitch.

The sum of this leads to one result: greater tension. That in turn gives less freedom but greater amplitude of vibration. Hence the sonority is less resonant, colourful and transparent; more powerful, covered and opaque. That is in itself neither an improvement nor a deterioration; it is simply a change brought about by the changing desires of composers and performers. But for the purposes of baroque music, it is a deterioration.

(c) Whenever it is possible in baroque music to use string instruments with baroque fittings, the advantages of getting the more suitable sonority are very considerable. There is a warmth, an openness and a piquancy of tone-colouring which are extremely attractive, and extremely appropriate to the baroque textures.

This, however, will not be possible in most ordinary circumstances. String instruments with modern fittings are capable of doing an excellent job of work in baroque music, and as is so often the case, the conception in the performer's mind is really very much more important than the implement in his hand. There will be a certain loss in colourfulness and transparency, but a performer who knows what he should be aiming at can very largely, although not wholly, restore this loss by the proper use of technique.

(d) One possibility in some circumstances is to put back a baroque type of stringing, or partly so.

On the violin, a plain gut top E string at once gives a slight rawness to the colouring which is very agreeable. It has the disadvantage that on a sticky night, it will occasionally break in the middle of a concert: no great catastrophe, but tiresome, and modern audiences are no longer used to it. However, the steel E now customary (it came in a decade or two into the twentieth century) gives a very pure, sweet and ringing tone. The difference is substantial, but by no means crucial.

The bottom G string of the violin ought always to be covered (normally silver wire on a gut core). The earliest baroque violins used uncovered gut, but this has to be so thick that it does not speak very readily or very well, and for this reason, there was a distinct tendency in most early baroque violin music to avoid the G string. Covering (gimping) the lower strings of bowed instruments became habitual sometime perhaps in the second half of the seventeenth century, and is acoustically and technically very advantageous indeed.

The bottom string of the violin, the bottom two of the cello and probably of the viola, the bottom two or three (depending on the individual instrument) of the six-string gamba: in all these cases, covering is obviously desirable. But for the middle strings of the violin, and the top strings of the viola and of the cello, the advantages are in no way so obvious. Plain uncovered gut really does sound very much better.

It is now customary to use covered strings throughout, and of course they can be made to sound very fine. But always there is a slight metallic hint of grossness, perfectly noticeable to anyone who remembers what fine violin tone was like somewhat earlier in the twentieth century. It can also be heard by comparison with early recordings of the violin or the string quartet, from Joachim's remarkably pure but sonorous unaccompanied Bach (G minor Prelude, recorded at an age over 70, in 1903, on G and T, 047903) right down through the glorious Lener Quartet recordings of late Beethoven quartets in the 1920s and early 1930s. Joachim would have been using a gut E as well as A and D.

It is therefore very advantageous in baroque music to use gut strings so far as is practicable. But, of course, it is quite impractical to change strings back and forth at short notice: the whole instrument would become hopelessly unsettled. Only when another instrument can be kept at hand is it practicable for busy professionals, at any rate, to use a gut-strung violin, and perhaps a violin with its original baroque fixtures restored.

(e) If an additional instrument is kept at hand, a bridge of *slightly* lower arch than the modern standard may be found desirable by violinists or cellists particularly interested in J. S. Bach's unaccompanied suites and similar works (though less complex) by other baroque composers. But the lowering must only be slight, since it is essential to retain the ability to play at full strength on one string at a time without touching the adjacent strings unintentionally.

(f) Violins and violas were not fitted with chin-rests in the baroque period; hence old instruments ordinarily show wear in the varnish on one or (usually) both sides of the tailpiece. The absence of a chin-rest can only result in a slight (and if noticeable, undesirable) damping of vibration. Nothing seems to be gained in modern performance by dispensing with a chin-rest; and the player is recommended to retain precisely the type to which he is accustomed.

(g) Cellos, like gambas, were supported on the calves of the legs in the baroque period and later; but the modern end-pin is considerably more comfortable, and there are no musical disadvantages whatsoever in retaining it.

(h) Mutes were used on bowed instruments throughout the baroque period, but only for rare special effects, since the acoustically veiled and filtered tone which they produce is the very opposite of the open sonorities ordinarily characteristic of baroque music.

3. CHANGES IN THE BOW

(a) Some baroque bows were longer than modern bows, or about the same; perhaps the majority were two or three inches shorter; some, again, especially if used for dance music, were very short indeed. Some had a considerable outward curve; most had a very slight outward curve, virtually straight when brought to proper playing tension; some, again, had no curve or a very slight inward curve, and this last became common in the course of the eighteenth century. Late in the century the youngest (François) of the three celebrated bow-making members of the Tourte family perfected the logarithmic inward curve which has

79

since become standardized, as has the length within relatively small deviations.

(b) It is impossible to date with certainty the development of the movable nut adjusted by a screw and eyelet. Early pictures with bows often show a knob, which may have been attached to a screw; or the knob may be merely ornamental. Late baroque bows certainly had screw nuts; some early baroque bows may perhaps have had screws, but fixed nuts are found in some surviving specimens. Other devices for adjusting the tension were common, but we do not know how common (wedge nuts, ratchets).

Only one aspect of this matter is of musical importance, and that is to realize that the playing tension of a baroque bow should be really quite tight. It is possible that Sol Babitz, in his somewhat exaggerated articles, and even David Boyden, in his magnificent *History of Violin Playing . . . to 1761* (London, 1965), have not made altogether sufficient allowance for this fact. Thus David Boyden (p. 71) writes: 'The yielding hair of the old bow naturally tended to produce a somewhat yielding bow stroke from the player, and this method of tone production contributed to the more relaxed and smaller tone of the old violin, as well as to a more clearly articulated sound.'

The hair of the old bow is not, in my experience, more 'yielding' if the stick is a good one and is screwed up to its normal playing tension (as can actually be seen in early pictures). A modern bow, because of its inward curve, has to be screwed up very much less, and a modern player with an old bow in his hands hardly ever realizes at first how much more it needs to be screwed up to reach the equivalent tension. Nor is the bow-stroke more yielding. On the contrary, it is the rigidity of the bow and the crispness of the bow-stroke which contribute to what David Boyden correctly calls the 'more clearly articulated sound'.

(c) If an old bow is acquired of which the nut is fixed (which is occasionally though not very often found) or is detached from the stick and meant simply to be wedged under the hair (which is quite often found), it is bad antiquarianism but tempting in practice to drill out the end of the stick, fit a screw and allow the nut to be adjusted at will in the ordinary way. Old bows with a ratchet and loop for adjusting the nut can be very well used just as they are, and should not be altered to a modern fitting. Many, of course, will feel that no old bow should.

Whether the bow is an old one or a modern reproduction, it is essential to make sure that it has a good stick: i.e. laterally straight (in the sense of not being warped to either side); resilient (in the sense of retaining full and ample elasticity); and strong (in the sense of being decidedly stiff and resistant to bending).

(d) Whereas the fittings and stringing of bowed instruments have a significant influence on the sonority, the bow has a significant influence on the articulation. Both are important factors in getting a baroque quality and texture of sound. But whereas it is expensive, and may not very often be practicable, to have at hand an additional violin fitted up especially for baroque music, it is much less expensive and very advantageous to have at hand an old (or more probably a reproduction) outcurved bow.

(e) There is an implement called (quite correctly) the Vega Bow, and also (very incorrectly indeed, in common with certain others of its kind) 'Bach Bow'. It would have considerably astonished J. S. Bach, who never saw anything remotely resembling it. On the contrary, it is a purely modern invention, evolved under the singular and readily disproved misapprehension that Bach's unaccompanied solos for the violin and for the cello are meant to be played in full chords simultaneously sustained in all their parts. True, many of them are written to look as if they were; but the evidence is quite explicit that they are meant to be arpeggiated as necessary.

4. THE DOUBLE-BASS

(a) The modern double-bass inherits some aspects of its structure from the very large and heavy violin contra-bass sometimes encountered in baroque pictures and descriptions and rare surviving specimens; other aspects from the smaller and lighter viol contra-bass generally preferred in refined baroque performances. The modern double-bass is, in fact, an extremely satisfactory compromise, and serves very well in baroque music if sensitively played.

(b) The viol contra-bass, commonly called violone, which was the usual baroque string double-bass, had its own special charm and silkiness. Doubling cello or gamba at the octave below, it gives a beautiful warmth and depth with less robustness and massiveness than a modern double bass. It is thus a pleasant as well as an authentic alternative; but it is not a necessity.

(c) The word *violone* is simply the Italian for 'big viol' (from which *violoncello* becomes, oddly but lucidly, 'little big viol'). *Violino* is 'little viol'; and '*viola*' is 'viol'. *Viola da braccio* is 'viol of the arm', i.e. member of the violin family, played on the arm in a horizontal position, yet including (illogically but conveniently) the cello and the double-bass. *Viola da gamba* is 'viol of the leg', i.e. member of the viol family (in all sizes, treble, alto, tenor, bass, double-bass) played on the legs in a vertical position; all are (quite properly) called 'gambas' in America (*Gamben* in Germany); but in England, they are called treble viol, alto viol, tenor viol, bass viol (which size in particular is also familiarly called gamba) and violone.

But observe well that in baroque scores, part-books, records of payments to orchestras (as first and second violins, violas, violones and contrabasses), etc., the word violone does not always mean double-bass; it more commonly just means bass, in the sense of cello (or gamba).

5. HOLDING THE INSTRUMENT

(a) Contemporary pictures and descriptions show many variations. Dance-fiddlers, rebec-players and the like tend to set the violin against the chest, where it cannot be steadied by the chin or the cheek. Their vigorous tunes had no need to take them out of the first position: i.e., they stopped all the notes they needed without moving the hand along the fingerboard. They could have shifted up the fingerboard with ease, since the instrument is then merely pressed more against the chest; but getting back again tends to pull the instrument away; and though this technique is possible, it is inclined to be insecure.

But more serious musicians commonly held the violin on or against the shoulder, where they could and did steady it with the chin or the cheek when required (not necessarily, to judge from many pictures, as continuously as a modern violinist). A chin-rest was not used nor required. The chin or cheek could be placed either on the right side or the left side of the tailpiece, or even across it. All these holds are satisfactory when sufficiently practised. Very little pressure is needed (or indeed desirable) to secure the violin during the shifting of the hand; and the good baroque violinists had certainly a complete mastery of high positions, which their virtuoso music necessitates.

(35) Francesco Geminiani, *The Art of Playing on the Violin*, London, 1751, p. [2] (*sic*):

'Observe also, that the Head of the Violin must be nearly Horizontal with that Part which rests against the Breast, that the Hand may be shifted with Facility and without any Danger of dropping the Instrument.'

(b) In modern performance, there seems no advantage in departing from the modern hold of the violin and viola, nor in dispensing with a chin-rest.

(c) For cellos and gambas, and even double-basses, early pictures show some strange postures (for example, across the knees); but in modern performance, modern holds are normally the most advantageous.

6. HOLDING THE BOW

(a) There was also much greater variety in ways of holding the bow.

(b) The modern grip is right at the nut (heel, frog), with the fingers on top of the stick (the little finger may optionally be raised), and the thumb under the stick. This is very satisfactory for baroque music also.

(c) The modern grip can be seen in many late renaissance and baroque pictures.

But in other pictures and descriptions, the grip is more or less inwards from the nut along the stick.

This gives very much the same effect as using a shorter bow. Folk fiddlers and tavern fiddlers have always done it in vigorous dances where short, powerful strokes are needed. In a brisk allegro by Corelli or the like, a baroque fiddler might have shifted his grip up the stick to get greater incisiveness; in a slow movement he might have shifted his grip to the end of the stick to get as long an effective hair-length as possible. It is open to a modern performer to do this if he so desires; but not necessary.

(d) A quite different baroque grip also appears in pictures and descriptions, particularly of French violinists. Here, too, the fingers are above the stick, but the thumb grips, not under the stick, but under the hair. This grip can easily be mastered with practice, but it seems on the whole better suited to dance music than to serious music.

There is no baroque evidence whatsoever supporting the (modern) suggestion that with this French grip, the tension of the bow can be controlled by varying the pressure of the thumb on the hair. It cannot, as a very brief experiment will demonstrate. Watch out; you may drop your bow.

(e) For the cello bow or double-bass bow, the commonest baroque grip was underhand, as with the viol. An overhand grip, as in modern use, is however also to be seen in pictures, together with other variants; it matches violin articulation better, and is therefore desirable.

7. FINGER TECHNIQUE

(a) During the sixteenth century, the violins, then a new family, were in the main regarded as assertive instruments better suited to the dance and the theatre than to refined virtuosity or chamber sensitivity, like the older family of viols.

Sylvestro di Ganassi, in his *Regola Rubertina* (Venice, 1542; Part II as *Lettione seconda*, Venice 1543) presents instructions for a very advanced virtuoso technique on the viol, which does not seem to have been equalled on the violin until well into the seventeenth century. We find an advanced violin technique developing early in Italy and (with a typical polyphonic bent) in Germany. We find it causing surprise in England as late as the middle of the seventeenth century, when Anthony Wood mentioned in his *Diary* (24 July, 1658) his 'very great astonishment' at seeing Thomas Baltzar 'run up his Fingers to the end of the

Fingerboard of the Violin' [probably seventh position]. But Christopher Simpson, in his *Division-Violist* (London, 1659) takes the gamba, of which bottom note is *D* (or optionally *C*, the lowest note of the cello— or on seven-string gambas, *A*), up to *a″* above the treble stave, a range of three and a half octaves and the equivalent of eighth position on the gamba's top *d′* string. The difficulty of the music probably equals that of any baroque violin music with the exception of Bach's unaccompanied suites.

(b) We must draw distinctions here:

(i) Violinists of the streets, the taverns, the dance and the theatre: a large class, and no doubt ranging from wretched to very excellent in their kind, but neither needing nor presumably possessing an extensive technique.

(ii) Regular orchestral string players: also a class liable to great variations of standard, but certainly of solid professional ability in such famous and well-drilled orchestras as Lully's in Paris and Corelli's in Rome. Their orchestral parts show them as needing a sound technique based almost entirely on the first, second and third positions, with some fourth-finger extension, and an occasional shift to fourth position or fifth position. The half-position is also useful.

(iii) Virtuosos of bravura brilliance, such as Vivaldi and Tartini and Geminiani: as a class, showy and resourceful in very high degree. These used positions up to the seventh on all strings regularly; and this is taught by Geminiani in his *Art of Playing on the Violin* (London, 1751), and recommended by Leopold Mozart in his *Versuch einer gründlichen Violinschule* (Augsburg, 1756). Joseph Barnabé Saint-Sevin (L'Abbé le fils) in his *Principes du violon* (Paris, [1761]) shows a French use of eighth, ninth or even tenth positions; and Locatelli soars dizzily to the fourteenth in his Opus 3, *L'Arte del Violino* (Amsterdam, [1733]).

(c) It is very desirable, in ordinary orchestral and chamber string parts of the baroque period, to keep the fingering basically within the third position (with fourth position or fourth-finger extension to take in *e‴*).

The purpose of this is to help in keeping the tone of that forward and transparent quality to which contemporary descriptions point ('an honest and virile tone', Leopold Mozart calls it in his *Violinschule*, Augsburg, 1756, II, 5; and at V, 12, 'a good, steady, and as it were round, fat tone'), and which the implications of the music require.

The positions higher than the third should mainly be avoided in orchestral parts, and even in trio sonata parts and similar chamber music, not because they were not taught and used at the time, but because their veiled colouring, beautiful as it can be, is too special an effect for everyday baroque use.

Open strings, as a rule, need not be avoided; their ringing quality does not at all come amiss.

(d) But in solo music of a virtuoso character, everything on the fingerboard, and even off the top end of it, is appropriate. Baroque fingerboards were usually about long enough to accommodate seventh position; but in higher positions than this, it is quite feasible to stop the string by fingering without any finger-board beneath.

(36) Leopold Mozart, *Violinschule*, Augsburg, 1756, VIII, i, 2:

'Consistency of tone-colouring is achieved by [high positions of the bottom and middle strings] as well as a more even and singing execution.

'[V, 13: A virtuoso] soloist will do well to allow his open strings to sound rarely or not at all. [He] should make a point of taking all feasible passages on one string, in order to keep them in one tone-colouring.'

(e) Harmonics, both natural and artificial, were familiar in the baroque period, and were occasionally exploited as a showy gimmick. Otherwise, they do not really fit into baroque ideals of string colouring, and are best avoided.

(37) Leopold Mozart, *Violinschule*, Augsburg, 1756, V, 13:

'The result [of natural or artificial harmonics] is a quite ridiculous kind of music and one which fights nature herself with its incongruity of tone-colouring.'

(f) Thumb positions on the cello (and even, which we do not now do, on the violin) were familiar for solo work in the later baroque period. They have also been tried in modern times for high passages on the gamba, and there is no reason why not, if they are found convenient.

8. VIBRATO

(a) Vibrato, at least in some degree, comes naturally to most string instruments; and it is repeatedly mentioned by contemporary authorities through the sixteenth, the seventeenth and the eighteenth centuries.

The contemporary evidence for vibrato goes back at least to the 'trembling' of the fingers described for the viol by Sylvestro di Ganassi (*Regola Rubertina*, Venice, 1542, Ch. II): by Martin Agricola (*Musica Instrumentalis Deudsch*, Wittenberg, 1529, ed. of 1545, pp. 42–3); for the violin and for the lute by Marin Mersenne (*Harmonie Universelle*, 2 pts., Paris, 1636–7, trans. R. E. Chapman, The Hague, 1957, Bk. II, section of Lute Ornaments, p. 24 and p. 109).

(b) There is, however, an apparent contradiction in these and subsequent instructions for vibrato on string instruments. Some baroque (and indeed some classical and romantic) authorities recommend it for intermittent use: i.e. as a special effect of expression. Others recommend it for continual use: i.e. as a general contribution to expressiveness.

(i) Most authorities discuss vibrato (done either with two fingers, or, as now, with one) under the classification of an ornament, variously called 'Close-shake . . . when we shake [a second] Finger as close and near the sounding Note as possible' (Christopher Simpson, *Division-Violist*, London, 1659, I, 16); 'The Sting . . . wave [the stopping finger] downwards, and upwards' (Thomas Mace, *Musick's Monument*, London, 1676, p. 109); '*Batement* . . . made when two fingers being pressed one against the other, the one is held on the string, and the next strikes it very lightly' or '*Languer* . . . made by varying the [stopping] finger on the fret' (Jean Rousseau, *Traité de la Viole*, Paris, 1687, pp. 100–1); 'Close shake . . . you must press the Finger strongly upon the String of the Instrument, and move the Wrist in and out slowly and equally' (Geminiani, *Art of Playing on the Violin*, London, 1751, p. 8); 'Tremolo . . . when the finger is pressed strongly on the string, and one makes a small movement with the whole hand' (Leopold Mozart, *Violinschule*, Augsburg, 1756, XI, iff.).

(ii) But on the one hand, Jean Rousseau (in 1687) recommends that the vibrato should be 'used in all contexts where the length of the note permits, and should last as long as the note'; Geminiani (in 1751) likewise wants vibrato to be 'made use of as often as possible'. And on the other hand, Simpson (in 1659) wants vibrato used 'where no other Grace is concerned'; Leopold Mozart (in 1756) considered it 'a mistake to give every note' a vibrato, though admitting that 'there are performers who tremble on every note without exception as if they had the palsy'. (References as in previous paragraph.)

(c) Nevertheless, it seems very probable that this contradiction is no more than apparent.

All through the nineteenth century, and even into the twentieth, the same theory went on being advanced that vibrato should be treated as a special effect of expression, for intermittent but not continual use. Louis Spohr, for example (*Violinschule*, Vienna, 1832, II, 20), wrote of the vibrato: 'Avoid however its frequent use, or in improper places'. Carl Flesch (*The Art of Violin Playing*, trans. F. H. Martens, Boston, 1924, ed. of 1939, II, 40) wrote that: 'The vibrato, as a means for securing a heightened urge for expression, should only be employed when it is musically justifiable.'

But I myself attended Carl Flesch's master classes in the late 1930s. Neither he nor his pupils dispensed with the more or less continuous vibrato habitual among violinists, as I imagine, of any period; we learnt its use primarily as a more or less continuous but not excessive left-hand colouring of the tone, which brings the sound to life without degrading it; and secondarily as an intermittent intensification (needing musical justification) of certain notes requiring broader expression than the majority.

Recordings of late nineteenth- and early twentieth-century violinists show a very similar situation. Joseph Joachim (1831–1907), for example, even in the austerely beautiful Bach recording (in 1903 on G and T, 047903), used a very restrained but more or less continual vibrato, intermittently intensified.

Joachim's near contemporary, Pablo de Sarasate (1844–1908) can be heard with all his rather flashy virtuosity, including a virtuoso vibrato, in recordings of which a dazzling example is of his own *Capriccio basque* (recorded 1904, on Black G and T, 37929). In the same way, the Lener Quartet, for example, played Beethoven much more dramatically, and with a much more prominent vibrato, than the Capet Quartet at the same date; while the still older Flonzaley Quartet (in the most crisp yet poetical style imaginable) came somewhere in between.

On not one early recording known to me is there any violin playing in which the vibrato is not more or less continuous, despite the apparently clear instructions to the contrary in contemporary treatises.

Thus we have:

(i) A conspicuous vibrato, which in the baroque age was regarded as an ornament, and which in any age is treated (according to temperament) with a greater or lesser degree of circumspection.

(ii) An inconspicuous vibrato, which in the baroque as in any other age was taken for granted as the natural enlivening of string tone, of vocal tone, and to some extent of wind tone, and which though variable in extent is never altogether absent.

9. BOW TECHNIQUE

(a) All types of bow-stroke currently used, both plain and fancy, were also used in the baroque period.

But we have again carefully to distinguish between different situations. Most baroque orchestral parts should be kept to plain and simple types of bowing. Most baroque chamber music needs very little more elaboration in the bowing technique; and the same is true of many of the more straightforward solos. But the solos and concertos of the great virtuosi not only admit but require every variety of fancy bowing, to the development of which the baroque violinist-composers, above all in Italy, made so eloquent a contribution.

(b) The following advice by the Italian virtuoso Tartini is addressed to a talented amateur, and that by his German disciple, Leopold Mozart, is also meant as fairly elementary instruction.

(38) Giuseppe Tartini, *Letter to Signora Maddalena Lombardini*, 1760, transl. by Dr. Charles Burney, London, 1771, 2nd ed., reprint. London, 1913, p. 11:

'Your first study, therefore, should be the true manner of holding, balancing and pressing the bow lightly, but steadily, upon the strings; in such a manner as that it shall seem to breathe the first tone it gives, which must proceed from the friction of the string, and not from percussion, as by a blow given with a hammer upon it. This depends on laying the bow lightly upon the strings, at the first contact, which if done [at once]' [Burney has 'gradually', but Tartini's word is *subito*], 'can scarce have too much force given to it, because, if the tone is begun with delicacy, there is little danger of rendering it afterwards either coarse or harsh'.

(39) Leopold Mozart, *Violinschule*, Augsburg, 1756, V, 3:

'Every note, even the most powerfully attacked, has a small though barely audible softness at the start of the stroke; for otherwise no note would result. This same softness must also be heard at the end of every stroke.'

These are normal and elementary instructions for securing a smooth start and not a scratch. Leopold Mozart calls the softness 'barely audible'; and David Boyden (*History of Violin Playing . . . to 1751*, London, 1965, p. 393), doubting if it is strictly audible at all, cites but rightly disagrees with Sol Babitz' inference of a basic 'crescendo-diminuendo stroke' in baroque music (which leads to very unmusical results). The rounded moulding of a sustained and unflagging *cantilena* line is more important to baroque music than any detail; and gimmicky interruptions of it are apt to be disastrous.

(c) As a special (not a basic) effect, however, a 'crescendo-diminuendo' stroke was derived, by direct imitation, from that peculiarly vocal effect known to singers as the *messa di voce*, which was described in vocal treatises and practised in vocal performances throughout the baroque period and subsequently. The sound is started as softly as possible, swelled to the greatest volume, and diminished to the softest possible conclusion. It requires, therefore, a note of quite considerable length for its successful execution.

Geminiani, for example, describes approvingly what he calls the 'Swelling of the Sound' (*Art of Playing on the Violin*, London, 1751). He seems to attach it indiscriminately to short notes as well as to long notes. The *messa di voce* is not possible on short notes; and the kind of unpleasantly lunging sforzando which results from attempting it could certainly not be described, in Leopold Mozart's words, as 'barely audible'. Geminiani may have had in mind here simply a somewhat emphatic attack which, in his brilliant allegros, is appropriate and even dazzling, though it would not always be appropriate or even tolerable in the subtler melodies characteristic of J. S. Bach, of François Couperin, or of Henry Purcell.

(d) A very smooth and sustained cantabile is often desirable in slow movements.

(40) Leopold Mozart, *Violinschule*, Augsburg, 1756, V, 10:

'The [legato] stroke has necessarily to be started gently and with a certain moderation, and, with no lifting of the bow, taken with so smooth a join that even the most powerful stroke carries the already vibrating string over one motion into another and different motion imperceptibly.'

(e) Considerable slurring (whether or not shown or partly shown in the notation) is often desirable in cantabile passages.

(41) Leopold Mozart, *Violinschule*, Augsburg, 1756, V, 14:

'You must therefore be at pains, where the singingness of the piece requires no separation, not only to leave the bow on the violin at the change of stroke, in order to bind one stroke to another, but also to take many notes in one stroke, and in such a way that the notes which belong together shall run one into another, and be distinguished in some degree merely by loud and soft.'

(f) But in an average allegro (as opposed to one in virtuoso style) comparatively few slurs, sometimes none, are likely to be desirable; and these for the most part including only two notes, or four, or in triple rhythms, three or six. Fancy slurrings of unsymmetrical durations are perfectly characteristic, however, in passages of a more virtuoso kind.

(g) For the separately bowed notes of moderate rapidity common in an average allegro, the so-called *détaché* of the modern violinist is apt to be a little too heavy and much too smooth.

For us, legato tends to be the standard; for them, something between legato and staccato tended to be the standard.

Geminiani (*Art of Playing on the Violin*, London, 1751) recommended average fast passages 'to be play'd plain and the Bow is not to be taken off the strings', as opposed to 'a Staccato, where the Bow is taken off the Strings at every Note', which he recommends only as a special effect, and only on notes of moderate rapidity.

But Geminiani's 'plain' bow-stroke is not necessarily intended to be altogether legato either. It requires a motion very relaxed and very easy, yet quite distinctly articulated. To acquire this clear yet flowing manner of linking long passages of short or rather short notes in the typical baroque allegro is one of the most important steps which can be taken towards a good fiddling style for the period.

A loose wrist and forearm are part of it; but the upper arm can take a little share, provided that it is kept relaxed enough. The strokes, neither very long nor very short, ripple along with a quiet momentum, avoiding everything that is stiff or heavy. The bow is kept not too fast, and well into the string, but it lightens a little at each change of stroke. Not so much that it springs right off the string (as in a spiccato); just so much that the natural resilience of the bow is allowed to ease off the pressure. A possible term for this very characteristic and useful baroque stroke is *sprung détaché*.

(h) It is often though not always desirable to give the sprung détaché a little extra crispness of articulation by starting each stroke with a momentary pressure of the forefinger on the stick of the bow, which is immediately released as the bow gets into motion.

The degree of pressure can be varied from a slight sharpness to a marked accent. It is a matter of the hair of the bow biting into the string; but how sharply it bites can be controlled at will. When it does not bite at all, but gently slides into motion, the effect may be the normal legato which a modern violinist will ordinarily understand by the word *détaché*.

(42) Leopold Mozart, *Violinschule*, Augsburg, 1756, XII, 18:

'Gay and playful passages must be lifted up with light and short strokes, cheerfully and rapidly; while in slow and sad pieces, you perform them with long bow strokes, simply and expressively.'

(i) Spiccato on separately bowed notes, and spiccato runs in one bow both up and down, form part of the virtuoso technique though not of the plain technique of baroque fiddling. Jean Rousseau (*Traité de la Viole*, Paris, 1687, p. 73) spoke (though with disapproval even on the violin, and still more on the viol) of 'those runs up and down the instrument with rebounding bow which are called "Ricochets" '.

Leopold Mozart (VI, 11) gives pairs of notes in spiccato both up-bow and down-bow, but longer groups only up-bow. The prolonged down-bow spiccato is indeed a difficult stroke to perfect; but it is legitimate in a virtuoso baroque context.

(j) Staccato, as ordinarily understood both then and now, is produced by a momentary stopping of the bow between strokes, without lifting it. If this is done with light pressure or none, the sound is not abruptly stopped, but to some extent carries through. If it is done with firm or heavy pressure, the sound is more or less damped out. The first gives the lighter varieties of staccato, the second gives the heavier varieties. All these are useful in baroque music.

(k) There is, however, one variety of staccato which had no place in baroque technique, though it is common today; and of which the effect, when it is misapplied to baroque music, can be extremely bad. It is a kind of *martelé* (hammered) stroke leaving the string and returning to it with a violent impact (a stroke for which David Boyden could find no evidence before the late eighteenth century, and allows no place before 1750 at the earliest).

A baroque allegro taken (as is not uncommon today) with this massive stroke, at the heel of the bow, becomes far too assertive and weighty; and indeed it is extremely doubtful whether short strokes of any variety were ever taken continuously at the heel of the bow. In the celebrated letter from Tartini to Signora Lombardini, already quoted above at (38), the great violinist advises his pupil to practise short strokes assiduously at different parts of the bow: at the point; in the upper middle; in the middle; in the lower middle; but not (and this is very interesting) at the heel.

(l) By far the best part of the bow for continued passages of moderately rapid notes is in the upper middle: i.e. about half-way between the point and the middle of the bow. There they can ripple along very easily, neither too light nor too heavy, but just agreeably solid.

At the point gives greater delicacy; at the middle gives greater solidity. The lower middle gives the most weight which will generally be wanted.

Modern violinists, and above all modern cellists, do far too much of their work (for baroque purposes) in the bottom half of the bow. They need to use the middle and the upper half far more. This change of technique is of the utmost importance.

(m) For average baroque purposes, the bow should be pressed well into the string, and moved at a moderate speed. These, too, are crucial factors.

A very fast-moving bow, at rather light pressure, produces a rather tenuous tone, good in baroque music only for special effects.

A fast bow but at heavy pressure, on the other hand, can be very brilliant, and again is useful in baroque music only where a special brilliance in the music calls for it.

The bow is usually to be kept fairly well up to the bridge. Fingerboard bowings have their place, once again, only as special effects.

The best advice to give is often just to use less bow.

(n) It cannot be too often reiterated that to get the right quality of string tone is the very foundation of good and authentic baroque performances.

An elementary test of orchestral string tone is whether it lets the harpsichord sound through. Of course, it has to be a fine and sonorous harpsichord, finely and sonorously played, in a hall not too outsize to be suited to ordinary baroque performances at all. But then the crisp edginess of the continuo harpsichord should cut through, not conspicuously, which is not its role, but effectively in sharpening the entire sonority to a keener brilliance. If a good harpsichordist, using a good instrument, can be seen but not heard working away, it is generally too much thickness in the string tone which is covering him.

(o) Pizzicato was a familiar resource throughout the baroque period, though used, on the violin family, only for special effects and not as a regular recourse. Long passages of pizzicato bass though occasionally indicated are not much in character *and are normally to be avoided*, particularly in early baroque music.

On the viol, pizzicato (including left-hand pizzicato), mingled with bowed notes, was a regular recourse. We have to remember that medieval string instruments (and to some extent, renaissance string instruments) were not so sharply divided into plucked and bowed.

Ganassi (*Regola Rubertina*, Part II as *Lettione seconda*, Venice, 1543, Ch. 11) taught pizzicato on the viol as *percotere la corde* ('striking the string'–the normal term used by lutenists and others). Monteverdi indicated pizzicato in his *Combattimento* of 1624 as 'here one leaves the bow and one plucks (*strappano*) the strings . . . Here one takes up the bow again.' Other early indications include Carlo Farina's *Ander Theil* (Dresden, 1627). It is not necessary, of course, to wait for a notated indication, in an appropriate place.

(p) Chords and polyphonic part-writing are found, sometimes in great density, and particularly in unaccompanied music such as Walther's and Biber's and the solo violin suites and the solo cello suites of J. S. Bach.

No attempt should be made to hold down all notes, or any more of them than can comfortably be sustained. The technique is comparable to that of the lute: a full polyphonic texture is sketched incompletely in the actual sounds, but completed mentally by the ear.

It is usual in modern performances of unaccompanied Bach to strain much too hard in the vain attempt to sound everything that is written. But the written notation represents the music as it will *mentally* be heard, i.e. complete. The idiom of the violin, as of the lute, is to play as much of this as is practicable and comfortable, thereby *suggesting* the whole without any sense of strain. Nothing is gained by strenuously *forcing down* the strings with a violent pressure of the bow. A relaxed and easy style makes far more out of this tremendous music than any amount of grinding and driving. The less the effort and the stress, the bigger the reward in beauty and impressiveness.

One proof of this was well suggested by Sol Babitz ('The Vega Bach Bow', *Musical Times*, May, 1955): numerous passages in J. S. Bach's unaccompanied violin suites actually cannot be fingered as they are notated, since the fingerings do not all exist simultaneously on the instrument. We have also a direct statement by Jean-Philippe Rameau (*Pièces de clavecin en concerts*, Paris, 1741, preface) that on the violin, 'at places where one cannot easily perform two or more notes together; either one arpeggiates them, stopping on that [note] from the side of which the melody continues; or one gives the preference, sometimes to the notes at the top, sometimes those at the bottom'. Jean-Jacques Rousseau likewise mentions (*Dictionnaire*, Paris, 1768, entry 'Arpeggio'), this 'manner of performing the different notes in rapid succession', where 'a chord cannot be produced except by arpeggiation [as on] the violin, the cello and the viol . . . because the convexity of the bridge prevents the bow from pressing on all the strings at once'.

10. THE FAMILY OF VIOLS

(a) The viols share their basic construction and even their basic name with the violin family.

By *viole da braccio* (viols of the arm) are understood members of the violin family, the smallest members of which, at least, are held up by the player's arm. By *viole da gamba* (viols of the leg) are understood members of the viol family, all members of which (even the smallest) are held resting on the calves or thighs, or on the ground.

The important aspect musically is that the small members (and later, all members) of the violin family are bowed overhand; but all viols are played underhand. This influences the articulation.

(b) The construction and acoustics of the violin and viol families are essentially the same: the only essential difference is in the tension. The viols have thinner wood (the table is where this chiefly matters) and slacker (because thinner) strings.

Some modern makers are using too much thickness in the table. The instrument should feel quite light when picked up.

(c) Gut frets are tied at semitone intervals round the necks of viols. The finger, to get a good tone, should press firmly on the fret from behind; and it can and must control fine intonation by pulling a little upwards or downwards.

An excellent vibrato (best done, cello-wise, from the arm) is both possible and desirable. The frets are no impediment to shifting, if the thumb is kept relaxed behind the neck. Knot the fret, however, behind the side of the neck away from the hand.

The frets also give an added sharpness to the sound, somewhat like an open string. Since this is part of the character of the viol, it is undesirable though possible to play a viol without its frets.

The French term *doigt couché*, laid finger, describes a single finger,

93

especially the forefinger, laid flat across several strings behind one fret for certain chords, or other fingerings, as on the viol, lute, guitar and other fretted instruments.

(d) It is likewise undesirable though possible to hold and bow the smaller viols violin-wise, or the larger viols cello-wise. There is no point in using a viol at all unless its peculiar sonority and articulation are fully retained, by means of its own fittings, accessories and technique.

(e) When a viol is correctly constructed, fitted up and played, it is capable of a light but cutting tone of remarkable colourfulness, clarity and beauty. If its tone sounds weak, it is either a poor specimen, or in bad condition, or not being well enough played.

The strings, being thinner, go more readily out of tune, and the frets limit the amount of correction possible by the fingers. But except under adverse conditions of temperature and humidity, a good player can and should play extremely well in tune.

He should also be able to produce an excellent volume of sound. This, as on other bowed instruments, depends not on force but on the purity, the accuracy, and the fine control of the bowing. When the string is brought into the freest and steadiest vibration possible, the sound, like that of a finely produced voice, may remain relatively small under the player's own ears, but it will carry strongly to the back of the hall, and will there sound unexpectedly big and loud.

The instrument must, however, be set up with enough clearance between the strings for a full bow pressure to be used without fouling an adjacent string. It is necessary to play very well into the string.

It is perfectly possible to get a gamba to match up to a pair of violins and a harpsichord in trio sonata work. On no account should the violinists be inhibited by being asked to reduce their volume in order to balance with the gamba.

(f) The French preference for the gamba over the cello as a standard bass instrument continued at least until the middle of the eighteenth century, at the end of the baroque period. This was particularly true for chamber music and solos. Virtuoso composer-gambists like De Caix d'Hervelois, Marin Marais and Antoine Forqueray (le père) stand in the same relationship to French baroque music as composer-violinists like Corelli, Tartini and Geminiani stand to Italian.

In Italy, the cello took a much earlier lead; yet gamba parts can still be found specified throughout the seventeenth century.

In England, the gamba remained the preferred bass and soloist through most if not all of the baroque period, with the composer-gambist Christopher Simpson the most brilliant figure of a brilliant school.

In Germany, the gamba was a favourite soloist, as well as a common

94

inner part in chamber music. J. S. Bach composed outstanding obbligato parts for gamba in his Passions and Cantatas, for which the cello affords no satisfactory substitute; brilliant parts for two gambas in his Sixth Brandenburg Concerto, where substituting cellos makes too thick a texture; and three magnificent sonatas for gamba with obbligato harpsichord, which all cellists pardonably play; but these sonatas have a more brilliant sparkle and a finer balance on their own instruments.

(g) The English chamber music for the complete consort of viols in the first half of the seventeenth century is one of the great schools in the history of music. Its simpler examples in three or four parts can often be played effectively on the violin family; but not its complex examples in four, five or six parts.

The German dance music for consorts of viols in the seventeenth century is less interesting, but more accommodating instrumentally.

The French early lost interest in the consort of viols; but they retained the treble viol (and even the little *pardessus de viole*, built smaller and tuned higher) for solos of a sensitive and rather sentimental charm, much of which is lost by substituting a violin. But like the English and the Germans, the French composed their finest and most serious viol solos for the gamba (bass viol), which in this family has (because of its relatively light construction and tension) the finest solo tone and capabilities, being nearer in these respects to the violin than to the cello.

11. PLUCKED INSTRUMENTS

(a) Apart from keyboard instruments (discussed later), the most important baroque plucked instruments are lutes of various sizes and stringings.

The baroque lute, like the late renaissance lute, has a large and excellent solo literature, which is even less capable of being transferred successfully to other kinds of instrument than the best literature of the viols.

The lute, both in its standard (tenor) version, and in larger and lower versions such as the theorbo (with added bass strings) and the archlute (the same, or larger still), has also an important function as one of the many harmonic continuo instruments of the baroque period.

The technique of the lute is subtle and exacting; considerable virtuosity is required to do it full justice. The test is not simply the player's agility and capacity for catching difficult chords and counterpoints, but above all his ability to do this with good intonation and a finely sonorous and ringing tone.

One factor is to come up as firmly and closely on to the frets as possible with the left-hand fingers; the tone is duller when the finger merely comes down between the frets. Another factor is great precision with the 'striking' (plucking) by the right-hand fingers, the tips of which should press the strings (pairs except for the top string which is single) and release them vertically, rather than pulling them to one side.

An alternative, sharper sound is achieved with the finger nails; but though legitimate as a variant in lute technique, this is perhaps best in combination with the fleshy finger-tip plucking. The point at which the string is plucked also has a great influence in varying the tone.

Many modern lutes (especially among those made in Germany) have, like many modern viols, too much thickness in the wood, which changes their character. The whole instrument should feel very light in the hands, and the table especially should be thin and delicate. The resonance should not be massive, but the freest possible.

The volume of the lute's tone can never be increased by normal means (electrical amplification changes its intimate character and may not be desirable). But when well produced, it has very great warmth and considerable carrying powers. The lute is a fine soloist, and a lovely accompanist for a solo voice or a small ensemble.

Larger ensembles can have several lutes, and even (as in some masques) massed lutes up to a dozen or so.

(b) Baroque guitars, like baroque lutes, were as a standard double strung. In addition to their valuable solo literature, they were continuo instruments of accompaniment, particularly for the solo voice. It was, at least in seventeenth-century Italy, considered that the lute or the harp was the more suitable accompaniment for serious songs, but that the guitar was particularly excellent in a lighter vein.

(c) There were a number of celebrated harpists in the baroque period; and the harp, in a variety of forms, was quite important for solos, accompaniment and orchestral colouring.

The modern orchestral harp, a splendid instrument, serves well in baroque orchestral contexts, but less well for baroque solos and chamber accompaniments. In any case, its sonority is very different; and the more ringing and transparent sounds of the baroque instruments are more suitable when they are available.

CHAPTER ELEVEN

Wind and Percussion

1. THE WINDS MORE VARIABLE THAN THE STRINGS

(a) Unless the strings are playing transparently and incisively, the whole mass of the sound is incongruously heavy; and to remedy this requires an intelligent and deliberate effort. But somehow the winds seem to have more the habit of clarity. They are more naturally inclined to a translucent sonority and an open articulation.

(b) On the other hand, the changes both in timbre and in technique have been much greater in the wind department.

Wind instruments are capable of almost unlimited gradations of timbre. Every modification in the design, and especially in the bore, and in the reed or the mouthpiece (and there have been many such), produces corresponding differences in the harmonic content, that is to say in the timbre; yet these differences can merge so imperceptibly one into another that classification is much less exact and meaningful than it is in the string department.

Moreover, the modifications which can be produced by the player's own individual technique and preference are astonishingly wide. More than ever it is true that the concept in the player's head is of primary importance; for within limits, he can influence almost any implement in the direction which he desires.

2. THE FLUTES

(a) The renaissance and early baroque transverse flute is soft and cooing; the later baroque flute, altered in bore, sounds louder and more focused. Each is excellent in its own music; but except in small halls, there can be a problem with volume, and it may not be desirable to use early wind instruments unless the acoustics are sufficiently resonant.

Intonation is always a problem on early wind instruments, with their few keys and many cross-fingerings; but it can be overcome, in reasonable tonalities, with sufficient skill and practice. This has now been shown by a number of first-rate performers.

97

Whether early flutes or other early wind instruments are to be used or not, it is always very advantageous for the player to have had some considerable experience of them. He may then, knowing their timbre, be able to produce a passable approximation to it on a modern instrument. Not, however, quite the gorgeous baroque colourings.

(b) The recorder, in its different timbre, was also soft and cooing as a renaissance and early baroque instrument, and also underwent a comparable change of bore, resulting in a somewhat louder and more focused tone, towards the end of the seventeenth century.

The accuracy of intonation and the beauty of tone from a good recorder depend crucially upon the excellence of the breath-control, which needs the steady support and easy amplitude of a fine singer. The difference can be very great: a really pure, sustained and melting tone from a recorder is not very common, but it can be a perfect delight.

Some baroque parts can be regarded as more or less interchangeable between flute and recorder; others not. The effect is always different; but if it is good both ways (not otherwise), a baroque musician would not have hesitated to use his normal performer's option, and we need not hesitate to do the same.

On the other hand, where a recorder is actually specified, it seems a pity not to enjoy the very pleasant and distinctive personality possessed by this excellent instrument, provided players as excellent are available. In J. S. Bach's Fourth Brandenburg Concerto, for example, the music is in no way spoilt by using two transverse flutes; but there is something in the way the parts are written which is still more enchanting on two recorders.

It is important to remember that *Flauto* (etc.) ordinarily means recorder in baroque music. The ordinary baroque term for our orchestral flute is *Traverso* (etc.).

(c) Both on the flute and on the recorder, a greater variety of articulation syllables was employed than is standard today. This factor has a most significant influence on the attack, the phrasing and the articulation, and it should be carefully studied, by players of these instruments concerned with baroque music, in the early treatises and the modern discussions mentioned in my Bibliography.

3. THE REEDS

(a) The oboes of the early baroque period were not much altered from the shawms and pommers of the renaissance: broad in bore and probably in reed, they were raw and powerful instruments, more colourful than sensitive, and eminently suited to the outdoor occasions for which they were commonly employed.

The same refinement was given the oboe by late seventeenth-century makers (particularly French, with the Hotteterre family in the lead) as was given the transverse flute and the recorder. The bore of the oboe was narrowed, and its bell-flare lessened; but the reeds seem to have remained broader than ours, and the tone more pungent or quacking, though amply sensitive and not particularly loud.

There are still to this day divergencies of oboe tone; but the modern French school seems to head the fashion (perhaps less decidedly than a few years ago). This has carried the sensitive aspects of oboe tone almost to the point of emasculation. The modern orchestra could well do with some more pungent oboe sounds again (perhaps as an alternative); the baroque orchestra positively needs them.

The late baroque oboe has been successfully recovered now by many talented players; and both in sonority and in articulation it is wonderfully suited to its function. In much baroque orchestral music (whether indicated in the score or not) it doubles with violins; and to be effective, this calls for a fairly rich though rounded oboe colouring. In obbligato, chamber and solo parts, this baroque pungency is particularly desirable.

As so often with wind instruments, the player can do a great deal, even on his modern oboe, to modify his reed, his lip and thereby his tone in the desired direction, so soon as he appreciates that it is desirable. 'Equally mellow and piercing', François Raguenet (*Comparison*, Paris, 1702, ed. Strunk, *Mus. Quart.*, XXXII, 3, p. 45) wrote of the oboe; 'gay', wrote Jean-Laurent de Béthizy (*Exposition*, Paris, 1754, 2nd ed., 1764, p. 304); 'particularly suited to open-air entertainment'–and (p. 305) of the bassoon, 'strong and brusque' yet capable in good hands of 'very sweet, very gracious and very tender sounds'.

(b) The bassoon has always been, and still remains, the most idiosyncratic of reed instruments, with much variety both between individual bassoons and between individual players. Robust and colourful sounds, but well rounded, are again the sounds to aim at in most baroque parts.

The primary function of the baroque bassoon was continuo work: either as a single melodic bass instrument in chamber music; or doubling with string instruments (or occasionally replacing them for entire passages or movements) in the orchestra. And once more, this orchestral doubling of the bass line by bassons (as many as four or even six in big ensembles) was taken for granted, in suitable movements, without necessarily being indicated in the score. There are some fine obbligato parts.

(c) The position of the clarinet in the early eighteenth century needs further exploration. Handel, Vivaldi, Rameau and Telemann are among the late baroque composers known to have made some use of it; but oboe players seem more frequently to have doubled on the clarinet than has until recently been realized.

4. THE BRASS

(a) The *cornetto* or *Zink* (in English sometimes spelt cornett to distinguish it from the modern cornet), is normally made of wood, with a narrow conical bore and a small cup-shaped mouthpiece. It is a lip-blown instrument, and therefore belongs with the 'brass' (the actual material seems not to be of crucial importance). It is indeed, as its name states, a 'little horn'.

The cornetto, in skilful hands, has a tone of light but silvery brilliance and an agility of almost vocal flexibility. From Monteverdi to J. S. Bach, it has a baroque role of the utmost value; and there are now some modern performers well on the way to recovering its once dazzling feats of virtuosity.

But when indifferently performed, the cornetto is of a melancholy sound and an uncertain intonation. The best modern substitute, when necessary, is the orchestral trumpet. This gives the necessary brilliance, although not the strangely poignant and almost distant quality which lends the cornetto its peculiar poetry. Imagine high horn tone brightened by an edging of trumpet tone: that is the cornetto at its exacting best, and difficult as it is to play really well, it is worth recovering.

The serpent is not strictly a bass cornetto, having a proportionately wider conical bore and larger mouthpiece; but it shares the same remarkable agility in skilful hands, cooing gently or bellowing massively as the case requires. The tuba is its modern heir, but the serpent, too, is well worth recovering for its rather more woody personality.

In baroque practice, since true cornettos of bass register proved impracticable, other instruments took the lower parts: most usually, sackbuts (trombones).

(b) Hunting horns make rare appearances in the scores of appropriate scenes of the earlier baroque operas, and were perhaps used more often than the scores reveal; but not till the age of Bach and Handel have we to consider the horn as a fairly regular orchestral instrument. The bore is conical, but long and narrow; the mouthpiece narrow but more or less tapered; the tone as colourful as a trumpet, but mellower, with a refinement of poetical sensitivity all its own.

But the late baroque horn differs considerably from the modern horn. It could be crooked in different keys, but is without valves, and depends for its virtuosity on a very remarkably developed technique for playing the high harmonics (at least to the twentieth and sometimes beyond).

Hand-stopping to get notes in between the lower harmonics replaced this technique of high harmonics during the classical period; and horn parts became simpler and less exacting. The valve horn established itself during the romantic period; and horn parts grew difficult and interesting again, but altogether in a different style. The double horn (in F and B flat) of our modern period makes the horn-player's arduous duties so much more secure that it is now generally preferred; and if he is skilled enough in unifying the tone of its two sections, he can do very much as he wants with it. However, some first-horn players prefer to retain a B flat alto horn.

The higher valve horn (or section of a horn), even with great skill, cannot sound quite like the longer and lower unvalved baroque horns (especially when crooked low); and another factor contributing to this unlikeness is an evergrowing and rather unfortunate tendency to broaden the bore for greater ease and sureness (but less poetical colouring). For the more elaborate and lofty of the baroque horn parts, we really need (and have begun to get) excellent players of the natural horn, with a mastery of the exceedingly specialized technique of playing securely up into the very high harmonics.

(c) The trombone (for which one early English name was sackbut) has a moderately narrow cylindrical bore (wider for more power, or narrower for more colour) and a mouthpiece varying, to taste, anywhere between the cup-shaped and the tapered. From the renaissance to the modern period, no radical alteration has occurred. A baroque trombone (sackbut) has a much less flaring bell, but no other structural difference which can be certainly ascertained as standard practice. The mouthpiece was probably always cup-shaped.

Yet the character of baroque trombone parts undoubtedly suggests a more reticent quality, in the main, than we are used to now; and this must lie with the player still more than with his instrument. There are varying trombone styles in modern orchestras, the Germans leaning towards a more massive force and the French and English towards a keener edge. It is both possible and desirable for a modern trombonist using a modern trombone (preferably a narrow or medium bore) to cultivate for baroque parts the right quality and quantity of clear yet mellow sound: warm in sonority, soft to moderate in strength, and by turns crisp and singing in articulation.

Reproductions of baroque trombones are extremely desirable when the instrument can be thoroughly mastered; but it is the player's conception of his part which is going to be the decisive factor.

(d) The trumpet, with its narrow cylindrical bore and more or less shallow and cup-shaped mouthpiece, is acoustically in the same family as the trombone, and was likewise musically operative throughout the baroque period.

The early baroque trumpeters favoured a long, 8-ft instrument in C; the later baroque period had a standard 7-ft instrument in D. These were at the ideal relationship of bore to length for the greatest possible production of high harmonics: both as timbre, and as high notes. There is no trumpet sound (and therefore no orchestral sound) quite so brilliantly colourful as the long baroque natural trumpet.

Throughout the baroque period, trumpeters specializing on high (*clarino*) parts (but using the same long instrument) rejoiced in a technique whose virtuosity is shown by the extraordinary floridity and soaring compass (again to the twentieth harmonic or beyond) of their most exacting music. It was a commonplace that what a singer could perform, a trumpeter could match. Not every trumpeter; but every *clarino* player worthy of the name.

There was again a history of declining high technique, resulting in simplified parts (late eighteenth century); and then the development of valves, resulting in renewed complexity of a different kind (early nineteenth century onwards). The decrease in average length, however, has gone much farther with orchestral trumpets in A, or especially in B flat; also in C, or higher still for very high baroque parts (taken with lower harmonics sounding higher notes). There is further a tendency towards increasing the proportion of conical tubing near the mouthpiece (almost like the modern cornet). The mouthpiece varies at the player's taste.

The cumulative difference in sound and character between a modern and a baroque trumpet has now grown too great to be ignored (the nineteenth-century medium-length F trumpet was a much nearer and, as many still believe, a much nobler instrument; but it, too, has gone out). There have been various attempts to design modern trumpets at or approaching baroque length and sonority, but usually with valves (or recently tiny side-holes) for help in correcting intonation and increasing security. Some of these attempts have now met with outstanding success.

5. THE DRUMS AND OTHER PERCUSSION

(a) Throughout the baroque period, there was a traditional association of trumpets and kettledrums (timpani). Both were part of the retinue of royalty and high nobility, from whom they were commonly borrowed when required for musical performances. Though baroque drum parts are not very common in notation, they can ordinarily be assumed to have been improvised, as the habit was, in performance, whenever trumpeters were present (which itself happened more often than the notated scores reveal).

The ordinary baroque provision was two drums tuned to the tonic and dominant of the trumpet tonality: especially C in the earlier baroque period and D in the later baroque period. In trumpet fanfares, more or less elaborate, the bass part might be entrusted to the drums alone.

In an orchestra, the drums would mainly improvise (with distinct strokes more often than with rolls) a simplified version of the notated bass line, such as can easily be written out for them under modern conditions, where they should be brought in with the trumpets whether so indicated or not. Drum solos also occurred (e.g. in Handel's *Semele*).

More numerous drums might be used for special purposes: Mersenne (*Harmonie Universelle*, Paris, 1636–7 II, vii, p. 54) shows a group of four, tuned c', e', g', c'', and of eight tuned to a diatonic C major scale.

Modern kettledrums meet baroque requirements so well that there need be no hesitation in using them, though very successful experiments with early kettledrums have now been carried out.

(b) Smaller drums, particularly the narrow, two-ended tabor with or without snares, were necessary in almost every sort of renaissance or baroque dance music. The part was and should be improvised to suit the rhythm of the dance.

(c) Castanets, clappers, cymbals, triangles, wooden bars and other percussion (including side drums and bass drums), though in use throughout the baroque period, only came into prominence with the fashion for 'Turkish music' early in the eighteenth century, which spread from military music into the orchestra mainly in the second half of that century.

(d) Our main obligation today is to see that enough percussion (particularly the kettledrums) is introduced into baroque performances, even where no indication is shown in the notated scores.

CHAPTER TWELVE

Keyboards

1. CHANGING PREFERENCES IN KEYBOARD INSTRUMENTS

(a) Changes of fashion in keyboard instruments have been far-reaching since the baroque period. The piano replaced the harpsichord through the nineteenth and early twentieth centuries because its dynamic flexibility and surging power exactly suited the kinds of musical romanticism then flourishing. The harpsichord has returned in course of the twentieth century because its dynamic steadiness and ringing clarity exactly suit the kinds of impassioned baroque classicism now once more in demand.

Similar fluctuations of preference have affected the design of organs to a remarkable degree; and there has been a similar return to more or less baroque types both of instrument and of registration. To get really satisfactory performances of baroque organ music (either in solo or in accompaniment), an instrument which includes reasonably baroque capabilities, and an organist with an effectual appreciation of them, are both indispensable.

(b) Where a harpsichord is unavailable (or where only a very inadequate harpsichord is available), a piano may have to serve for baroque accompaniment. To play it drily and inexpressively is no remedy; a warm tone, decided phrasing and a keen ear for balance give much more musicianly and enjoyable results.

Where a piano is used for harpsichord solos, a complete re-thinking of the music in pianistic terms is better than trying to get the best and ending by getting the worst of both worlds. There is great pleasure to be had from it, although the original instrument is really very much more satisfactory.

For regular baroque performances a good harpsichord should have first claim on any funds available.

(c) Organs are so variable that a good organist can often hope to find some quite successful registration even on an instrument with no actually baroque or baroque-style provision. He will aim at contrasted

104

and clear rather than at merging or veiled sonorities; and his articulation and his phrasing will both be highly conspicuous.

But organs wholly or partly in baroque style, with low wind-pressures and mechanical tracker actions, are growing commoner, and the change both in the instruments and in the understanding of baroque organ-music has become quite phenomenal in recent years.

2. THE HARPSICHORD

(a) In choosing a harpsichord, it may be noticed that:

(i) An instrument built more or less along traditional lines is certain to be superior to an instrument modernized by heavier construction of the frame and sound-board, heavier stringing, quilling and action or any other attempt to get more power, which may indeed give a louder sound under the player's ear, but not at the back of the hall where the real test comes. Many of the commercially-produced modern harpsichords are very poor.

(ii) Leather, well selected and properly cut, is admirable material for the plectra, giving a warm and rounded quality of sound. Quills cut from feathers can be excellent, but are harder to get and may give trouble sooner; they give a sharp and brilliant quality of sound. Plastic, properly used, sounds marvellous, can be satisfactory in every respect, and is now being adopted by the best makers.

(iii) Proper scaling (relation of string lengths, materials and gauges to pitch) is the maker's affair; but it is better to spend money on a simple instrument of adequate length and good scaling than on numerous and complex registers (variations of stop and colouring).

(iv) The 16-foot is an unnecessary and most undesirable luxury. It puts added pressure on the frame and the sound-board, so that the instrument tends to sound much less bright throughout; it brings more weight into the tone, but very little more effectual loudness: it adds some variety of colour, which is not missed if it is not there.

The 4-foot, on the other hand, is of value, since it glitters piquantly, when alone, and adds a splendid brilliance, when in combination.

The lute stop (separate jacks plucking the same 8-foot strings nearer to the end, with a more pungent sound) is a fairly expensive extra, but a pleasant one.

The harp stop (also called buff, or sometimes lute, but bringing felt or leather dampers gently up to the strings so as to lessen their resonance) is hardly ever so musicianly in practice as the player fondly imagines, since it reduces the sonority far too much out in the hall. It can well be dispensed with; if present, it should hardly be used, and never for long at a time.

Two keyboards are very desirable if funds allow, even if only with a single (but differently voiced) 8-foot on each. A coupler enormously enhances their value.

(v) Foot-pedals for stop-changing were uncommon in the baroque period; and the complicated registration which they permit is harmful to any but the most virtuoso music. Hand-stops and a sliding coupler do all that is needed.

(vi) A good harpsichord in good adjustment and played with good technique should have a very ample volume for all ordinary concert work, provided that the bowed strings are playing with proper baroque transparency. In very large ensembles, two or even more harpsichords can be used. Electrical amplification never sounds altogether natural but should be used if needed. Remember that a continuo harpsichord in a big ensemble is not meant to be heard separately, but simply to give a sharper cutting edge to the sound as a whole.

(b) The following three factors are the foundation of a good harpsichord touch:

(i) The fingers should grasp the keys, not daintily, but with considerable prehensile strength. Too light a touch plucks the strings feebly and ineffectually, and sounds like it. On the other hand, too raised a touch, with the fingers dropped or thrust down on to the keys from some distance above, sends the jacks flying past the strings too rapidly to get a proper grip of them, and a tone of indescribable tinniness results, even from the best of harpsichords. Couperin (*L'art de toucher le clavecin*, Paris, 1716, ed. of 1717, p. 7) warns us that 'a hand which falls from a height gives a drier stroke than if it touches from close; and the quill draws a harder sound from the string'. Qua tz (*Essay*, Berlin, 1752, XVII, vi, 18) recommends: 'a certain force which puts the strings into sufficient vibration'. This forcefulness of grip is of the utmost importance to a good sound. Beginners at the harpsichord often sound feeble from not realizing the basic strength of harpsichord touch.

(ii) All chords of more than two or three notes should be spread: the bass note *taking the beat* (this is important) with great punctuality; the remaining notes *following* in quick, ascending order. So quickly will this spreading be ordinarily done that it will not be heard as a spreading at all, but simply as a chord of rich sonority. The chord is whipped down strongly, from the bass note up; the ear does not detect this, however, but is deceived into hearing the chord as simultaneous although in fact it is not. If, on the other hand, the chord really is simultaneous, the ear is assaulted by a metallic clash altogether foreign to the true nature of the harpsichord. It is also possible, for musical reasons, to spread chords perceptibly in any desired degree and direction; but this is additional to the basic spreading which ensures a good sonority.

(iii) Since the harpsichord has no damper-raising pedal to allow a

106

building up of sympathetic vibrations, it is essential to hold down all notes, after striking them, for so long as fingers remain available, the harmony remains the same, and no necessity of phrasing or articulation intervenes. (This is so basic to the technique of the instrument that it scarcely ever appears in notation; but the reader may like to compare Couperin's own rather more complete notation of 'Les Bergeries' in his *Livre II*, 'Ordre 6', with the sketchier but more ordinary notation of the same piece in the *Klavierbüchlein für Anna Magdalena Bach*, both given in the *Neue Bach Ausgabe*, Ser, V. Bd. 4, p. 85, and its 'Kritischer Bericht'.) If all possible and suitable notes are not thus held on to, the harpsichord has no chance to gather cumulative sonority, and the tone sounds dry and evanescent. If they are, the harpsichord at once begins to ring and to sing.

(43) Michel de Saint-Lambert, *Principes du clavecin*, Paris, 1702, p. 41:

'There are passages, which without being chords, become such by the manner in which the notes are managed, and by the rule which obliges one to hold down certain ones, until others have been touched.'

To sum up: a powerful, gripping touch; no quite simultaneous chord of more than three notes; every possible and suitable note held on (even though notated short) so as to build up sonority.

(c) Spreading chords perceptibly on the harpsichord (i.e. more than the basic spreading) is good and idiomatic where there is need to fill out the sounds or to provide a more interesting figuration; and this figuration may, if there is room for it, be quite elaborate, going up and down and back again, and including a few non-harmonic passing notes.

If, however, the ensemble between the harpsichord and other parts sounds a little ragged, although it appears to be punctual, there is probably too much perceptible spreading, which can give a rather untidy effect where much rapid movement is going on in the main parts. It is very necessary to watch out for this effect of untidy ensemble. The remedy is to close up the spreading so that it is scarcely perceptible or not at all; and to make certain that its *first* note (normally the bass) is on the beat (*not* before the beat).

The last chord of a movement can often be filled out by a considerable arpeggiation, perhaps up and down again more than once (commonly ending at the top); but the degree must still be proportionate to the character of the movement.

(d) Registration on the harpsichord can be showy, up to a point, if the music is showy; but even in the most brilliant of harpsichord music, such as the toccatas of J. S. Bach, or the sonatas of Domenico Scarlatti, few changes but bold ones are nearly always the most effective. It is

107

often possible to set up one registration on each keyboard, and to do all that is required merely by changing keyboards at appropriate moments.

We may recall the words of that greatest of French harpsichordists, François Couperin (whose music J. S. Bach so much admired), already quoted at (5) above: 'I declare in all good faith that I am more pleased with what moves me than with what astonishes me.'

3. THE CLAVICHORD

(a) A good clavichord may be either single-strung or double-strung; but the latter tends to be the more sonorous and expressive instrument, especially if big.

Even the best and best-played of clavichords has a tone so quiet that it can be properly heard only in a room, or at the most (with an audience exceptionally quiet and concentrated) in a very small hall. The ear has first to adjust itself to the minute volume; but if the tone still seems too small to hear in perfect comfort, the instrument is not a good one, or it is not being well played, or both.

If the sound is electrically amplified, the sense of inwardness and intensity is lost. Since this is the real point of the clavichord, that course does not seem to be a very desirable one, even though it can overcome the volume difficulty. Broadcasting and recordings, however, can be fairly successful.

(b) Clavichord touch, though sensitive, is much stronger than might be supposed. Quite a powerful attack is needed for the loudest sounds, and a very delicate attack for the softest sounds. But never violent enough to send the string too sharp; and never a weak or a flabby attack, since this merely sounds tinny and ineffectual. Good clavichord tone, however soft, is always vibrant and colourful. There is just a certain firm and purposeful way of grasping the keys, without hitting them, which brings it out.

(c) The vibrato on the clavichord needs fine control, especially when used to bring out one contrapuntal part of several. It can be amazingly expressive, but must stop short of sounding unduly out of tune. The strings must be so scaled as to be fairly taut, so as not to go sharp too easily; yet not so taut as to sound hard.

(d) The clavichord is not an instrument on which to rattle through a showy allegro; but it can sing in slow movements like no other keyboard instrument. It can also sound (though it is not) extraordinarily powerful in a big, romantic piece such as J. S. Bach's Chromatic Fantasy and Fugue, where its capacity for startling dynamic contrast can be shown to the fullest effect.

4. THE ORGAN

(a) Two branches of the organ family are concerned in the recent baroque revival. One is big church or concert organs of varying capacities and designs, for solo recitals and for accompanying music on a large scale; the other is small, more or less portable chamber organs (flue and reed) for some solo work, and for accompanying small or moderate ensembles, as an alternative to the harpsichord, where the music suits. Such portative organs have been most valuably revived.

(b) Idiomatic organ technique is an art in itself; but two points may be stressed briefly here:

(i) Silences of articulation are of quite paramount importance. Every good organist of the newer schools knows that in baroque music, it is particularly essential to break down phrases into comprehensible patterns, not only by making sufficient silences of articulation, but also by making these silences sufficiently long to get across to the listeners (and, of course, the longer the reverberation period of the building, the longer the silences need to be, not to get swallowed up in echo).

There is nothing in the above which is not also true for good harpsichord playing; but the inherently sustained character of organ tone requires even firmer measures to clarify the articulation and the phrasing.

(ii) And just as on the harpsichord, so also on the organ, good baroque registration is mainly a matter, not of merging different colourings imperceptibly into one another, but of contrasting them decisively at not too frequent intervals.

The only important exception to this is echo effects, which were popular in some styles of baroque music, and which may require quite a brief loud phrase to be immediately repeated soft.

The swell-box was known, but not much exploited, in the late baroque period. Crescendos and diminuendos produced by opening and shutting it, or by the imperceptible addition and subtraction of stops, have really nothing to do with the basic styles of baroque organ music, any more than they do with harpsichord music when produced by modern pedal-work.

But to build up by distinctly graded steps to a climax, and perhaps to take it down again by the same means, can in the proper places be magnificently in the baroque style.

PART THREE

THE NOTES

CHAPTER THIRTEEN

The Problem of Accidentals

1. WHY BAROQUE ACCIDENTALS ARE DIFFICULT

(a) Accidentals are among the choices, largely left to the performer, which affect the actual notes.

Early baroque accidentals, though easier than renaissance or medieval accidentals, are still a big problem. This problem diminishes, though it does not disappear, in later baroque music.

(b) Medieval theory recognized only diatonic notes, illogically but conveniently including B flat, as an alternative to B natural for preventing augmented or diminished octaves, and augmented fourths or diminished fifths (i.e. the tritone).

F sharp, though serving the same purpose, remained admittedly chromatic, as did other sharps and flats, the growing effect of which was (especially by sharpened leading notes) to destroy the absolute (stable) tonality of mode and to establish the relative (mobile) tonality of key: already in practice, though not yet in theory, by the late renaissance.

The baroque period inherited (and so, to our still greater disadvantage, do we) a legacy of notation by which only the 'white' notes of the keyboard have names and diatonic positions of their own; the 'black' notes, whether used diatonically or chromatically, can only be named or shown as chromatic modifications. We inherit the confusion (it never was a system) of *musica ficta*, feigned music; and that is why we have a problem of accidentals.

(c) The late renaissance ambiguity about accidentals may be gathered from the following somewhat contradictory statements:

(44) Pietro Aaron, *Thoscanello de la Musica*, Venice, 1523, p. 1 of additions following Ch. 41:

'There are, among students of music, many arguments as to flats and sharps, that is whether composers should mark such accidentals.'

(45) Stephano Vanneo, MS treatise 1531, trans. Vincentio Rosseto, *Recanetum de musica aurea*, Rome, 1533, III, 37:

113

'The ears are considered the best interpreters, which can help you most [with accidentals].'

(46) Gioseffo Zarlino, *Istitutioni armoniche*, Venice, 1558, ed. of 1589, III, 252:

'There are some who in singing sharpen or flatten a melody in a case which the composer never intended.'

(47) William Bathe, *Briefe Introduction to the Skill of Song*, London [? 1590], on accidentals:

'Thappendancy of the flat by the sharp, and of the sharp by the flat is taken away, though by negligence and ignorance of prickers, we are oft driven to gather thappendencie by the course of the song.'

(48) Thomas Morley, *Plaine and Easie Introduction to Practicall Musicke*, London, 1597, p. 88:

'Because I thought it better flat than sharpe, I have set it flat. But if anie man like the other way better, let him use his discretion.'

(d) In the early baroque period, composers who wanted performers to confine themselves to the notated accidentals were still in the minority, and found it necessary to draw special attention to their wishes in the matter.

(49) Crescentio Salzilli, (a) *Il primo libro de madrigali a cinque voci*, Naples, 1607; (b) *Il secondo libro de madrigali a cinque voci*, Naples, 1611:

(a) 'The singers are notified that they should not sing ♯ or ♭ except where they are marked.'
(b) 'One does not have to sing ♯ or ♭ except where it is marked.'

2. BAROQUE SIGNS FOR ACCIDENTALS

(a) Our ♭ (originally meaning B flat) had in baroque music the function of lowering any note by a semitone.

Our ♮ (originally meaning B natural) had in baroque music its modern function of restoring a previously altered semitone (theoretically only on B), but was infrequent in the seventeenth century though more frequent in the eighteenth.

Our ♯ (originally a *signum cancellatum*, in the shape of a cross because used to cancel or cross out the influence of a previous flat) had in baroque music the function of raising any note by a semitone.

The standard seventeenth-century cancellation of ♭ is by ♯, and of ♯ is by ♭. In the eighteenth century, some musicians (including Bach and Handel) showed more preference than others for ♮; a typical inconsistency, from Rameau, is shown at Ex. 50 below.

(b) Notice that in the baroque period, the sign X can stand either for sharp, or for double sharp (it can also be a sign for an ornament).

(c) We ordinarily place accidentals before their notes. In baroque prints, this is the commonest placing, but (especially when the notes are crowded) accidentals may also appear above or below their notes. In baroque manuscripts, accidentals may be placed very variably indeed, wherever there happens to be room for them. There is no difference of meaning intended.

(d) In figured bass, however, there is (subject to numerous mistakes) a difference of meaning between accidentals before notes (which they affect), and above or below notes (whose harmonization they affect).

3. KEY SIGNATURES

(a) The Dorian mode (no flat in signature) underlies our D minor (one flat in signature); the Dorian mode once transposed (one flat in signature) underlies our G minor (two flats in signature); etc.

There was therefore a baroque tendency to notate key signatures with one flat (or, by false analogy one sharp) too few.

The intention was to supply the missing flat or sharp by notated accidentals; but mistakes in this respect are numerous.

(b) As an added precaution (to us, a confusion), the same flat or sharp may be shown twice, at the octave distance, in one key signature: see Ex. 1(a) and Ex. 1(b) below. There is no difference of meaning.

Ex. 1. Key signatures (a) of three apparent but two actual flats; (b) of seven apparent but four actual sharps.

Ex. 1

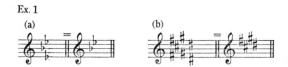

4. BAROQUE ACCIDENTALS AFFECTED BY CONTEXT

(a) Modern accidentals *fix* a note: they give it an absolute position within the tonal framework.

But baroque accidentals *inflect* a note: they give it a position relative to that which it would otherwise have had.

(49a) Christopher Simpson, *Compendium*, London, 1665, ed. of 1732, p. 5 (but all eds. have it):

'That ♭ takes away a *Semitone* from the Sound of the Note before which it is set, to make it more *grave* or *flat*: This ♯ doth add a semitone to the Note to make it more *acute* or *sharp*.'

115

(b) Thus if a baroque musician wanted to raise a B flat to B natural, he might give it a sharp (♯) and call the result 'B sharped' (Ex. 2a). He would say that G major has a 'sharp third'; and he would therefore call this key a 'sharp key' (whereas he would call G minor a 'flat key'). In this case, what looks to us like B sharp means B natural.

And if a baroque musician wanted to lower a B sharp to B natural, he might give it a flat (♭) and call the result 'B flatted' (Ex. 2b). He would say that G sharp minor has a 'flat third'; and he would therefore call that key a 'flat key' (whereas he would call G sharp major a 'sharp key'). In that case, what looks to us like B flat means B natural.

Again, if a baroque musician wanted to raise a C flat to C natural, he might give it a sharp (♯) and call it 'sharped' (Ex. 2c); and if he wanted to lower a C sharp to C natural, he might give it a flat (♭) and call it 'flatted' (Ex. 2d). In the first case, what looks to us like C sharp means C natural; and in the second case, what looks to us like C flat means C natural.

Furthermore, if a baroque musician wanted to restore B double-flat to B flat, he might give it a sharp (♯) and call it 'sharped' (Ex. 2e); and if he wanted to restore C double-sharp to C sharp, he might give it a flat (♭) and call it 'flatted' (Ex. 2f). At the one extreme, therefore, what looks to us like B sharp means B flat; and at the other extreme, what looks to us like C flat means C sharp. (But equally, he might do nothing at all in notation to restore a double-flat to flat, or a double-sharp to sharp; or possibly he might notate one sharp or one flat, as we might do; but only the context can tell us with what intention.)

Ex. 2(g) and Ex. 2(h), and (less commonly) Ex. 2(i) and Ex. 2(j), are standard baroque notation. Ex. 2(k) and Ex. 2(l) show Jean-Marie Leclair using ♮ to *restore* a previously cancelled sharp or flat (not standard practice). Ex. 2(m) shows Johann Philipp Treiber (*Der accurate organist*, Jena, 1704, Ex. xii) using a not uncommon enharmonic substitution, also shown in Ex. 2(n) (Alfonso Ferrabosco, *c.* 1575–1628, in Nomine as scored in Oxford, Christ Church, MS2, 2nd half of 17th cent., f. 248 v. to 250, Tr. II, m. 36).

Ex. 2. Accidentals altering but not defining a note.

Ex. 2

5. HOW FAR FORWARD DO BAROQUE ACCIDENTALS WORK?

(a) The modern convention is: one bar, one accidental. The baroque convention is: one note, one accidental. A bar-line *has no influence either way* on baroque accidentals.

(49b) Christopher Simpson, *Compendium*, London, 1665, ed. of 1732, p. 5 (but all eds. have it):

[A flat or a sharp] 'serves only for that particular Note before which it is placed'.

(b) That is always the theoretical basis in baroque music. But in practice, certain not very consistent, but nevertheless recognizable exceptions were commonly made and occasionally described.

For example, when the same note is repeated immediately, any accidental tends to influence the repetitions.

(50) Domenico Mazzocchi, *Partitura de' madrigali a cinque voci*, Rome, 1638, Preface:

'They are written in accordance with the usage, and in accordance
117

with the notice that I gave already in the Catena d'Adone [Venice, 1626, having the same instructions in the preface], namely, that alterations are not to be made, unless they are found marked; excepting, however, the notes immediately following on the same degree, which for less complexity, and not to multiply things without necessity, are understood [as if they were] marked, and of the same value, as the first [note] preceding them, until another new sign is found, which differentiates them, which in this case, and for no other purpose will be placed there.'

Domenico Mazzocchi was, for his period, exceptionally careful in his notation, and the 'usage' he mentions was not yet by any means established. Nor did Mazzocchi himself follow his own rule consistently (Ex. 3a, Ex. 3b).

Ex. 3. Domenico Mazzocchi, *Partitura de' madrigali*, Rome, 1638, (a) pp. 63–74, 'Pian piano', m.17, (b) pp. 52–62, 'Oh se potreste mai', m.22, inconsistent accidentals:

Ex. 3

(51) Jacopo Peri, *Euridice*, Florence, 1600, Avvertimento:

[An accidental] 'is never to be introduced except on that note alone on which it is shown, even though there may be several repetitions of that note'.

The above instruction, which is the opposite of what Mazzochi at (50) above described as 'in accordance with the usage', was no more consistently followed by Peri in his own notation (Ex. 4a, Ex. 4b, Ex. 4c).

Ex. 4. Jacopo Peri, *Euridice*, 1600, (a) p. 34, m.17; (b) p. 36, m.16;

(c) p. 54, m. 13; inconsistent accidentals:

Ex. 4

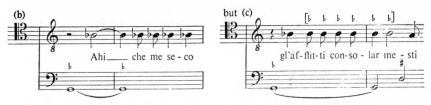

In Ex. 5, source (b) has a page-turn where the asterisk is marked, and repeats the accidental perhaps as a reminder after the page has been turned; whereas source (a) has no page-turn there, and does not repeat the accidental. On such slight factors, or none, might a baroque copyist's whim depend.

Ex. 5. [? Luigi Rossi] oratorio, *Un peccator pentito mi son fatto nemico* (mid-17th cent.), (a) in Rome, Vatican Lib., Barb. Lat. 4191, f. 13 v., accidental notated once; (b) in Rome, Vatican Lib., Barb. Lat. 4201, f. 84 v., the same accidental notated twice, perhaps because the page turns over in between (at*):

Ex. 5

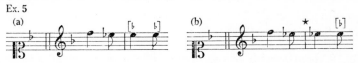

(c) Even if one or more other notes come in between, the repeated notes *may* still fall under the influence of a previous accidental (Ex. 4a, Ex. 6a, Ex. 6b).

In Ex. 6, source (a) carries the influence of the flat over two other notes in between, and source (b) over one other note in between, while source (c) notates the flat each time, thus confirming that its influence was likewise meant to persist in source (a) and source (b).

Ex. 6. Giacomo Carissimi, cantata, *In un mar di pensieri* (mid-17th cent.), m. 12, (a) in London, Brit. Mus. R.M. 24. i. 11, No. 5; (b) in Vienna, Österreichische Nationalbibliothek, MS 17765; (c) in Oxford, Christ Church Lib., MS 51; same accidentals differently notated:

Ex. 6

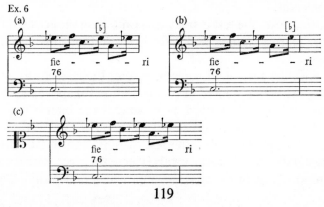

But in Ex. 7, the musical sense depends upon a chromatic sequence which *precludes* carrying the influence of the accidentals forward over the notes in between, whether cancelling accidentals are notated, as at (b), or not, as at (a).

Ex. 7. J. S. Bach, 'Coffee Cantata', autograph MS, Berlin, Preussische Staatsbibliothek (c. 1732), (a) p. 10, m. 5; (b) p. 11, m. 10; inconsistent accidentals:

(d) When the chord changes although the note does not, the influence of the accidental may be treated as cancelled or at least weakened by the change of chord, and the accidental may therefore be renewed.

In Ex. 8, at (a) the notes with accidentals are repeated without change of chord, and one accidental for each suffices. But at (b), the chord changes and the accidentals, though still to the same repeated notes, are renewed. See also Ex. 10(c) below.

Ex. 8. Jean-Joseph Mondonville, *Pièces de clavecin avec voix ou violon*, Paris [1748], (a) p. 14, m. 10, repeated notes influenced by single accidentals; (b) p. 14, m. 12, accidentals renewed on repeated notes at change of chord:

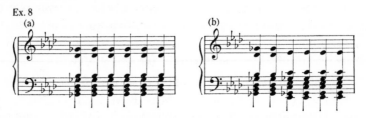

(e) A rest coming between repeated notes tends to *cancel* the influence of an accidental.

In Ex. 3(b) above, the rest is treated as cancelling the accidental, which is therefore renewed immediately after the rest, though not on the other repetitions.

In Ex. 9(a), the accidental is renewed after the rest, consistently with Peri's own instruction quoted at (51) in section (b) above, which would have required it to be renewed even without the intervening rest. At Ex. 9(b) (in appearance inconsistently with Peri's own instruction) the accidental is not renewed, and the rest does not cancel the influence of the accidental (but that is because this is merely a precautionary accidental, due to an E flat in the bass three measures previously). The sharp over the C in the bass is likewise precautionary, to ensure E natural in the harmonization.

Ex. 9. Jacopo Peri, *Euridice*, Florence, 1600, (a) p. 14, m. 11, rest helping to cancel the influence of an accidental, which is therefore renewed; (b) p. 25, m. 22, precautionary accidental not needing to be renewed after a rest:

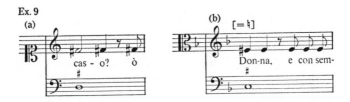

In Ex. 10, at (a) the rest is treated as cancelling the accidental, which is therefore renewed. At (b), either the rest is *not* treated as cancelling two out of the three accidentals, since these two are not renewed after the rest, though the other is inconsistently renewed; or more probably, the missing two have been left out by mistake, since mistakes in this treatise are numerous. At (c), two accidentals are (consistently) renewed, with no rest intervening, because the chord has changed though the two repeated notes have not; see section (e) and Ex. 8(b) above.

Ex. 10. Johann Philipp Kirnberger, *Grundsätze des Generalbasses*, Berlin [1781], Fig. LI, realization of the Andante in J. S. Bach's trio sonata in the *Musical Offering*, mm. 14–15, (a) rest treated as cancelling the influence of an accidental; (b) rest not cancelling two out of three accidentals (or unintentional omission); (c) accidentals renewed because chord changes:

(f) The start of a new phrase also strongly tends to *cancel* the influence of an accidental.

At Ex. 11, the first two D's in Tenor II are sharp, as leading notes in a normal ornamental resolution of the suspended E. But the third D is not a leading note. It is the start of a new phrase, and is therefore no longer under the influence of the previous accidental. This is confirmed by the lute tablature, which shows the fingering for D natural, and also by the

121

need to avoid an improbably augmented second to the C natural next
following.

Ex. 11. John Dowland, *Lachrimae*, London [1605], 'Lachrimae
Verae', m. 22, influence of accidental cancelled by start of new
phrase, though the note is immediately repeated.

At Ex. 12, the first G is correctly marked sharp as the leading note of
A minor; but the next G is the start of a new phrase, and is therefore
no longer under the influence of the previous accidental. It is G natural,
as the harmony confirms by progressing into C major.

Ex. 12. Giacomo Carissimi, cantata, *Deh, memoria* (mid-17th cent.),
in Rome, Vatican Lib., MS Chigi Q. IV. 18, ff. 43–8 v., and also in
Rome, Vatican Lib., MS Chigi Q. IV. 11, ff. 1–6 v., m. 29; influence
of accidental cancelled by start of new phrase (rather than by the
different note in between):

(g) A rest and the start of a new phrase together tend still more
strongly to *cancel* the influence of an accidental.

In Ex. 13, the first phrase is in D minor, with the leading note and the
sixth of the scale both sharpened. The second phrase is in F major,
which confirms that the C which starts it after the rest is natural.

Ex. 13. John Jenkins, 'Fantasia 21', Treble I, in London, Brit.
Mus. MS Add. 17192 (mid-17th cent.), f. 50; influence of accidental
cancelled by rest and start of new phrase.

TABLE I

The Hexachordal System

Pitch in Helmholtz' notation	HARD HEX'D*	NAT'L HEX'D†	SOFT HEX'D‡	HARD HEX'D*	NAT'L HEX'D†	SOFT HEX'D‡	HARD HEX'D*	THE BASIC GAMUT
e″							E la	E la (Ela)
d″						D re	D sol	D re sol (Delasol)
Treble c″						C sol	C fa	C sol fa (Cesolfa)
b′						b fa B	B mi B	b fa B (Befa) mi or mi / B (Bemi)
a′					A la	A mi	A re	A la mi re (Alamire)
g′					G sol	G re	G ut	G sol re ut (Gesolreut)
f′					F fa	F ut		F fa ut (Fefaut)
e′				E la	E mi			E la mi (Elami)
d′			D la	D sol	D re			D la sol re (Delasolre)
Middle c′			C sol	C fa	C ut			C sol fa ut (Cesolfaut)
b♭ b♮			b fa B	B mi B				b fa B (Befa) mi or mi / B (Bemi)
a		A la	A mi	A re				A la mi re (Alamire)
g		G sol	G re	G ut				G sol re ut (Gesolreut)
f		F fa	F ut					F fa ut (Fefaut)
e	E la	E mi						E la mi (Elami)
d	D sol	D re						D sol re (Desolre)
Tenor C	C fa	C ut						C fa ut (Cefaut)
B	B mi							B mi (Bemi)
A	A re							A re (Are)
G	Γ ut							Γ ut (Gamma Ut)

* *Hexachordum durum*, because it includes *b durum* or *quadration, i.e. B mi (B natural).*
† *Hexachordum naturale*, including no B.
‡ *Hexachordum molle*, because it includes *B molle* or *rotundum, i.e. b fa (B flat).*

(h) The influence of baroque accidentals has often a certain tendency to *persist* while the part remains within the compass of one hexachord.

Baroque theory long continued to organize scales by the hexachord of six diatonic notes rather than by the octave of eight. A hexachord is any portion of a diatonic scale which will include one semitone but will not include two. The position of the semitone is always in the middle, between *mi* and *fa*.

The compass of a hexachord is exceeded by transmuting mentally into another hexachord; and the position of the semitone is altered by transmuting into another hexachord. When an accidental is introduced, mutation into another hexachord is presumed, and this presumption tends to continue until a further accidental, or an exceeding of the six-note compass, again implies mutation.

In Ex. 14, the compass remains that of the hard hexachord from *G sol re ut* to *E la mi*, and the influence of the B natural persists, as the marked B natural in Treble I confirms.

Ex. 14. John Dowland, *Lachrimae*, London [1605], 'M. Giles Hobies Galiard', m. 21, continued influence of accidental within the compass of one hexachord:

In Ex. 15(a), the piece begins in D minor (to us), with notated Csharp (as leading note) and B flat (as descending sixth of the scale). The presumption (to a baroque musician) was therefore the untransposed soft hexachord. The first B in the right hand has no accidental notated, but is by hexachordal tendency a flat, like the next B, which is notated flat. (To us, the tonality is F major, with the same implication.) At m. 10, the melody exceeds the compass of a hexachord, and the B is natural. This is confirmed by the need to avoid an improbable (in this context, impossible) augmented second from the notated C sharp immediately before.

In Ex. 15(b), the hexachordal tendency is to keep the second B as a B flat; but this tendency is overcome by the stronger tendency to take it as the leading note to C, and therefore natural.

Ex. 15. Anonymous keyboard pieces from the Gresse MS (17th-cent. Dutch), in *Dutch Keyboard Music of the 16th and 17th Centuries*, ed. Alan Curtis, Amsterdam, 1961, (a), p. 108, LXXX, 'Menuets du Dauphin', mm. 4–10; influence of flat prevailing because of the soft hexachord; (b), p. 100, LXIX, 'Courante', mm. 4–5; influence of flat not prevailing:

Ex. 15

6. WHERE DO BAROQUE ACCIDENTALS WORK BACKWARDS TOO?
(a) The influence of a baroque accidental may extend backwards as well as forwards. In such cases, we may speak of a *retrospective* accidental. (See also Ch. XIV, Sect. 7d, below.)

In Ex. 16 (a), an entry is shown of a theme which is apparently chromatic; but at Ex. 16 (b), an entry of the same theme is shown occurring at a pitch requiring no accidental, from which it is seen that the theme is not chromatic but diatonic. At (a), therefore, the meaning is not G, F, F sharp, but G, F sharp, F sharp.

Ex. 16. Giovanni Pierluigi da Palestrina, Mass, *Confitebor tibi Domine*, retrospective accidental as noticed though not followed up by Knud Jeppesen, *The Style of Palestrina*, tr. M. W. Hamerik,

Copenhagen and London, 1927, 2nd ed. 1946, p. 36, (a) with accidental, (b) not needing accidental.

In Ex. 17, the bass note E has a sharp above it to indicate the major third, G sharp, thus confirming that the sharp before the second G in the melody is retrospective, influencing also the first G in the melody.

Ex. 17. Jacopo Peri, *Euridice*, Florence, 1600, p. 14, m. 13, retrospective accidental:

In Ex. 18, the bass note A is preceded by a sharp in the C space a third above, which is a common placing in very early figured bass for an accidental showing the major or the minor third as harmony. Cantus I sounds D against the E in Cantus II, and against the C sharp thus shown in the accompaniment; this D resolves ornamentally on to C sharp (i.e. the disonance D is sounded together with its note of resolution C sharp, a progression favoured in early baroque though not in later baroque practice). The C sharp in the accompaniment confirms that, in Cantus I, the first C, which is not marked, must be sharp, as well as the second C, which is marked. The sharp which is marked against the second C in Cantus I must therefore be exerting a retrospective as well as a prospective influence.

Ex. 18. Lodovico (Grossi da) Viadana, *Cento concerti ecclesiastici*, Venice, 1602, IV, 'Laetare Hierusalem', m. 3 (of bass):

In Ex. 19, at (a), the sharp before the second G in Treble I is retrospective, influencing also the first G; this is confirmed by the lute tablature, which shows the fingering for G sharp on both notes. But at (b), a very interesting passage, the sharp before the last G in Treble I is not retrospective, and does not influence the G immediately preceding it; this is confirmed by the harmony, by the coincident G natural in Tenor I, and by the lute tablature.

Ex. 19. John Dowland, *Lachrimae*, London [1605], 'Lachrimae

Amantis', (a) m. 3, retrospective accidental; (b) mm. 9–11, accidental not retrospective.

In Ex. 20, (a) and (b) are from the aria 'Possente spirto', in which Monteverdi has notated two alternative versions: the upper is left plain for the singer to ornament at will; the lower is already ornamented and needs little if any further ornamentation. At (a), the first sharp in the lower version is retrospective, as the upper version confirms. At (b), the first sharp in the lower version is normally retrospective, but exceptionally interesting in being crossed by a tie; the remaining sharps are erratically notated, but all the Fs are sharp, both as leading notes and by hexachordal tendency; the upper version has no Fs. At (c), which is a duet, the sharps in either voice are retrospective, and the sharp in the upper voice is persistent, both as leading note and by hexachordal tendency.

Ex. 20. Claudio Monteverdi, *Orfeo*, perf. Mantua, 1607, publ.

Ex. 20

Venice, 1609, (a) f. 56 m. 5, and (b) f. 58 m. 7, Act III, aria, 'Possente spirto', (c) f. 95 m. 7, Act V, duet, 'Saliam cantand' al Cielo'; accidentals retrospective and persisting.

(b) The retrospective accidental can occur in figured bass.

In Ex. 21, the sharp on the F line above and to the left of the second D in the bass indicates F sharp as major third in the harmony. But a voice part has F sharp notated over both Ds in the bass. This confirms that the sharp shown in the figuring influences retrospectively the harmonization of the first D, as well as indicating prospectively the harmonization of the second D before which it is actually placed.

Ex. 21. Stefano Landi, *La morte d'Orfeo*, Venice, 1619, p. 23, m. 3, retrospective accidental in the figuring:

Ex. 21

(c) That the effect of a retrospective accidental (influencing backwards as well as forwards) is no different in kind from the effect of a normally prospective accidental (influencing forwards) is shown by the one being often substituted for the other in matching passages or different sources for the same passage.

In Ex. 22 (i), at (a) the sharp against the second G in the voice part is retrospective; this is confirmed by the matching passage at (b) where the corresponding C is notated sharp, with the same effect. At (b), however, the second C is not marked sharp, but becomes so (under the prospective influence of the previous sharp) both as leading note, and by hexachordal tendency.

Ex. 22 (i). Giacomo Carissimi, cantata, 'Apritevi, inferni' (mid-17th cent.), Modena, Bibl. Estense, MS Mus. G. 32, dated 1662, (a) m. 89, retrospective accidental; (b) m. 101, matching accidental confirming the former, and persisting, as confirmed by the former.

At 22 (ii), a complicated situation arises, involving considerations of melody, of harmony, of hexachordal persistence, and of the retrospective accidental. The problem first makes itself felt at the words *E'l bel mese*. Here the acting bass is a thrice-repeated B flat, above which the two top lines pass one across the other through a notated E natural; the second part (now the higher) then returns by a notated E flat. This makes an improbable melody; E flat up as well as down is much more agreeable and unartificial. Moreover, the harmony is also more agreeable and unartificial if the passing Es above the B flat bass are flat, as befits that key (B flat major).

In the second part, the singer could see the flat coming on the descending E, and might well be moved to take that, retrospectively, also on the ascending E. But there is no such E flat coming in the first part from which the singer might take a retrospective hint. What is there to put E flat into his mind?

There is hexachordal persistence. E flat was notated in his part at the previous occurrence, some distance back, it is true; but his part has remained meanwhile within the soft hexachord once transposed. He will have solmized the previous phrase as *re, fa, mi* (i.e. C, E flat, D, as notated): he will therefore be disposed to solmize the present phrase as

129

sol, fa, mi (i.e. F, E flat, D, although not so notated); for there has been no cause for him to mutate into a different hexachord.

Where the second singer, then, could be alerted by the retrospective potentialities of his coming flat, the first singer could be alerted by the hexachordal potentialities of his previous flat; thus they could meet and cross parts happily on a common E flat above the second B flat in the acting bass. And if this did not happen at the first run through, it could quickly have been sorted out in rehearsal. What are rehearsals for?

The best solution therefore seems to be as suggested between square brackets in Ex. 22 (ii). I have to thank Mr. Bernard Bailly de Surcy for drawing my attention to this problem; and he agrees with my suggested solution for it.

Ex. 22 (ii). Claudio Monteverdi, *Madrigali a cinque voci*, First Book, Venice, 1587, X, 'Almo divino raggio', Second Part, accidentals not notated but suggested by a combination of considerations:

Ex. 22 (ii)

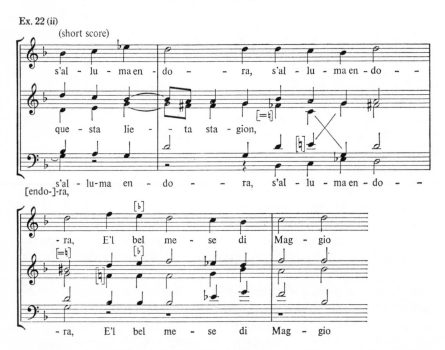

(d) The retrospective accidental ceased to be standard notation in course of the later baroque period.

In Ex. 23, at (a) it can be argued that the first G in the alto part belongs to an ornamental resolution of the suspended A, and that it should therefore accept, as leading note, the retrospective influence of the sharp before the second G, exactly as in Ex. 18 above. The passage

130

certainly runs more smoothly in that form. But at (b), we can compare a somewhat corresponding measure in the first half of this piece, without the suspension, but with the same bass and the same progression. Unlike (a) as notated, (b) as notated runs quite smoothly. The first two Gs in the treble part must surely be natural, both from the melody and from the G naturals in the tenor part; the sharp before the third G cannot, therefore, be retrospective; nor are we in any way tempted to make it retrospective. This is not a conclusive obstacle to making the sharp before the second alto G in (a) retrospective, since the passages do not altogether match; but it strongly casts a doubt.

It could also be argued that a sharp was left out by mistake before the first alto G in (a); but the sources, which do not agree on all the accidentals in this piece, do agree in this passage. A more realistic line of argument is that, under the fluid conditions of baroque notation, a performer who preferred to take the first alto G in (a) as a sharp was likely to have done so in any case.

So, then, may we; it could not be wrong. Yet to follow the notation exactly as it stands, and take the first alto G in (a) as written, could not be wrong either; and it is, very possibly, the better choice.

We have to remember how uncommonly rich such passing inflections of the tonality are in J. S. Bach – not just here, not just in a few undoubted passages, but over and over again. Not even in Bach should we try to assert that one solution is right, and all others wrong; for on prevailing baroque principles, any solution is right which lies within the boundaries of style. But this is not to say that one solution is not better than another. The literal solution almost certainly seems to be the better in this particular instance.

However, in Ex. 23(c), Bach's autograph shows (unless it is merely a slip) a genuinely retrospective accidental, as is confirmed by the posthumously printed edition.

Ex. 23. J. S. Bach, (a) Sarabande to the French Overture (Partita in B minor), second half, m. 4, apparent but doubtful retrospective accidental; (b) first half, m. 6, comparison casting doubt; (c) Art of Fugue, first fugue, m. 32, retrospective accidentals in autograph confirmed by first edition, Berlin, 1750, shown at (d):

Ex. 23
(a)

Retrospective accidentals cannot altogether be excluded from the age of Bach and Handel; but they were no longer a standard feature of notation, as they had been in the age of Palestrina and the age of Monteverdi. They were no longer standard, yet they were still quite common, in the age of Blow and Purcell. (Blow's *Venus and Adonis, c.* 1685, shows many cases, though not all are such which look as though they might be here.)

7. WHEN DID OUR BAR-LINE CONVENTION COME IN?

(a) The essential characteristic of our modern notation for accidentals is the convention by which an accidental does not exert any retrospective influence, but does exert a prospective influence up to the end of the bar in which it appears: i.e. so far as the next bar-line, but not beyond.

At no time within the baroque period had this modern convention for governing the influence of notated accidentals by the bar-line come into being. Thus Geminiani in 1751 still reiterated the same basic rule that Simpson gave in 1665, as quoted at (49a) above. The only differences are, first that he admits its insufficiency, and second that he adds a reference to the natural sign (♮), by then in common though not universal use for cancelling a previous accidental.

(51a) Francesco Geminiani, *The Art of Playing on the Violin*, London, 1751, p. [3]:

'A Sharp (♯) raises the Note to which it is prefixed, a Semitone higher ... A Flat (♭) on the Contrary renders the Note to which it is prefixed, a Semitone lower ... This Rule concerning the Flats and Sharps is not absolutely exact; but it is the easiest and best Rule that can be given to a Learner. This Mark (♮) takes away the Force of both the Sharp and the Flat and restores the Note before which it is placed to its natural Quality.'

132

Geminiani's own music examples show an unquestionable tendency not to repeat an accidental before a repetition of the same note *within* the same bar. But they also at times allow the force of an unrepeated accidental to carry *across* a bar-line. We may see in this stage, therefore, the beginnings of a transitional stage.

(b) This transitional stage appears quite explicitly in Türk's great treatise of 1789.

(51b) Daniel Gottlob Türk, *Klavierschule*, Leipzig and Halle, 1789, p. 46:

'[Accidentals] are valid only through one bar; yet one must not wish to observe this rule too strictly, for such a modifying sign often remains valid through several bars, or indeed so long, until it is cancelled by a ♮. Above all, the sharp and the flat are valid still further on, when the first note of the following [bar] and the last [note] of the previous bar stand on one degree [i.e. are the same note repeated].'

'[p. 47:] One still finds now and again, especially among the French and in older works, pieces in which a ♯ stands in place of our sharpening ♮ . . . In the same way one finds ♭ for a flattening ♮.'

See Ex. 49 and Ex. 50 below for cases of somewhat archaic French notation in the music of Rameau; we learn from Türk that it went on later.

Inconsistent reliance on the bar-line convention can still be found in Beethoven. But by the nineteenth century, the general intention was to notate accidentals according to the modern conventions.

CHAPTER FOURTEEN

The Treatment of Accidentals

1. CERTAIN CONSIDERATIONS HELPFUL OVER ACCIDENTALS
(a) In deciding how to interpret, correct or supply baroque accidentals notated misleadingly, wrongly or not at all, there are a number of considerations which can helpfully be taken into account.

2. ACCIDENTALS IN FIGURED BASS
(a) We get to recognize certain typical mistakes in the accidentals of *figured bass*.

(b) In Ex. 24, the flat before the low C should, at that very early baroque period, have been placed one line higher, to show the minor third (E flat). Its misplacing makes nonsense, and is therefore readily detected; but similar misplacings may be less obvious elsewhere.

Ex. 24. Claudio Monteverdi, *Orfeo*, perf. Mantua, 1607, publ. Venice, 1609, Act III, obligato for the double harp in the aria 'Possente spirto', misplaced accidental in bass part:

Ex. 24

(c) Later, when the correct placing of accidentals as part of the figuring was above or below the bass note, similar mistakes still occurred, as at Ex. 25.

Ex. 25. Giacomo Carissimi, cantata, 'In un mar di pensieri' (mid-17th cent.), in London, Brit. Mus., MS R.M. 24, i. 11, No. 5, m. 29, misplaced accidental:

134

Ex. 25

me sem-pre, sem-pre   di   pian -

(51c) D. Delair, *Traité d'accompagnement*, Paris, 1690, p. 21:

'One sometimes finds in opera basses, a flat, or a sharp, before a figure but the said flats or sharps, do not modify at all the said figures, they only indicate that the natural chord has to be major or minor.'

(d) Another recurrent and very easy mistake, in figured bass, is ♭ in place of 6 or 6 in place of ♭, as at Ex. 26.

Ex. 26. Giacomo Carissimi, cantata, 'In un mar di pensieri' (mid-17th cent.), in Vienna, Nat. Lib., MS 17765, ff. 41–8 v, (a) mm. 7–8, 6 for ♭ and ♭ for 6; (b) mm. 45–46, corresponding section correctly notated:

Ex. 26

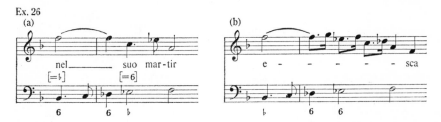

(a) nel___ suo mar-tir   (b) e - - - - sca

3. TABLATURE AS A CHECK ON ACCIDENTALS

(a) *Tablature* can help with accidentals. This is because it notates indirectly, by showing the fingerings which (with the tuning intended) will produce the notes desired.

Since all notes (diatonic or chromatic) have their independent fingerings, neither key signatures nor accidentals are required. Mistakes are just as possible as in staff notation – but not misnotated or omitted accidentals.

(b) Thus it is often useful to check the accidentals in voice or string parts against lute parts. In Ex. 27, the top string part shows a sharp before the second G, but the lute tablature shows the fingering for G natural, which the progression confirms. This is a Phrygian cadence with B flat dropping to A in the bass; a suspended A resolves on G natural before rising to A. It would still be possible to change to G sharp in the second measure, and might look desirable to a player seeing only the top line; but not in the harmonic context shown by the tablature.

135

Ex. 27. John Dowland, *Lachrimae*, London, [1605], 'M. Giles Hobies Galiard', mm. 20–1, lute tablature used to correct wrong accidental in string part:

Ex. 27

4. CONSISTENCY AS A GUIDE TO ACCIDENTALS

(a) Mere *consistency* can sometimes be a useful guide. For example, many sequences obviously require consistent accidentals: see Ex. 7 above.

(b) Some matching phrases obviously require consistent accidentals, as at Ex. 28.

Ex. 28. J[an Pieterszoon]. S[weelinck?]., 'Praeludium', LXXI in *Dutch Keyboard Music of the 16th and 17th Centuries*, ed. Alan Curtis from the Gresse MS (17th-cent. Dutch), Amsterdam, 1961, p. 101, matching phrase transferred from right hand to left hand, and therefore requiring matching accidentals (added editorial accidental is mine):

Ex. 28

(c) Some imitations obviously require consistent accidentals: see Ex. 29 (i) below, at (a), where the C sharp notated in the bass of m. 2 implies a G sharp in the voice part.

(d) Some corresponding passages and sections obviously require consistent accidentals.

In Ex. 29 (i) below, at (a) the G in the voice part requires a sharp to match its imitation by the bass in the same measure; and this is confirmed by this G sharp serving momentarily as leading note to the A. The two As in the bass need a sharp third figured. At (b), the C requires a sharp to be consistent with (a). At (c), the two Cs, the F and the G in the voice part, and the C in the bass, all require sharps to be consistent with (a). The two As in the bass again require a sharp third figured. At (d), the two Fs and the C in the voice part require sharps, and the bass requires a sharp third figured, to be consistent with (b). The only other source at present known (Naples, Bibl. del Conservatorio di Musica 'S. Pietro a Majella', MS 33.4.17 II, ff. 145–56) is virtually identical with the source quoted, and shows no variants in this passage.

Ex. 29 (i). Giacomo Carissimi, cantata, 'Apretivi, inferni' (mid-17th cent.), in Modena, Bibl. Estense, MS Mus. G. 32 (a separate MS, dated 1662), (a) mm. 95–6; (b) m. 104, corresponding passage; (c) mm. 153–4, section corresponding to (a) in the written-out da capo repetition; (d) m. 165, passage corresponding to (b) – all requiring consistent accidentals:

Ex. 29 (i)

(e) A simpler case is Ex. 29 (ii) at (a), which confirms that the accidental in subsequent matching passage at (b) is to be taken as retrospective.

Ex. 29 (ii). Giuseppe Giamberti, 'O belle lagrimette', in *Raccolta d'arie spirituali*, Rome, 1640, retrospective accidental confirmed by matching passage:

Ex. 29 (ii)

5. INDICATIONS FROM THE MELODY

(a) Considerations of *melody* are often indicative. For example, baroque melody in the minor tends to go up with sharps and down with flats.

Ex. 30. Claudio Monteverdi, *Orfeo*, perf. Mantua, 1607, publ. Venice, 1609, Act II, violin parts in the aria 'Possente spirto', sharp in ascent not influencing subsequent descent:

Ex. 31. Antonio Vivaldi, violin concerto in A minor, Op. 3 (*L'Estro armonico*, Amsterdam, 1712), No. 6, 1st movt., m. 55, solo violin, ascending sharps not influencing subsequent descent in a minor melody:

But there are exceptions, as at Ex. 13 above.

(b) Again, augmented seconds and diminished thirds are relatively uncommon in early baroque melody: see Ex. 11 and Ex. 15(a) (at m. 10).

But likewise there are exceptions. Thus at Ex. 32(a), the second measure shows a clearly notated augmented second from E flat to F sharp; and others as clear occur elsewhere in *Orfeo* to emphasize words of grief or compassion. We may therefore take the influence of the sharp as extending to the other Fs, which gives matching augmented seconds.

At Ex. 32(b), the diminished third is confirmed by the bass, of which the tritone progression (also found elsewhere in *Orfeo*) is in turn confirmed by the melody.

At Ex. 32(c), the clearly notated augmented second is matched to the grievous words.

138

At Ex. 32(d), on the other hand, the words are happy, and also the shape of the melody precludes an augmented second.

Ex. 32. Claudio Monteverdi, *Orfeo*, perf. Mantua, 1607, publ. Venice, 1609, (a) Act III, harp obligato in the aria 'Possente spirto', (b) Act IV, (c) Act V, unusual but correct melodic intervals; (d) Act V, usual interval correct:

(c) In Ex. 33, the notation shows the first B as natural. The second
B is not marked, and might therefore be mistaken by a modern performer, relying on the modern bar-line convention, for B natural also;
but in baroque music there is no bar-line convention, and as this
phrase is descending in the minor, B flat is more probable. The A next
following is (by the key signature) notated flat; but in the third measure
the matching A of the sequence, an octave lower, is (by an accidental)
notated natural, and the first A in the first measure has probably had a
similar accidental left out by mistake. But the second A in the first
measure, also notated flat (by the key signature) is confirmed as flat
by the precautionary accidental (the flat) on the matching A of the
sequence, an octave lower, in the fourth measure. If, in the first measure,
we take the second B as natural and the first A as flat (which a performer relying literally on modern conventions would be bound to do),
we get a melodically unconvincing augmented second here (though not
in the matching passage of the sequence an octave lower). Melodic
considerations seem decisive, and the best solution is as shown below.

Ex. 33. Antonio Vivaldi, *Il Cimento dell'Armonia e dell'Inventione*,
Op. 8, Paris [*c*. 1730] and Amsterdam [*c*. 1730] No. 4, 'The Four
Seasons' (violin concertos), 'Winter', 3rd movt., mm. 80–3, accidentals
suggested by melodic considerations:

6. INDICATIONS FROM THE HARMONY

(a) Considerations of harmony may likewise be indicative; but here,
considerable caution is required. Thus Ex. 32(b) above, like many others
in Monteverdi and his contemporaries, is a bolder use of key tonality
than could be found in Corelli or Lully; but it is, of course, intended.
Even Blow and Purcell were too bold for subsequent eighteenth-century
taste.

THE TREATMENT OF ACCIDENTALS

(51d) Charles Burney, *A General History of Music*, 4 Vols., London, 1776–1789, ed. F. Mercer, 2 Vols., London, 1935, repr. New York, 1957, p. 352:

[Blow has] 'licenses in the harmony which look and sound quite barbarous.' [f.n.] 'But the passing-notes, and notes of embellishment of the composers, in general, of this period, were uncouth in melody and licentious in harmony.' [Three pages of 'Specimens of Dr. Blow's Crudities' follow in musical examples, and *some* truly are crude!]

Ex. 34. John Blow, passages quoted by Dr. Burney, as above, pp. 353–4, harmony unacceptable to Burney but certainly intended by Blow:

Ex. 34

At Ex. 34 (a) above, Burney's objection was to the augmented second between G sharp in the melody and F natural in the bass; but the progression was one familiar in Monteverdi, and habitual in Blow and Purcell. At (b), the scale in the melody ascending with sharps clashes with the scale in the bass descending with flats – see Section 5 at (a) above – but this was likewise a familiar idiom of the seventeenth century though hardly of the eighteenth. At (c), a particular form of the same clash is shown, which was a regular idiom in the English school of Byrd and others, and also in Monteverdi and other Italian composers of the late renaissance and early baroque periods (but in most instances, the sharp in the bass, which is in fact a leading note, rises a semitone to its tonic–which would here be D; in this instance, the bass falls to the 2 of a 4–2, thereby becoming still more incomprehensible, no doubt, to Dr. Burney). At (d), the same clash was aggravated, for Dr. Burney, by the upwards resolution of the suspended A, in place of the normal downwards resolution.

(b) The diminished octave shown in Ex. 34 above at (c), and the augmented octave shown at (b) and at (d), are also shown below. In Ex. 35, the clash of the diminished octave, C sharp in the lower against C natural in the upper part, is reached by stepwise contrary motion outwards, and resolved by stepwise contrary motion inwards, which is the most frequent, the most logical and therefore the most comprehensible and convincing form of this idiom. The B's all seem best taken flat.

Ex. 35. Giovanni Coperario (John Cooper), fantasy 'Che Pue Mirarvi' [sic] (early 17th cent.), Christ Church Lib., Oxford, MS 21, m. 5 on p. 163 (no variant accidentals here in Christ Church, MS 2, f. 170 v):

Ex. 35
(short score)

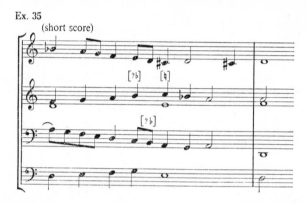

(c) In Ex. 36, the diminished octave clash is reached by leap in similar motion, which is a much harsher variant, but one greatly favoured by Monteverdi.

Ex. 36. Claudio Monteverdi, *Orfeo*, perf. Mantua, 1607, publ. Venice, 1609, Act V, diminished octave approached by leap:

Ex. 36

non so - ra il duol   con - for - me

(d) In Ex. 37, a similar progression, but with the sharp leading note in the upper part, and the flattened peak of the phrase in the lower part, produces an augmented octave, in a manner frequently encountered in renaissance music and in early baroque music but hardly in late baroque music.

Ex. 37. Nicholas Carleton, 'Gloria Tibi Trinitas', Mulliner MS (English, 2nd half of 16th cent.), ed. Denis Stevens, *Musica Britannica*, I, London, 1951, p. 5:

Ex. 37

(e) In examples such as those above, harmonies or progressions which are, to some extent, exceptional are nevertheless correct, and no change of the notated accidentals is required or acceptable.

But in other instances, a change in the notated accidentals is required or at least desirable, simply because the harmony or the progression itself suggests it. With every precaution against making anachronistic changes, we should nevertheless take these harmonic considerations fully into account, even where none of the practices so far discussed seems quite to cover them.

(f) In Ex. 38, the vertical combination is decisive, both at (a) and at (b).

At Ex. 38(a), the first F in bar 2 of the lower voice is notated sharp; but the second F, which is not given an accidental, must be taken natural, since it is plainly the tonic of an F major triad, in root position, with the F natural an octave below already sounding in the bass. Contrast this situation carefully with those shown above at Ex. 34, Ex. 35, Ex. 37 and, especially, Ex. 36.

At Ex. 38(b), the first C in the second part from the top would, other things being equal, probably be best taken sharp by retrospective influence from the second C, which, as leading note, is (correctly) notated sharp; the B before being then taken natural as sixth of the scale. But other things are not equal; for the progression decisively precludes it. The first C is plainly functioning as the fifth (i.e. the dominant) in a six-three inversion of an F major triad (the D which persists in the lower part but one becoming an 'added sixth' to this inverted triad). We therefore know here that the sharp notated is not retrospective. Compare Ex. 19(b) and Ex. 23(a) above; but contrast Ex. 16(a), Ex. 17, Ex. 18, Ex 19(a), Ex. 20(a), (b) and (c), Ex. 21 and Ex. 22(i) (a).

Ex. 38. Claudio Monteverdi, *Orfeo*, perf. Mantua, 1607, publ. Venice, 1609, (a) Act V, accidental proved by the harmony not to persist; (b) Act III, accidental proved by the harmony not to be retrospective:

Ex. 38

(a)

do - ve ha vir - tù ve - ra - ce de - gno

do - ve ha vir - tù ve - ra - ce de - gno

(b) (short score)

(g) At Ex. 39(a), considerations of harmony are negative and prohibitive. The progression is from A minor to C major. Therefore the influence of the sharp notated before the first G cannot persist on the subsequent Gs, all of which are to be taken natural.

At Ex. 39(b), on the other hand, considerations of harmony are positive and mandatory. The progression is from F major to G minor, by way of a Phrygian-type cadence or half-close on the notated bass E flat to D. To this progression, E flats are harmonically appropriate: E naturals are not. Therefore the influence of the flat notated before the E in the bass must be regarded as extending retrospectively to the previous Es in the voice part, all of which are to be taken flat. This is confirmed (indeed, would in any case be suggested) by the melodic contour of the voice part.

Ex. 39. Giacomo Carissimi, (a) cantata, 'Deh, memoria' (mid-17th cent.), in Rome, Vatican Lib., MS Chigi Q. IV, 18, ff. 43–8 v, and (virtually identical), MS Chigi Q. IV. 11, ff. 1–6 v, mm. 29–30, non-persistence of accidental confirmed by harmonic progression; (b), cantata, 'Nella più verde età dell'anno' (mid-17th cent.) in Florence, Conserv., MS 3808, ff. 71–94 v, Oxford, Christ Church, MS 51, pp. 116–28, Bologna, Bibl. del Conserv., X 235, No. 2, Naples, Bibl. del Conserv., 33.5. 16, ff. 104–20 v (all identical with regard to these accidentals); retrospective influence of accidental confirmed by harmonic progression and melodic contour:

Ex. 39

7. PRECAUTIONARY ACCIDENTALS

(a) Precautionary accidentals occur freely in the baroque period, often helpfully, and sometimes with interesting implications.

(b) At Ex. 40, the implication is that Peri, who gave notice–see Ch. XIII, Section 5 (b), quotation (51) above–that he wanted an accidental to influence 'that note alone on which it is shown', nevertheless did not trust his own instruction (and indeed he was not consistent in applying it–see Ex. 4 above). It is, however, a desirable precaution here in view of the progression, which could easily be mistaken as leading to a major triad.

Ex. 40. Jacopo Peri, *Euridice*, 1600, p. 30, mm. 3–5, precautionary accidental, theoretically unnecessary:

(c) Ex. 41 shows a precautionary accidental, the flat notated before the first B in the bass, which was absolutely necessary to prevent a contemporary performer from taking it as natural by retrospective influence from the sharp (i.e. natural) notated before the second B. He would have been all the more inclined to fall into that misinterpretation since it avoids the augmented second between this note and the C sharp immediately before it. By notating the precautionary B flat, however, Monteverdi made it plain that the augmented second, though unusual, is intended, and that the sharp after it is not retrospective.

In this same Ex. 41, however, Monteverdi (or his printer) left out (probably by oversight) another precautionary accidental which would have been desirable. There is a sharp correctly notated before the first G in the lower voice-part. The remaining Gs, however, are natural, as a comparison with the next measure shows; for here, the upper voice-part has the same phrase in imitation, with a sharp correctly notated before the first C, and a (to them) precautionary or (to us) cancelling flat (i.e. natural) notated before the second C. Moreover, the augmented second between G sharp and F natural which would result in the lower voice-part from not taking the remaining Gs as natural surely makes (unlike the augmented second in the bass) no sort of musical sense whatsoever.

145

Ex. 41. Claudio Monteverdi, *Orfeo*, perf. Mantua 1607, publ. Venice 1609, p. 45, mm. 7–8 (Act II), two precautionary accidentals (and one more needed which is conspicuous by its absence):

Ex. 41

(d) Ex. 42 shows another example of a precautionary accidental which was necessary at the time, although to us it may look rather bewildering at first sight. The flat notated before the first D in the Cantus part lowers it by a semitone; but not from D natural, which would give an impossible D flat. The lowering can only be from D sharp, giving a perfectly possible D natural. But why would this first D have been (but for the precautionary accidental) regarded as a D sharp? That can only have been because of a retrospective influence potentially exerted by the sharp notated before the second D.

The precautionary accidental was therefore necessary in order to *prevent* this potentially retrospective influence. The second D, notated sharp, is the leading note to E minor. We might well conclude, from the harmonic progression, that the first D is already part of this cadence: i.e. likewise a leading note, and therefore sharp. To prevent this misunderstanding, Viadana, not being in the habit of using natural signs for general cancellation, could only use a flat. This makes perfect sense on the assumption that otherwise the note was to all intents and purposes D sharp, and almost certain, in the absence of a precautionary accidental, to be so regarded. But only retrospective influence from the notated sharp could account for that.

This is one of the neatest proofs that retrospective accidentals (for which see Ch. XIII, Sect. 6 above) were not merely an occasional aberration, but an established though inconsistent convention which had to be taken into consideration then, and which has to be taken into consideration now in preparing baroque music for performance.

Ex. 42 Lodovico (Grossi da) Viadana, *Cento concerti ecclesiastici*, Venice, 1602, II, 'Peccavi super numerum', m. 10 (counting by the bass), precautionary accidental to prevent retrospective influence:

Ex. 42

(e) When a clearly precautionary accidental is notated, it should (if interpreted correctly) be decisive; but no reliance should be placed on finding precautionary accidentals, clear or otherwise. A good instance of notational casualness in this (as in so many other) respects will be found at Ex. 33 above.

8. CERTAIN SITUATIONS REQUIRING ACCIDENTALS

(a) There are certain situations in baroque music (as there are similar though not identical situations in earlier music) which more or less strongly suggest or even necessitate accidentals, whether or not these are notated in the written text.

9. SHARPENING THE LEADING NOTE

(a) The most prevalent and important element in these situations is the leading note.

(b) The leading note is that sharp or sharpened (or natural or naturalized) seventh note of the scale which, with one of the most powerful attractions in the whole tonal field of force, draws the mind across the narrow interval of a semitone to a point of arrival on the tonic.

Perhaps it costs the human voice a little less effort to change vibration by this smallest of diatonic intervals; for on such little differences the ingrained associations of tonality may well be built. A fourth, or a fifth, will have the same ease, because of the simple relationship of their vibrations to those of the tonic.

When a leading note moves to its tonic, and when at the same time the bass reaches it by leaping (from the dominant) up a fourth or down a fifth, the strongest forces in key tonality are present; and it was the growing preference for this situation which did most to weaken mode and develop key, until by the late renaissance, this great revolution was achieved in all but name.

(c) Even in the sixteenth century, and still more by the seventeenth, sharp leading notes were standard practice.

(51e) Thomas Morley, *Plaine and Easie Introduction to Practicall Musicke*, London, 1597, p. 144:

'In your third note you have a flat *Cadence* in your counter Tenor, which is a thing against nature, for everie *Cadence* is sharpe [with exceptions described as] passing closes and not of the nature of yours, which is a kind of full or final close.'

(52) Agostino Agazzari, *Del sonare sopra 'l basso*, Siena, 1607, p. 7:

'All cadences, whether intermediate or final, demand the major third; some people, therefore, do not mark it, but as an added precaution, I recommend using the sign.'

(53) Charles Butler, *Principles of Musik*, London, 1636, p. 83:

'Nevertheless the *La Cadence* [with unsharpened leading note] is sometimes admitted; as in these examples.'

Ex. 43. Charles Butler, *loc. cit.*, 'Phrygian cadences', leading note not to be sharpened:

Ex.43

(54) Matthew Locke, *Melothesia*, London, 1673, Rule 3:

'[Where the bass] riseth Four, or falleth five Notes . . . the Thirds are *Thirds Major*, and are so to be Play'd . . .'

(d) But notice that the last of Butler's three examples at Ex. 43 above is an exception to Locke's statement of the rule at (54), being, in fact, one form (though not the most usual form, which Butler's first example shows) of Phrygian cadence. The Phrygian cadence, known by its falling semitone, never has its rising element (the whole tone D to E in Ex. 43) sharpened by *musica ficta*, and must not have (the German sixth which results was not unknown to baroque composers, but hardly lies within the performer's proper option).

It is not, of course, a Phrygian cadence when the falling element is a whole tone, even if this happens in the bass (instead of the more usual leap by a fourth up or a fifth down). In Ex. 44, the D in the voice part needs to be sharpened, as a normal leading note; and this is confirmed by a subsequent matching passage, where the sharp on the D is in fact notated.

Ex. 44. Giacomo Carissimi, solo cantata, 'Bel tempo per me se n' andò' (mid-17th cent.), Rome, Vatican Lib., MS Barb. lat. 4136, ff. 43–52 (identical for these passages in Bologna, Conservatory, MS X234, ff. 69–76 v), (a) sharpened leading note required though not marked; (b) matching passage confirming this by marking the required sharp:

Ex. 44

(a)   (b)

[-e] - ra-no a   -   miei   [-ba] - va non tur - ba - va

(e) Ex. 45 shows a normal dominant to tonic passing close, from E major triad to A major triad. It is necessary to supply editorially a sharp on the two Gs, although none appears in the notation. For the sharp supplied editorially on F, see (c) below; for the sharp supplied editorially as a figuring of the bass A (rendering this unmarked triad major instead of minor), see (e) below.

Ex. 45. Claudio Monteverdi, *Orfeo*, perf. Mantua, 1607, publ. Venice, 1609, Act I, duet, leading note G unmarked but requiring to be sharpened (also sixth of scale F unmarked but requiring to be sharpened; also Picardy Third unmarked but required in the accompaniment):

Ex. 45

[ve-] - - - - - ste di fior   la pri-ma - ve [-ra]

[ve-] - - - - - ste di fior la pri-ma -ve - - - [-ra]

10. SHARP SIX IMPLIED BY SHARP SEVEN

(a) When the seventh of the scale, as leading note, is sharp or sharpened, then the sixth of the scale, in any ordinary circumstances, also requires to be sharp or sharpened: i.e. sharp seven ordinarily implies sharp six.

(b) In Ex. 32(d) above, the last two Fs (in the top part) are correctly marked sharp. The E immediately before them, as sixth note of the scale, is natural (and is so shown), the flat before the first E of the previous beat remaining in force for the second E in that beat but not beyond. This is confirmed by the necessity to preserve a good melodic contour, since in this instance there is neither musical nor verbal justification for an augmented second from E flat to F sharp. No good baroque singer would have been likely to go wrong here.

(c) In Ex. 45 above, a similar situation occurs, except that the G, as leading note, itself requires to be sharpened although not so marked. The F also requires to be sharpened, although not so marked, to avoid

149

the musically and verbally unjustified augmented second which would otherwise result between F natural and G sharp. (For musically justified augmented seconds in Monteverdi, see Ex. 32(a); and for others both musically and verbally justified, see Ex. 32(c), and the remarkable bass of Ex. 41.)

(d) In Ex. 46 below, the C as leading note requires to be sharp, and is so marked; the B as sixth of the scale requires to be sharpened (i.e. taken as B natural) although not so marked. This is necessary to avoid a musically and verbally justifiable augmented second from B flat to C sharp. Confirmation in this instance is provided by the fact that the speed of these quite short notes would make an augmented second not only unjustifiable but virtually unsingable.

Ex. 46. Claudio Monteverdi, *Orfeo*, perf. Mantua, 1607, publ. Venice, 1609, Act I, sixth of the scale requiring to be sharpened where the seventh of the scale is sharpened as leading note:

(e) In Ex. 47, the first alto G, as leading note, is shown sharpened; but the F which immediately follows it as the sixth note of the scale (in the ornamental resolution of the suspended A) must also be sharpened, although not so shown, and although it clashes quite sharply against the F natural (which falls to E) in the tenor. All this is confirmed by the accompanying lute tablature. The whole piece is full of similar instances. And indeed, early baroque music abounds in them.

(f) We may sum up this aspect of the situation by saying that any preparation to and any resolution from a suspended dominant fourth (i.e. the tonic) on to the dominant third as leading note (i.e. the seventh of the tonic scale) normally requires that dominant third to be major; and that any ornamental preparation or resolution thereof involving the dominant second (i.e. the sixth of the tonic scale) normally requires that dominant second to be major also. Sharpened 7 implies sharpened 6.

A variety of examples (some more typical than others) may be seen at Ex. 13, Ex. 29(i) (c), Ex. 32(d), Ex. 34(b), Ex. 34(d) and Ex. 45 above. But notice also the very unusual and interesting exceptions at Ex. 32 above.

Ex. 47. John Dowland, *Lachrimae*, London, [1605], 'Lachrimae Coactae', m. 2, sixth note of the scale requiring to be sharpened when the seventh note is sharp as leading note:

Ex. 47

(g) In Ex. 48, m. 2, the alto enters (and is correctly shown as entering) on a G natural against the G sharp correctly shown (as leading note) in the treble. The F in the alto is also correctly shown as natural; but the ornamental resolution in m. 3 of the lute tablature (here transcribed into staff notation) correctly shows F sharp as the sixth of the scale to the correctly sharpened G as the seventh of the scale. Thus the solution here, bold as it may appear, is simply to follow the notated accidentals as written, with no editorial modification whatsoever.

Ex. 48. John Dowland, *Lachrimae*, London, [1605], 'Lachrimae Antiquae', concluding measures, accidentals as notated bold but correct:

Ex. 48

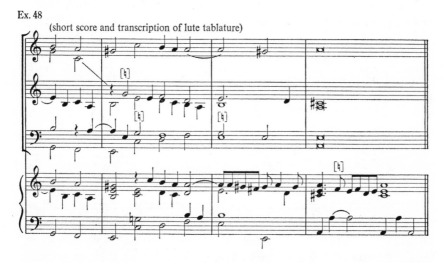

(h) Casualness in notating (though not in performing) the required sharpening of the sixth of the scale, in conjunction with the sharp or sharpened seventh of the scale as leading note, continued to some extent throughout the baroque period, and may therefore have to be corrected by a modern editor or performer.

Ex. 49 shows an example in the bass part of a printed opera score, where the notated E flat before the notated F sharp requires to be taken as E natural to avoid the musically unjustified augmented second which would otherwise result. This can be confirmed from a separate source, namely a manuscript part-book, which shows the required accidental correctly notated.

Ex. 49. Jean-Philippe Rameau, *Castor et Pollux*, Paris, 1737, (a) printed score, accidental requiring to be supplied on the sixth of the scale rising to the correctly sharpened seventh of the scale as leading note; (b) confirmation from the same accidental correctly notated in the 'Basse Continuë Generalle', Paris, Bibl. Nat. Vm² 335:

Ex. 49

(i) That Ex. 49 shows a genuine instance of old-fashioned notation, rather than a mere slip of the pen, is perhaps rather confirmed by the occurrence of other, unmistakable archaisms. Thus in the surviving manuscript part-books for the same opera (the set is not complete), both sharp and natural signs are used for cancelling flats in the signature, evidently with no distinction intended, as at Ex. 50.

Ex. 50. Jean-Philippe Rameau, *Castor et Pollux* (printed Paris, 1737), manuscript part-book, Paris, Bibl. Nat. Vm² 335, (a) 'Sᵈ Violon D'acc. [concertino] hautbois et flûte', chorus 'C'est à toi', m. 7, natural sign used to cancel flat in signature; (b) one copy of 'Sᵉ Violin [ripieno]', *ibid.*, playing the same notes in unison, sharp sign used to cancel flat in signature (another copy of this ripieno part, however, is notated like the concertino part):

Ex. 50

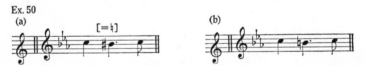

Ex. 50 also to some extent supports the statement concerning archaic French notation by Türk, quoted in Chapter XIII, Section 7(b) above, at 51(b); but it is from Türk that we learned that half a century later, similar habits of notation continued, by which time they were much more archaic still.

11. FLATTENING AT THE PEAK OF A PHRASE

(a) When at the top of a phrase there is the rise of a single note, which then falls back again, that note tends to be at the interval of a semitone rather than of a tone, whether so marked or not.

(b) There was an old medieval and renaissance mnemonic for this: *Una nota super la Semper est canendum fa,* one note above *la* is always to be sung *fa.* In hexachordal terms, this means that one note above (for example) A is always to be sung B flat and not B natural.

(c) Ex. 51 shows a fairly late though perfectly normal example of *Una nota super la Semper est canendum fa,* at (a) as left unnotated in most copies, and requiring to be introduced by the performer; and at (b) as notated in one copy, which thereby confirms the necessity of introducing it. Example 51 (c) shows a similar passage, not very much earlier, where it seems evident that the same principle applies, since the case is very typical.

> Ex. 51. (a) Henry Purcell, second phrase of 'Fairest Isle' (late 17th cent.), as shown in *Orpheus Britannicus,* one note rising and at once falling again at the top of the phrase, and therefore requiring to be taken flat although not so marked in most copies; (b) the same phrase as it is printed in *Apollo's Banquet, Second Book,* London, 1691, additional sheet, with the requisite flat notated, and also with the conventional though optional inequality notated, for which see Chapter XIX below; (c) Giacomo Carissimi, 'Amor mio', Bologna, Civico Museo Bibliografico Musicale, MS V 289, ff. 139–42 v, m. 7 on f. 140 v (and identically here in Harvard Univ., Houghton Lib., MS Mus. 106; Modena, Biblioteca Estense, MS Mus. G. 30; Venice, Conservatorio di Musica, MS 11), one note rising and falling again at the top of the phrase, and therefore requiring to be taken flat although not so marked:

Ex. 51
(a) [all] isles ____ ex - [celling]
(b) [isles ____ ex - celling]
(c) [commer-] - - - - cio ___

(d) This principle of flattening a single note which rises and falls again can apply in any part, including the bass. Ex. 52 shows, at (b), a bass-part rising from D to E and falling back. No flat is notated, but E flat is required, and this is confirmed by the E flat notated against it in an upper part, as well as by an E flat in the bass correctly notated in the following measure; also by the notation, at (a), of the corresponding bar of which this is a varied repeat.

153

Ex. 52. William Randall, setting of Dowland's 'Lachrimae Pavan', in *Tisdale's Virginal Book*, c. 1600, ed. Alan Brown, London, 1966, pp. 17–22, (a) m. 6, E flat correctly notated in bass; (b) mm. 13–16, corresponding passage, E flat in bass, etc., correctly added in bass by the editor:

Ex. 52
(a)

(b)

(e) Ex. 53 shows a precautionary sharp (i.e. natural) against two Es which would need no such precaution were it not that a baroque musician would otherwise have taken them as obvious cases of *Una nota super la Semper est canendum fa*: i.e. as E flats.

Ex. 53. Claudio Monteverdi, *Orfeo*, perf. Mantua, 1607, publ. Venice, 1609, Act II, duet, precautionary sharps notated to prevent an improvised flattening on single notes rising to and falling from the top of a phrase:

Ex. 53

[parti-] – ta in sul fio - rir de' gior – – ni

[gior-]-ni in sul fio - rir de' gior – – – – ni

Ex. 54 shows a typical key signature of two flats, for the key of C minor, where the A, though shown natural, is certainly required to be flat.

Ex. 54. Jean-Baptiste Lully, *Amadis*, Paris, 1684, Act V, 'Chaconne', passage of continuo bass requiring an added flat on melodic grounds (for the single note rising and falling at the top of the phrase) and on harmonic grounds (to conform with the prevailing key of C minor):

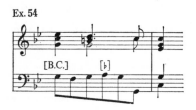

Ex. 54

12. SHARPENING AT THE TROUGH OF A PHRASE

(a) Likewise, when at the bottom of a phrase there is the fall of a single note, which then rises back again, that note tends to be at the easy interval of a semitone rather than of a tone, whether so marked or not.

But this tendency is not nearly so strong, unless the falling and returning note is in fact a leading note, and therefore requiring to be sharp in any case.

(b) The first F in Ex. 37 above could, as a result of the tendency just stated, be taken as a sharp, although not so marked. But it is not really functioning in the capacity of a leading note; and the choice is therefore quite an open one. At all events, the second F, which does not rise back but goes on descending, has certainly to be taken as a natural.

(c) But in Ex. 35 above, the treble C sharp, besides representing a fall and return at the bottom of a phrase, also functions as a leading note, and would certainly have to be sharpened if it were not (as it is) already so marked. And the alto C natural (which has momentarily crossed above the treble, representing as it does a single note rising and falling back at the top of a phrase), must remain natural (as it is marked) in spite of (or more truly because of) its clash with the simultaneous C sharp in the treble.

13. AVOIDING UNDESIRED TRITONES

(a) When the tritone ('three-tone') interval (either as augmented fourth or as diminished fifth) took on more prominence than medieval and renaissance musicians cared to give it (disliking not its dissonance,

155

which is mild, but its tonal ambiguity, which is extreme), they tended to make the imperfect interval perfect by a written or improvised accidental.

(b) On the other hand, the rather disturbing poignancy and instability of the tritone, both as melody and as harmony, were deliberately exploited for their expressive effect by many advanced composers of the late sixteenth and early seventeenth centuries, including Monteverdi.

Later in the baroque period, when its first revolutionary excitement was passing into a more classical restraint, the tritone relationship (as between E flat major and A major, much favoured by Monteverdi) grew less prominent as a harmonic progression, except in its disguised version as the Neapolitan Sixth. But the tritone interval itself had come to stay, as had diminished thirds and fourths.

(c) In Ex. 55 (a), in one manuscript, the A is notated as natural, though both melodic and harmonic considerations may incline us to take this as A flat, despite the prominent diminished fourth, from A flat to E. We can confirm our inclination, not only from matching passages in the same piece, but also from the same passage in another manuscript, which notates A flat, as at (b). A similar case, confirmed by a matching passage, is shown at (c) and (d), with prominent tritone.

Ex. 55. Giacomo Carissimi, (a) 'In un mar di pensieri' (mid-17th cent.), London, King's Music Lib. (Brit. Mus.), MS R.M. 24. i. 11, No. 5, m. 52, diminished fourth requiring to be introduced when not so notated; (b) the same passage in Vienna, Österreichische National-bibliothek, MS 17765, ff. 41–8 v, showing the required accidental notated; (c) same piece, Brit. Mus. MS R.M. 24. i. m. 68, melodic tritone requiring to be introduced although not so notated; (d) m. 74, confirmation from matching passage so notated:

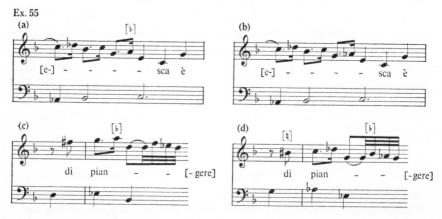

Ex. 55

(d) The only situation in which the older prejudice against tritone intervals can clearly be seen in baroque music is the general under-standing, for figured bass, that a fifth will ordinarily be taken to be perfect, not diminished, without the necessity to notate it so in the figuring; and even to this exception, there are many exceptions.

14. INTRODUCING THE PICARDY THIRD

(a) The minor third is acoustically so ambivalent an interval (because the major third always present in the overtones of its lower note clashes with it, however subliminally), that neither medieval musicians (who preferred a bare fifth) nor renaissance musicians (who preferred a major triad) regarded it as reposeful or conclusive enough for final or other important closes.

(b) When a final or other important close would otherwise reach a tonic triad with minor third, it remained standard early baroque practice to change it to major, either by a notated or by an improvised accidental. This change is known as the *Tierce de Picardie*, the Picardy Third.

The chief difficulty is to decide which closes are important and suitable enough to invite it. Many closes are quite optional in this respect.

(55) Francesco Bianciardi, *Breve regola per imparar' a sonare sopra il basso*, Siena, 1607, ninth rule:

'In the final closes, one always ends with the major Third.'

(56) Wolfgang Ebner, German translation by Johann Andreas Herbst in his *Arte prattica e poëtica*, Frankfurt, 1653, Rule 8:

'When it is a full cadence, the last note must always be taken with the sharp.'

(57) Lorenzo Penna, *Primi Albori musicali*, Bologna, 1672, Bk. III, Ch. V, Second Rule:

'On the last note, [introduce a] major third.'

(58) Friedrich Erhard Niedt, *Musikalische Handleitung*, I, Hamburg, 1700, Ch. VIII, Rule 6:

'[Close in the major regardless of what goes before, except that] French composers do the opposite, but everything is not good merely because it comes from France.' [Nor is this observation concerning French composers necessarily reliable.]

(c) The change to major which constitutes the Picardy Third may also be notated.

In that case, it is chiefly of importance for the performer to be aware that the very next chord, at the very beginning of the next phrase, may be the same chord, but in the minor; and that he cannot rely upon this being indicated in the notation, even if the previous change to major has been indicated.

Ex. 45 above shows two Picardy Thirds: the A major chord which starts the second measure has to be supplied by the accompanist without any indication notated into the figuring of the bass, though there is confirmation half way through the measure from the C sharp notated in the second voice part; the D major chord following is shown by the notated F sharp in the first voice part, but is not notated into the figuring of the bass.

(d) Ex. 56 shows at (a) a typical passing close with Picardy Third duly notated into the figuring of the bass, as a chord of E major although the passage, and indeed the piece, is in E minor. The pick-up to the new phrase, a quarter note later, has the return to the minor notated (as a flat) into the figuring of the bass; but there is no indication in the voice-part, although this enters simultaneously.

Four measures later, the piece ends, with an unfigured E in the bass and another E in the voice. Apart from the convention of the Picardy Third, there is nothing to tell the accompanist to take this chord in E major, with the G sharpened. But he undoubtedly should do so; and this is confirmed by the four parallel passages earlier in the piece, two of which show, in the same manuscript, the corresponding chord as major by a sharp in the figuring. One passage (ironically enough, the first) omits the sharp without apparent reason, although requiring it; and one (the fourth) has a flat in the figuring, as a precautionary accidental, in order to prevent the accompanist from introducing a G sharp here: see Ex. 56 (b). But this is because the voice part enters, this time, a beat earlier, with the start of the next phrase; and in each other case, though the cadence is major, the new entry of the voice is in the minor.

Nevertheless, in another manuscript of the same piece, the scribe preferred the Picardy Third, of which the tradition was evidently still extremely strong: see Ex. 56 (c).

Ex. 56. Giacomo Carissimi, 'Deh, memoria' (mid-17th cent.), in Rome, Vatican Lib., (a) MS Chigi Q. IV. 18, ff. 43–8 v, m. 88, voice-part entering in the minor immediately after the Picardy Third in the major, with no precautionary accidental to alert the singer, and none needed for a baroque singer; (b) the same MS at m. 79, precautionary accidental in the figuring of the bass, to prevent a Picardy Third otherwise sure to be introduced by a baroque accompanist; (c) the same measure in MS Chigi Q. IV. 11, ff. 1–6 v, Picardy Third notated in the figuring of the bass, by a scribe evidently preferring it that way:

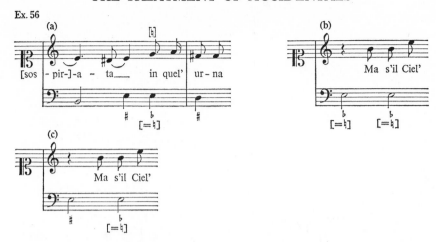

Ex. 56

15. TAKING RESPONSIBILITY FOR BAROQUE ACCIDENTALS

(a) Editors should interpret, correct and supply accidentals in baroque music, and especially in early baroque music, much more frequently than on the whole they do.

(b) Such editorial accidentals should, however, be put forward as provisional. They should be typographically distinguished by being above or below (but this is not possible with chordal music, nor on the bass line where there are figurings); in visibly smaller type (but the distinction of size must really be sufficient to be unmistakable); or within square brackets (much the clearest distinction where there is room for it, and the only one used in this book; or by footnotes; or some combination of these methods, as appropriate.

(c) It is then possible for the performer to share in the choice of accidentals.

We must appreciate that in many cases, there may well be more than one good solution. Any single choice of accidental is liable to commit us to other, consequential choices, often for an entire passage to come.

(d) Whether or not the editor has gone far enough in sorting out the accidentals, it is often quite reasonable, especially in early baroque music, to disagree with him.

Accidentals in baroque music, as a matter of principle, lie ultimately within the performer's responsibilities.

CHAPTER FIFTEEN

Ornamentation

1. ORNAMENTATION A NECESSITY IN BAROQUE MUSIC

(a) Ornamentation in music, as elsewhere, springs from a certain exuberance of the creative spirit, over and above what is structurally necessary.

Provided that the structural notes of a melody are kept reasonably intact and recognizable, the figuration can be varied without essentially altering the music.

Details of harmony within the main progressions can also be varied; and likewise details of rhythm.

The structural notes of a melody are chiefly its harmony notes, as opposed to its accented or unaccented passing and changing notes.

(b) Baroque ornamentation was heir to long ages of improvisation and tradition, originally without notation, later increasingly supported by notation, but never altogether replaced by notation.

By the late renaissance, the structure was commonly complete in the notation, and capable of sounding complete in performance; the figuration was left for the most part optionally to the performer; and the more or less improvised ornamentation by which he provided it was primarily melodic.

But in the baroque period, the structure, though commonly complete in the notation, was not always capable of sounding complete in performance; the figuration was for the most part supplied by the composer, but in so far as it was left to the performer to provide, it was obligatory rather than optional; and the more or less improvised ornamentation by which he provided it included (chiefly through the pervasive influence of the long appoggiatura) a harmonic element.

(c) Thus ornamentation is not a luxury in baroque music, but a necessity.

2. ORNAMENTATION IN THE RECITING STYLE

(a) The reciting style (*stile recitativo*) of the early baroque period ranged from free but melodious recitative, through more measured arioso, to lyrical aria of a symmetrical form whether simple or complex. But always, in Monteverdi's famous phrase (*Scherzi musicali*, Venice, 1607), the 'intention is to make the words the mistress of the music and not the servant'.

(b) In the reciting style, virtuoso ornamentation is very prominent, although restricted in theory and very largely in practice to places where it can support the meaning of the words.

(59) Giulio Caccini, *Le Nuove Musiche*, Florence, 1602 (actual date), Preface:

'[I have] placed the consonances on long syllables, and avoided short [ones], and observed the same rule in making [ornamental] passages although for a certain adornment I have sometimes used some few eighth notes up to the value of a quarter of a [whole note] beat or a half [at] the most over short syllables for the most part . . . long windings of the voice [are acceptable] in less impassioned music, and [also] over long syllables, and not short [ones], and on final cadences.'

This passage may be amplified as follows:
(i) The long syllables of the words should be set by the composer on harmony notes, as opposed to passing notes.
(ii) On such long syllables, long (but not too long) passages of ornamental figuration may be set by the composer (or introduced by the performer if not so set).
(iii) On short syllables, however, short segments (not exceeding two or at the most four eighth notes) of ornamental figuration may be composed or introduced 'for a certain adornment' of the passage (in practice, this means largely the ornamental resolution of suspensions).
(iv) These rules apply to the more impassioned kinds of music (chiefly recitative and arioso and the more emotional arias), in which the words are highly charged with emotion.
(v) But in the less impassioned kinds of music (chiefly the more lyrical arias) in which the words are rather graceful than emotional, a reasonable amount of ornamental virtuosity can be permitted purely for its own sake.
(vi) In Caccini's own published *Nuove Musiche* ('New Compositions') of 1602 and (also Florence) of 1614 (a different collection), the fairly extensive passages of composed ornamental figuration there notated should suffice, leaving only the smaller ornaments to the performer to introduce at will.

Ex. 57. Giulio Caccini, opening of 'Ardi, cor mio', (a) as notated plain in Florence, Bibl. Naz., MS Magl. XIX.66, p. 131 (and almost identically in Brussels, Bibl. du Cons., MS 704, pp. 77–8; (b) as notated ornamentally in Caccini's *Nuove Musiche*, Florence, 1602 (collated by H. Willey Hitchcock and reproduced here by kind permission):

Ex. 57

(vii) In the reciting style, the most appropriate places to ornament with more or less improvised figuration are important cadences: either on the last note but one; or on two or three notes before that (in which case, the last note but one may need a *trillo*, i.e. a tremolo-like vocal portato, or a *gruppo*, i.e. a trill).

The last note, being the point of arrival, *must not be ornamented.*

(60) Giovanni Camillo Maffei, *Delle lettere*, Naples, 1562, pp. 5–81, 3rd rule:

'One ought to make the ornamentation on the last but one syllable of the word, so that, with the ending of the word, the ornamentation also is ended.'

(61) Vincenzo Giustiniani, *Discorso sopra la Musica*, [c. 1628], ed. Angelo Solerti, *Le Origini del Melodramma*, Turin, 1903, p. 108:

'Articulate the words well in such a manner that one may hear even the last syllable of each word, which should not be interrupted or suppressed by passages or other ornaments.'

(c) Wherever the reciting style took root as a vocal idiom, similar ornamentation attached to it: particularly in France, from Caccini's visit to Paris in 1604 and de Nyert's return from Rome around 1638; and England, where Vincent Duckles (see my Bibl.) has found plain and ornamental versions of English songs of the early baroque period, contemporary with and similar to the Italian examples.

3. VOCAL ORNAMENTATION FOR ITS OWN SAKE

(a) Later in the baroque period, and above all in the eighteenth century, the ideal of expressing every sonorous inflection and emotional significance of the words in the music gave place, once again, to a pursuit of vocal virtuosity more or less for its own sake.

Only the general mood of the words, rather than their exact shades of sound and sense, might be reflected in the arias of an opera or a solo cantata by Handel and his contemporaries. Words themselves, or even syllables of words, might be repeated, for musical convenience, far beyond any dramatic or poetic validity, and sometimes to the point of verbal absurdity.

Vocal ornamentation shared in this common (though never complete) divorce of musical from dramatic or poetic considerations. It became more important to secure a good vowel on which to vocalize than to choose a word with a meaning appropriate to expressive prominence.

(b) Recitative of the later baroque period, in its characteristically Italianate varieties, was far more distinct from aria than in the early baroque period; and it is virtually incompatible with free ornamentation, *which should not be attempted there.*

(c) Late baroque Italianate arias, on the other hand, particularly of the *da capo* variety, lend themselves to a display of vocal ornamentation, more or less improvised by the singer, to an extent limited only by his innate musicianship and sense of propriety. Here, free ornamentation should usually be attempted, at least in the *da capo*. (Not too much.)

(62) Pier Francesco Tosi, *Opinioni*, Bologna, 1723, transl. Galliard as *Observations on the Florid Song*, London, 1742, p. 93:

'In the first [section of a *da capo* aria] they require nothing but the simplest Ornaments, of a good Taste and few, that the Composition may remain simple, plain and pure; in the second they expect, that to this Purity some artful Graces be added, by which the Judicious may hear, that the Ability of the Singer is greater; and in repeating the *Air* [i.e. the first section], he that does not vary it for the better, is no great Master.'

From examples surviving in writing (such as the two duets printed in Ernest T. Ferand's invaluable *Improvisation in Beispielen,* in the series *Das Musikwerk,* Cologne, 1956, Eng. transl. as *Anthology of Music,* Cologne, 1961), we know that the first time round, a *little* (but only a little) free ornamentation is appropriate, in addition to the customary small ornaments such as cadential trills, or appoggiaturas, or turns, or slides. The main consideration here is to allow the composer's own melody to appear almost unadorned, so that it can be the better recognized, under its greater adornment, the second time round at the *da capo* repeat.

The middle section, since it is often of a relatively contemplative character, may not stand very much ornamentation without damage to its contrasting function.

The *da capo* repeat of the first section allows greater scope (but still not too much) for the performer's invention in adding runs, roulades, changing notes and all manner of florid embellishment. The more unexpected these are to the hearer, the more he will enjoy the singer's daring and skill; but this enjoyment will be quite spoilt if the added embellishment is so excessive or so inappropriate as to disguise the original melody. The whole point is to recognize the original, while at the same time being surprised and delighted at its unforeseen modifications; which themselves should, however, be very similar to the original in their general idiom and style.

Dr. Burney (*History,* London, 1776, ed. of 1935, II, p. 545) wrote of an aria: 'such new and ingenious embellishments as, in Italy, every singer of abilities would be expected to produce each night it was performed'; and of the great castrato Farinelli, that: 'Of his taste and embellishments we shall now be able to form but an imperfect idea, even if they had been preserved in writing, as mere notes would only show his invention, and science, without enabling us to discover that expression and neatness which rendered his execution so perfect and surprising.' Nevertheless, the following, which has been preserved (among some others even longer and more florid), is interesting enough.

Ex. 58. Geminiano Giacomelli, *Merope,* Venice, 1734, opening of 'Quell' usignolo', (a) as written; (b) as sung with free ornamentation, including a relatively brief cadenza, by Farinelli (properly Carlo Broschi), repr. by Franz Haböck, *Die Gesangskunst der Kastraten,* Vienna, 1923, p. 140, from an unspecified manuscript in Vienna (actually Österreichische Nationalbibliothek MS 19111 No. 3):

Ex. 58

Ex. 59. George Frideric Handel, cantata 'Dolce pur d'amor l'affanno', early 18th century, facsimile of autograph in Cambridge, Fitzwilliam Museum, MS 30–H–2, by kind permission of the Syndics; ornamentation of voice part, and inconsistent notation of rhythms all

Ex. 59

(a)

(b)

meant as dotted (for which see Ch. XIX, esp. 5, below), (a) p. 10, end of aria; (b) p. 12, the same in another key, with similar but not identical notation of ornamentation (for start of this aria see Ex. 108 in Ch. XIX, 5 below).

(d) Vocal cadenzas, as in Ex. 58 (b) above, are often desirable on the dominant harmony leading to the last chord: slight, if at all, for the first section; not much more, if at all, for the middle section; more, but still not too much, for the *da capo* repeat of the first section. The cadenza should never be longer than can be sung in one breath: see (64) below. A fermata in the notation greatly increases the probability of a cadenza being required.

4. INSTRUMENTAL ORNAMENTATION

(a) In early baroque music, instrumental figuration more or less improvised by the performer occurred prominently (i) in operatic prologues, dances and ritornelli; (ii) in organ, lute and harpsichord playing; (iii) in trumpet fanfares; (iv) in divisions on a bass, etc.

Because of our interest in seventeenth-century opera, we are particularly concerned with (i), but it is for us more a problem of editing, and indeed of composing, than of impromptu performing.

(b) In later baroque instrumental music, either the editor or the performer or both will have to take action (i) in slow movements notated only with a structural outline of the melody, which it is obligatory to complete in performance with ornamental figuration, although the nature of this figuration is at the performer's option; (ii) in a variety of other situations where some such ornamentation is less obligatory, but nevertheless up to a point desirable, (iii) in situations more or less markedly calling for a cadenza, especially if a fermata appears.

Ex. 60. Arcangelo Corelli, Violin Sonatas, Op. V, Rome, 1700, No. 9, with free ornamental elaborations (first half of 18th cent.) by Francesco Geminiani, printed by Sir John Hawkins, *A General History . . . of Music*, London, 1776, ed. of 1875, II, pp. 904ff. (and in Hans-Peter Schmitz, *Die Kunst der Verzierung*, Kassel, 1955, 2nd ed., Kassel, 1965, pp. 62–9):

Ex. 60

Tempo di Gavotta Allegro

Ex. 61. Arcangelo Corelli, Violin Sonatas, Op. V, Rome, 1700, No. 1, opening slow movement, (a) as in first edition; (b) as in the ornamented playing version printed and attributed to Corelli in Roger's Amsterdam edition of ?1715, and Walsh's London edition pirated therefrom (slow movements only, of first six sonatas only, are thus ornamented; a full facsimile of this movement is given by Schmitz, *op. cit.*, pp. 55–61):

Ex. 61
(a)

(b) Grave

(c) Instrumental cadenzas are called for in many situations, where considerations similar to those calling for vocal cadenzas arise.

(63) Joachim Quantz, *Essay*, Berlin, 1752, XV, 1:

'[A cadenza is] that free ornamentation (*willkührlichen Auszierung*), which is made by a solo (*concertirenden*) part, at the close of a piece, over the last note but one of the bass part, namely over the fifth of the key in which the piece stands, according to the free will (*freyen Sinne*) and pleasure (*Gefallen*) of the performer.'

The baroque cadenza does not serve the architectural function of a classical or romantic cadenza, which is ordinarily of considerable length and substance, and leads into a final re-statement of the primary matter of the movement. The baroque cadenza has a more strictly ornamental function.

(64) Joachim Quantz, *Essay*, Berlin, 1752, XV, 5:

'The intention of the cadenza is no other than to surprise the hearer unexpectedly once more at the end, and in addition to leave a particular impression on his feeling.

'[8:] Cadenzas must flow from the principal feeling (*Hauptaffecte*) of the piece.

'[17:] Cadenzas for a singing part or a wind instrument must be so constituted that they can be made in one breath. A string player can make them as long as he likes, in so far as he is otherwise rich in invention. Yet he achieves more advantage through a reasonable shortness than through a tiresome length.'

Ex. 62. Joachim Quantz, *Essay*, Berlin, 1752, Table XX, (a) Fig. 1, cadenza faulted by Quantz because too square and repetitive; (b) Fig. 2, similar cadenza, but approved for Adagio; (c) Fig. 3, the same cadenza reduced to simpler form, for Allegro; (d) Fig. 8, cadenza suited for a 'very sad' piece:

Ex. 62

Quantz' creative talent was by no means the equal of his pedagogical ability, and the above examples are neither particularly inspired nor particularly craftsmanlike. Nevertheless they are reliable illustrations of the length and general style required.

Cadenzas in two parts simultaneously are proper (in vocal duets or in trio sonatas, for example). But Quantz very reasonably recommends that these should be worked out between the two soloists beforehand.

5. BAROQUE ORNAMENTATION IN PRACTICE

(a) The baroque preference for trusting so much of the figuration to the more or less improvised ornamentation of the performer is attested by ample contemporary evidence.

(65) Bénigne de Bacilly, *L'Art de bien chanter*, Paris, 1668, p. 135:

'The necessary embellishments . . . not marked at all on paper [because] too many marks encumber and take away the clearness of a melody.'

(66) Roger North, London, British Museum, MS Add. 32533, f. 106 v., c. 1700:

'The Manner of artificial Gracing an Upper part . . . is Incommunicable by wrighting.'

(67) Johann Adolf Scheibe, *Critische Musicus*, I, 12, Hamburg, 1737:

'All embellishments, all little graces [J. S. Bach writes in notation, and thereby] makes the melodic line utterly unclear.' [*Cf.* (65) above.]

(68) Charles Burney, posthumous article 'Adagio' in Rees' *Cyclopedia*, London, 1819:

'An adagio in a song or solo is, generally, little more than an outline left to the performers abilities to colour . . . if not highly embellished [slow notes] soon excite languor and disgust in the hearers.'

(b) Modern editors and performers can use their own judgement as to the amount and character of their ornamental figuration, so long as (i) they do enough to serve its necessary function; (ii) they keep within the bounds of discretion and the boundaries of the style.

It is far better to be on the short side than on the long side. For numerous surviving specimens on which to model our attempts, see my Bibliography under Ernest T. Ferand, Imogene Horsley and Hans-Peter Schmitz.

Ex. 63(i). (a) George (Georg) Frideric (Friedrich) Handel, Sonata in C major for Viola da Gamba (early 18th cent.) with Handel's own written-out accompaniment, plain text as notated, and suggested free ornamentation (fairly simple) by Robert Donington; (b) sample bars showing Handel's accompaniment. Ex. 63(ii) (a) Henry Purcell, Chaconne in G minor from the *Ten Sonatas in Four Parts* [i.e. Trio Sonatas for two violins, gamba continuo and keyboard continuo], London, 1697, mm. 91ff., plain text as notated, and suggested ornamentation (more elaborate) by Robert Donington; (b) mm. 79ff., plain text as notated, and brief cadenza by Robert Donington; (c) last two measures, plain text as notated, and longer cadenza by Robert Donington:

ORNAMENTATION

Ex. 63 (i)

(a) Adagio

171

Ex. 63 (i)
(b)

(first time: as notated by Handel)

(second time: as ornamented by R.D.)

(Handel's accompaniment: N.B. hold down all notes
in the right hand till the harmony changes)

Ex. 63 (ii)

(relax the rhythm approximately to triplets)

(relax the rhythm approximately to triplets)

(light and tranquil)

Ex. 63 (ii) contd.

(c) The last note of a phrase, a section or a movement, being a point of arrival and not of departure, must, in order to sound sufficiently reposeful and final, be left without free ornamentation. See (60) and (61) above, which refer to vocal music; but the principle is of a general validity and considerable importance.

(d) Whether written or unwritten in whole or part, the ornamental notes of the melody should sound graceful and flexible, as if improvised; and the structural notes should sound strong and solid, so as to make the main outline of the melody clear. The lightness with which the ornamental figuration is performed (whether from notation or not) is the essential feature.

(69) Jean-Jacques Rousseau, *Dictionnaire de Musique*, Paris, 1768, entry 'Passage':

'[Passage-work is] composed of many notes or divisions which are sung or played very lightly.'

It really does not matter how much or little, if at all, the performer is making up the ornamental figuration as he goes along. It only matters that he shall sound as though he is.

CHAPTER SIXTEEN

Ornaments

1. SIMPLIFYING THE COMPLEXITY OF BAROQUE ORNAMENTS

(a) Within that general and perennial disposition to ornamentation which so flourished throughout the baroque period, a large number of small, specific ornaments can be discerned, historically arising out of it, but achieving a more or less independent existence as units of embellishment.

These units are, for the most part, quite remarkably inconsistent in their names and their signs; but much less inconsistent in their manners of behaviour. A thorough study of them is very necessary for specialists in many particular idioms of baroque music. It is not necessary for the average performer.

It is only necessary for the average performer of baroque music to master the working principles of a very small number of extremely common ornaments, and to know well the musical contexts in which these may be desirable, or even essential, regardless of any signs or other indications which may or may not appear in the written notation.

(b) Certain rough working rules apply to baroque ornaments as a whole.

(i) Whereas most baroque ornaments are more or less optional, certain baroque ornaments are more or less obligatory. Those which are optional can be used by the performer, or not used, at his own well-trained discretion; and it need only be asked of him that, in idioms of which extensive embellishment is a normal element, a sufficiency of well-chosen ornaments shall appear. Those ornaments which are obligatory, however, must ordinarily appear wherever they are strongly implied by the musical context: they are the cadential trill; and particularly in recitative, the long appoggiatura.

(ii) The absence of any sign for an ornament should neither be taken as preventing the performer from introducing an optional ornament which suits the context; nor as excusing him from introducing an obligatory ornament which the context implies.

(iii) Conversely, the presence of any sign for an ornament should neither be taken as obliging the performer to introduce a particular ornament; nor as preventing him from introducing another ornament, or none.

(iv) By way of exception, some baroque keyboard music of the French school, or modelled upon it, shows ornaments notated by complex signs carefully applied, with the intention of their being taken more or less literally by the performer. Being contrary to the general spirit of baroque musicianship, this intention was commonly disregarded, as we know from Couperin's complaint of their 'unpardonable neglect' (*Pièces de clavecin*, III, Paris, 1722, preface). We may wish to follow the signs more closely in such a case (easily recognized in practice); but even then, the signs are never mandatory, and it would be an entirely unbaroque attitude to treat them as mandatory.

(v) Conversely, it is entirely the baroque attitude to regard signs for ornaments, not as commands, but as hints; and to be guided ultimately by taste, by context and by suitability. This precludes any over-use of ornaments; or any abuse such as gay ornaments in an expressive piece or expressive ornaments in a gay piece; or any use of ornaments against the natural idiom of an instrument.

(vi) Suitability further implies making ornaments consistent throughout fugal entries, imitations and matching passages. Thus C. P. E. Bach (*Essay*, Berlin, 1753, II, i, 28), teaches that 'all imitations must be exact to the last detail' (ornaments included). This rule is particularly reliable for fugal entries, which should normally carry identical ornaments (if any), regardless of any discrepancies in the signs (if any). It is less reliable for freer passages of imitation, and least reliable for matching passages, as will next be seen.

(vii) Conversely, this element of consistency in the choice of ornaments, though always necessary to good taste and sound musicianship, does not by any means necessarily have to be literal or identical. On the contrary, some diversity within the overall consistency may be needed to avoid monotony or anticlimax. Thus Quantz (*Essay*, Berlin, 1752, XIII, 29) recommends that in ornamenting sequences, 'the variations should not be continued in a single kind of notes; but one must soon depart from that, and try in the sequel to do something which is not like the foregoing' (including ornaments as well as free ornamentation).

(viii) Ornaments may fall between beats. They are then more or less unaccented passing or changing notes, including little notes of anticipation slipped in as lightly and as late as possible before the ensuing beat. These are *between-beat* ornaments.

(ix) Conversely, ornaments may fall upon the beat. They are then more or less accented passing or changing notes, and as such, they cannot anticipate the beat. These are *on-the-beat* ornaments.

179

(x) Some ornaments, such as turns, regularly occur either unaccented (between-beat) or accented (on-the-beat); others, such as slides, fairly often occur unaccented (between-beat) although they more often occur accented (on-the-beat); others again, such as trills and appoggiaturas, regularly occur accented (on-the-beat).

(xi) Baroque ornaments, when unattached to a beat, fall between beats. Baroque ornaments, when attached to a beat, mostly take the beat. It is this last rule which C. P. E. Bach meant when he wrote (*Essay*, Berlin, 1753, II, i, 23) that 'while the previous note is never curtailed, the following note loses as much of its duration as the [ornamental] notes take away from it'. To this he added (ed. of 1787), in words true both then and now: 'It might be thought unnecessary to repeat that the remaining parts including the bass must be sounded with the first note of the ornament. But as often as this rule is invoked, so often is it broken.' The rule is more reliable for late than for early baroque music, and at no time was accepted unanimously; but for the age of Bach and Handel it can never be wrong. It meets all ordinary situations in the strongest and most musicianly way. Those who are interested in alternative possibilities are asked to turn to my *Interpretation of Early Music*, New Version (1973). They will find there a very thorough consideration of the newest discoveries and arguments.

(xii) Many ornaments can be taken either diatonically (in the key momentarily prevailing), or chromatically (outside the key momentarily prevailing). As C. P. E. Bach puts it (*Essay*, Berlin, 1753, II, i, 17): 'the notes of an ornament adapt themselves to the sharps and flats [prevailing, but with modifications] which the trained ear at once recognises'.

(xiii) The interpretation of an ornament must be such as to make good harmony. This usually, but not always, means correct harmony. So far back as Diego Ortiz (*Trattado*, Rome, 1553, Introduction) we find the common instruction that incorrect progressions (such as consecutive fifths) are perfectly acceptable in ornamentation 'since at that speed they cannot be heard'; and as Michel de Saint-Lambert put it so well (*Traité*, Paris, 1707, VIII, 13, p. 126): 'Since music is made only for the ear, a fault which does not offend it is not a fault.'

(xiv) Between-beat ornaments, being unaccented, can hardly offend the ear by making bad harmony. They are primarily melodic (like most turns).

(xv) On-the-beat ornaments, being accented, may be either primarily rhythmic (like most mordents), with little or no influence on the harmony; or primarily harmonic (like most long appoggiaturas), with some or much influence on the harmony, and therefore needing more care from this point of view.

180

ORNAMENTS

(xvi) A few specific ornaments (especially: long appoggiaturas; half trills without termination; prolonged trills with or without turned endings; short mordents; prolonged mordents; lower appoggiatura with mordent; upper appoggiatura with trill) may be used, unlike free ornamentation, on the last note of a section or of a movement, provided that they increase rather than decrease the necessary sense of finality. This is, however, comparatively the rare exception; the common rule remains *to leave last notes plain*. See Ch. XV, Sect. 5(c) above.

(xvii) Ornaments serve as melody, as rhythm, as harmony, as colouration (like the long trills which help in sustaining the tone on the harpsichord), or in some combination of these functions. In deciding what functions the music requires, we can choose and interpret our ornaments to suit their contexts.

2. APPOGGIATURAS

(a) The appoggiatura (Ital. *appoggiare*, to lean) is an auxiliary note, more or less stressed, and commonly although not necessarily dissonant to the harmony on to which it resolves.

When dissonant, an appoggiatura is an element (both of melody and of harmony) structurally identical with a suspension except in not requiring to be (although it may be) prepared. When consonant, an appoggiatura is an element of melody, and perhaps of rhythm, but not particularly of harmony.

The influence of the long appoggiatura (with its liberation of un-prepared dissonance) upon the common progressions of harmony affords an excellent illustration of originally ornamental material becoming structural. Appoggiaturas in Bach, however necessary, are still ornamental. Appoggiaturas in Mahler, remaining such though no longer written as such, are structural.

(b) A brief silence of articulation *before* an appoggiatura is often very expressive, though it must never be exaggerated.

(70) Joachim Quantz, *Essay*, Berlin, 1752, VI, i, 8:

'It is a general rule, that one must make a small separation between the appoggiatura and the note which precedes it, above all if the two notes are at the same pitch.'

(c) Appoggiaturas take the beat. Any ornament which is called an appoggiatura, but which does not take the beat, is miscalled; for all true appoggiaturas are what their name calls them, i.e. leaning notes.

Appoggiaturas lean upon the remainder of the harmony proper to their beat.

(71) François Couperin, *L'Art de toucher le clavecin*, Paris, 1716, ed. of 1717, p. 22:

181

'Strike [appoggiaturas] with the harmony, that is to say in the time which would [otherwise] be given to the ensuing note.'

(72) J. E. Galliard, footnote to his English translation of Tosi's *Opinioni*, Bologna, 1723, as *Observations on the Florid Song*, London, 1742, p. 32:

'You lean on the [appoggiatura] to arrive at the [main] Note intended.'

(73) Friedrich Wilhelm Marpurg, *Anleitung zum Clavierspielen*, Berlin, 1755, 2nd ed., Berlin, 1765, I, ix, 4:

'All appoggiaturas . . . must come exactly on the beat . . .
'[8] the accompanying parts must not be delayed by that, but should be played at once with the appoggiatura, only the main note to which the appoggiatura is the accessory being delayed.'

(d) The length of appoggiaturas varies with the date.
Early baroque appoggiaturas are shown at a very moderate length, ranging approximately from one quarter of duple-time notes to one third of triple-time notes. Their effect on the harmony ranges from negligible to slight.
But from about the last quarter of the seventeenth century, longer appoggiaturas are shown, especially as one half of a duple-time note; and of these, the effect on the harmony becomes substantial.
By the eighteenth century, still longer appoggiaturas are in evidence; and their tendency was to grow longer as that century went on.
(e) The length of appoggiaturas also varied with the context. The standard eighteenth-century rules are as follows.

(74) Joachim Quantz, *Essay*, Berlin, 1752, VIII, vii–xi:

'Hold the appoggiatura half the length of the main note . . .
'[But] if the appoggiatura has to ornament a dotted note, that note is divided into three parts, of which the appoggiatura takes two, and the main note one only: that is to say, the length of the dot . . .
'When in six-four or six-eight time' [in fact any compound triple time] 'two notes are found tied together, and the first is dotted . . . the appoggiatura should be held for the length of the first note including its dot . . .
'When there is an appoggiatura before a note, and after [that note] a rest, the appoggiatura . . . is given the length of the note, and the note the length of the rest.'

(75) C. P. E. Bach, *Essay*, Berlin, 1753, II, ii, 16:

'[Sometimes the appoggiatura] must be prolonged beyond its normal length for the sake of the expressive feeling conveyed . . .
'Sometimes the length is determined by the harmony.'

Ex. 64. (a) Joachim Quantz, *Essay*, Berlin, 1752, end of book, Table VI, Figs. 11, 13, 15, 17, 23 to be performed as Figs. 12, 14, 16, 18, 24; (b) C. P. E. Bach, *Essay*, Berlin, 1753, II, ii, 11, noteworthy effect of appoggiatura on dotted rhythm:

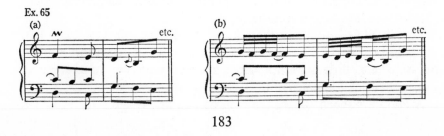

(f) In Ex. 65, the progression of the harmony is not only acceptable, but correct, since the second of the parallel fifths (in the second measure) is an accented passing note correctly resolved: the normal justification for this normal baroque and classical progression. Instances (some notated, others introduced by an ornament as here) are quite common in baroque music.

Ex. 65. François Couperin, *Pièces de Clavecin*, Livre I, Paris, 1713, Cinquième Ordre, 'La Tendre Fanchon', m. 9 (a) as notated; (b) as correctly interpreted, since the resulting consecutive fifths are justifiable as a normal baroque progression:

Ex. 65

(g) The character of every true appoggiatura as a leaning note, besides requiring it to come not before but on the beat, also requires it to take a certain greater or lesser degree of stress.

(76) C. P. E. Bach, *Essay*, Berlin, 1753, II, ii, 7:

'All appoggiaturas are performed more loudly than the ensuing note . . . and are joined with it, whether slurs are written or not.'

(77) F. W. Marpurg, *Anleitung zum Clavierspielen*, Berlin, 1755, 2nd ed., Berlin, 1765, p. 48:

'The note with which the [appoggiatura] is made should always be sounded a little louder than the main or essential note, and should be gently slurred into it.'

(78) Joachim Quantz, *Essay*, Berlin, 1752, VIII, iii:

'Swell [appoggiaturas] if time permits and slur the ensuing note to them more softly.'

The advice at (78) above should be taken cautiously, as the swelling is not always desirable even if time does permit. Geminiani (*Art of Playing on the Violin*, London, 1751, p. 7) gives the same advice without even the saving qualification; but then, Geminiani had a passion for swelling notes suitable and unsuitable, greatly exaggerating the prevailing fashion in that direction, which in any case belongs mainly to virtuoso music.

But that the appoggiatura should be louder than the main note on to which it resolves, is common ground. Above all is this the case when, as most often happens, the appoggiatura is a dissonance to which the main note is the resolution of the harmony; for it is a basic element of expression to stress a discord more than the concord upon which it resolves.

(h) The character of every true appoggiatura as a leaning note is further quite incompatible with any break *after* it, i.e. between the appoggiatura and its ensuing main note: see (76), (77) and (78) above.

(i) Besides the moderate appoggiatura of early baroque music, which did not die out, and the more or less *long* appoggiatura, which became much the most important for late baroque music, we have to consider the *short* appoggiatura, which acquired a distinct and independent character in late baroque music.

There will be nothing in the notation to distinguish these two main kinds of late baroque appoggiatura. (Little notes of very short notated duration, e.g. little sixteenth notes, may or may not hint at short rather than long appoggiaturas.)

A good approach, where the context permits, is often to try first a long, and then perhaps an even longer appoggiatura: if that does not do, to try next a short or a very short appoggiatura; if this works no better, to try an appoggiatura of moderate or intermediate length. If none of this makes good sense and good harmony, it is time to think of some other ornament or none. See, however, Sect. 3 below.

(79) C. P. E. Bach, *Essay*, Berlin, 1753, II, ii, 13:

'It is only natural that the [short] appoggiatura should appear most often before quick notes [and be] played so fast that the ensuing note loses hardly any of its length.

'It also appears before long notes . . . repeated [or] with syncopations.

'[14: also to] fill in leaps of a third . . . But in an Adagio the feeling is more expressive if they are taken as the first eighth-notes of triplets and not as sixteenth-notes . . .

'When the appoggiatura forms an octave with the bass it is taken short . . .

'[15:] If a note rises a second and at once returns . . . a [short] appoggiatura may well ornament the middle note.'

Ex. 66. C. P. E. Bach, suggested short appoggiaturas, (a) illustrating the above passage; (b) my interpretation of the last example, according to the above instructions, if in Allegro; (c) the same, if in Adagio:

In all respects other than length, short appoggiaturas (being true appoggiaturas) behave like long appoggiaturas, so far as their length permits (e.g. they cannot be swelled; but they can be stressed). Like all other true appoggiaturas, they take the beat.

(80) Joachim Quantz, *Essay*, Berlin, 1752, VIII, ii:

'[Short appoggiaturas] are performed very briefly . . . on the beat of the main note.'

(j) Appoggiaturas are frequently notated (especially in late baroque music), either by an inconsistent variety of signs, or by notes more or less misleadingly written or printed small (see Examples in this section). Still more frequently, they may be desirable or even necessary where they are not notated at all.

(81) Joachim Quantz, *Essay*, Berlin, 1752, VIII, 12:

'It is not enough to know how to perform the appoggiaturas according to their nature and difference, when they are marked; it is also necessary to know how to put them in suitably when they are not written.'

3. THE SO-CALLED 'PASSING APPOGGIATURA'

(a) Joachim Quantz (*Essay*, Berlin, 1752, VIII, 5) and Leopold Mozart (*Violinschule*, Augsburg, 1756, IX, 17) describe what they call a 'passing appoggiatura' (*durchgehender Vorschlag*), taken (writes Leopold Mozart) 'from the time of the note before'. This is, in fact, no true appoggiatura, since it does not lean on the ensuing main note, even when slurred to it.

To call these quite ordinary ornaments appoggiaturas was and is bad terminology, as was firmly emphasized at the time by F. W. Marpurg (*Anleitung*, Berlin, 1755, 2nd ed. Berlin, 1765, I, ix, 4); but they are perfectly good ornaments in their own right. They are simply one instance of passing notes used (as so often in free ornamentation) to connect disjunct notes with an agreeable smoothness and gracefulness.

(b) In French music of the entire baroque period, the so-called 'passing appoggiatura' appears (in fact though not in name) with much frequency, notated in a manner indistinguishable to the eye from a true appoggiatura. The interpretation is shown in Ex. 67.

Ex. 67. Jean-Jacques Rousseau, *Dictionnaire de musique*, Paris, 1768, Plate B showing though not naming the so-called 'passing appoggiatura':

Ex. 67
written:
performed:

4. APPOGGIATURAS IN RECITATIVE

(a) Recitative, in its *late* baroque Italianate varieties, is quite a special case both with regard to free ornamentation (which ought hardly to occur in it, because of its essentially unmelodic and declamatory character); and with regard to specific ornaments (which ought virtually to be confined to more or less obligatory appoggiaturas).

(b) *Early* baroque Italianate recitative is not by any means unmelodic, though it is certainly declamatory. It is open, like other branches of the reciting style, to moderate applications of free ornamentation, governed by poetic and dramatic considerations, as discussed in Chapter XV,

Section 2 above. It does not yet seem, however, to suggest obligatory appoggiaturas.

(c) French recitative, retaining (unlike Italianate recitative) an arioso melodiousness throughout the baroque period, permits both ornaments and (though Lully disapproved of this) free ornamentation; but it suggests obligatory appoggiaturas very much less, if at all.

(d) Appoggiaturas in late baroque Italianate recitative are obligatory:

(i) To fill in a cadential interval of a (descending) third.

(ii) To diversify a feminine (and sometimes a masculine) ending even with no such third to fill in.

(iii) To delay a cadential drop of a fourth on tonic six-four harmony.

Ex. 68 shows instances of the first two situations in an anonymous Italian cantata which may be so early as 1650, and can hardly be later than 1670; but no instance of the third situation. Notice well the appropriate words of this example!

Ex. 68. Anonymous Italian cantata, 'Se voi vi credete sentirmi cantare', c. 1650–70, Paris, Bibliothèque Nationale, MS Vm⁷.2, fol. 10 v, (a), interval of a third inviting an appoggiatura, to the actual word *accenti* (meaning 'appoggiaturas'); (b), (c), (d), plain feminine endings, suggesting other possible appoggiaturas but perhaps best without them; (e) recommended interpretation of (a):

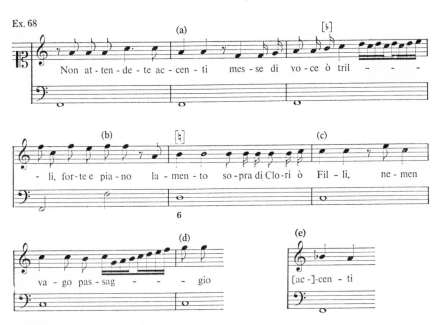

The third situation (delayed drop of a fourth on six-four harmony) can be found in the mid-17th century; later in the baroque period it became particularly characteristic, and it is specifically referred to in the following.

(82) Johann Mattheson, *Der vollkommene Capellmeister*, Hamburg, 1739, p. 177:

'The customary method of notation [i.e. C written twice at the phrase-ending, over a six-four harmony, is for purposes of illustration here written F dropping to C] as it would be sung.'

(83) J. A. Scheibe, in F. W. Marpurg's *Kritische Briefe*, Berlin, for 1760–2:

'The notation of the feminine cadence with the dropping fourth . . . differently from what is sung . . . is undoubtedly regrettable . . . because many untutored singers can be led astray by this, especially in the middle of a recitative.'

Ex. 69. J. A. Scheibe, illustration to the above:

It is easy to remember that a masculine cadence has the rhythm: 'I am a man'; and that a feminine cadence has the rhythm: 'I am a woman'. Scheibe, at (83) above, mentions only the feminine cadence, which has the stronger claim always to be given an appoggiatura. Nevertheless, we have grounds for thinking that an appoggiatura is ordinarily implied on the masculine cadence also. J. F. Agricola's examples added to his German translation as *Anleitung zur Singskunst* (Berlin, 1757, pp. 154, ff.) of Tosi's *Opinioni* (Bologna, 1723) confirm this; as does Ex. 70 following. See also Postscript on p. 206.

Ex. 70. Georg Philipp Telemann, *Harmonischer Gottes-Dienst, oder geistliche Cantaten*, 2 pts. [Hamburg, 1725–6], Preface, illustrations

showing (a) drop of a fourth, obligatory required appoggiaturas on masculine and feminine endings; (b) other situations (some obligatory, some optional).

There are two written-out realizations by Pasquali of accompaniments for recitative, in which the voice-part (no doubt for teaching reasons) shows some appoggiaturas notated which would ordinarily have been left unnotated. Not one of these, as it happens, is on a feminine ending; but this may be because in English (the language of the text here) feminine endings are much less common than masculine endings. Of the masculine endings shown, most have appoggiaturas notated; but a few of the more abrupt ones do not have appoggiaturas notated. If this is an intentional distinction (never a reliable inference in baroque notation) it might, and I think it does, hint at taking a few of the more abrupt masculine endings without appoggiatura. If so, such exceptions should at the most be rare. There is no doubt at all that far too few appoggiaturas are currently being sung in recitative.

Ex. 71. Nicolo Pasquali, facsimile from *Thorough-Bass Made Easy*, Edinburgh, 1757, sample realization of recitative, showing masculine endings some with and some without notated appoggiaturas (see p. 190).

(e) The standard length of an appoggiatura in recitative is one half of the written main note on masculine endings, and the whole of the first of the two written main notes on feminine endings (see Ex. 69 and Ex. 70 above).

There is always great flexibility of rhythm, however, in well-performed recitative; and there may be considerable drawing out on many of the cadences.

(f) The appoggiatura in recitative, having its true character as a leaning note, will receive the usual stress, and plenty of it.

(g) In the first two situations as here described, at (d) above, the performer has the choice of an appoggiatura by step from above or below; and from the same side as the note before, or from the other

189

Ex. 71

side. Thus Ex. 72 shows my own preferred solutions to certain of the illustrations from Telemann shown otherwise at Ex. 70 above. The one alternative is as correct as the other. The only incorrect solution would be neither.

Ex. 72. As Ex. 70, with alternative but equally correct solutions at the performer's option:

Ex. 72

In the third situation as here described, no such alternatives are available. The entire idiom consists in the appoggiatura descending from the same side as the note before (which indeed it repeats), by the leap of a fourth within the six-four harmony.

(h) In this third situation as here described, a further convention applies, no less arbitrary and no less obligatory. The subsequent resolution of the six-four harmony on to a dominant five-three, followed by the tonic five-three, is usually (although not always) misnotated in the figured bass. For the correct manner of accompaniment, see Ch. XVII, Sect. 12 below.

ORNAMENTS

5. THE ACCIACCATURA AND THE SLIDE

(a) The *acciaccatura* has two forms.

(i) An auxiliary note of dissonance is struck simultaneously with its main note: if time permits, the auxiliary note (i.e. the acciaccatura) is immediately released; but the main note continues to sound.

This is the simultaneous acciaccatura. It is an ornament primarily for the harpsichord, where it produces an effect of sudden sharpness and accent, and is excellent in very brilliant passages (e.g. in Domenico Scarlatti). F. W. Marpurg (*Anleitung*, Berlin, 1755, Fr. ed. as *Principes du clavecin*, Berlin, 1756, XIX, 2) describes it as 'frequently used in the bass'. Other references will be found in Geminiani (*Treatise of Good Taste*, London, 1749) and C. P. E. Bach (*Essay*, Berlin, 1753, II, v, 3). Since the simultaneous acciaccatura coincides with the start of its own main note, it is always and necessarily an on-the-beat ornament.

The simultaneous acciaccatura is also extremely effective on the piano, and was included in its nineteenth-century technique, not as a mere vague 'grace note', but correctly (i.e. simultaneously) executed, with all its old snap and verve.

(ii) An auxiliary note of dissonance is struck between two main notes, usually a third apart: the auxiliary note (i.e. the acciaccatura) is quickly, though not too quickly released; but the main notes on either side of it continue to sound. A certain lingering over the dissonance is effective here.

This is the passing acciaccatura. It is an ornament suitable for a keyboard (but no other) instrument. Since the passing acciaccatura differs from the simultaneous acciaccatura only and precisely in falling between the main notes on either side of it, the passing acciaccatura is always and necessarily a between-beat ornament.

The passing acciaccatura is the only acciaccatura discussed by Francesco Gasparini (*L'armonico pratico al cimbalo*, Venice, 1708, transl. F. S. Stillings, ed. D. L. Burrows, New Haven, 1963, pp. 80–1). But when the ornament comes singly he most confusingly calls it 'a mordent, sounded on, or rather a little before the beat and released immediately', whereas for several in a row he writes: 'Sometimes a certain dissonance is used which consists of an acciaccatura of two, three or four notes one close upon the next.' But this is a distinction without a difference, since Gasparini's musical examples all show normal, between-beat passing appoggiaturas (i.e. they are most accurately to be described not as 'a little before the beat' but as between the beats in the usual way).

Johann David Heinichen rebukes Gasparini for his confusion, in a passage otherwise derived from him, and itself not much less confused

191

(*Der General-Bass in der Composition*, Dresden, 1728, pp. 532–5, partly translated and discussed in George J. Buelow, *Thorough-Bass Accompaniment according to Johann David Heinichen*, Berkeley and Los Angeles, 1966, pp. 164–5). But both these great authorities of the early eighteenth century stress the immense value of the passing acciaccatura in filling out the sonority and enriching the harmony on the harpsichord, especially when accompanying recitative. Heinichen recommends 'even three or four adjacent notes in a slightly spread arpeggio while releasing the false, or non-chordal notes'.

Ex. 73. C. P. E. Bach, *Essay*, Berlin, 1753, III, 26, 'an arpeggio with an *acciaccatura*' (Tab. VI, Fig. XI):

Ex. 73

Ex. 74 shows passing acciaccaturas notated in two ways, of which the second is indistinguishable visually from an appoggiatura; and indeed those two ornaments are themselves related.

Ex. 74. J. S. Bach, Partita VI, Sarabande, passing acciaccaturas, (a) as written; (b) as it might alternatively have been written; (c) approximately as performed:

Ex. 74

The notation as at (b) in Ex. 74 above is perhaps the commonest, especially in Domenico Scarlatti. The chord always gets some slight spreading in good harpsichord playing; but when the chord is short and quick, there may in practice be no time to release the acciaccaturas first, so that one just hears a glorious tone-cluster.

Passing acciaccaturas may be freely introduced by the performer in suitable contexts; and especially, when accompanying recitative by that surge of imaginative (but not melodic) arpeggiation needed to give it sonorous (but not confusing) support from the harpsichord.

(b) The *slide* comprises a stepwise pair of auxiliary notes, regularly taken accented on the beat; and thereby delaying the main note on which it occurs, in the same manner as the appoggiatura.

The slide is equally excellent on melodic and on keyboard instruments; and though it is not on the whole very frequently notated, it may be very freely used.

On keyboard instruments, though not on melodic instruments, it is usually possibly and frequently desirable to hold the first auxiliary note of the slide, while releasing the second after just the main note arrives. So performed, the slide is identical with the passing acciaccatura, with which it has in any case an obvious relationship.

Ex. 75. Jacques Champion de Chambonnières, *Pièces de clavecin*, Paris, 1670, slide indistinguishable from passing acciaccatura:

Ex. 76. Jean Henri d'Anglebert, *Pièces de clavecin*, Paris, 1689, slides held and not held:

J. G. Walther ('Praecepta', 1708), a minor authority, shows slides interpreted as concluding the previous beat, i.e. as between-beat ornaments; J. D. Heinichen (*General-Bass*, Dresden, 1728, I, vi, 9), a major authority, also describes a variety of slide (*Schleifung*) equivalent to ordinary passing notes, and concluding the previous beat: i.e. as between-beat ornaments. It is also possible to slur the slide to the ensuing beat as a before-the-beat ornament. Walther shows such a version, but it was not much recommended and is rather weak.

The regular (on-the-beat) slide is described and illustrated from Giulio Caccini (*Nuove Musiche*, Florence, 1602), through John Playford (*Introduction to the Skill of Musick*, London, 1654, eds 1660 on);

Christopher Simpson (*Division-Violist*, London, 1659); Thomas Mace (*Musick's Monument*, London, 1676); Henry Purcell (or his editor in the posthumously published *Lessons*, London, 1696); the French harpsichordists shown at Ex. 75 and Ex. 76, and other Frenchmen; Georg Muffat (*Apparatus Musico-organisticus*, Salzburg, 1690); Gottlieb Muffat (*Componimenti musicali*, Augsburg, [?1735]; F. W. Marpurg (*Kunst das Klavier zu spielen*, Berlin, 1750); Joachim Quantz (*Essay*, Berlin, 1752, XVII, ii, 21); C. P. E. Bach (*Essay*, Berlin, 1753, II, vii); and so on to Daniel Gottlob Türk (*Klavierschule*, Leipzig and Halle, 1789, IV, ii, 18), which takes us to Haydn and Mozart; and Johann Nepomuk Hummel (*Anweisung zum Piano-Forte-Spiel*, Vienna, 1828), which takes us to Beethoven and onwards (so that, for example, the powerful slides which open Beethoven's last Quartet, Op. 135, are not meant weakly before the beat, but strongly on the beat).

Ex. 77. J. S. Bach, 'Trauer-Ode I', *Neue-Bach-Ausgabe*, I, 38, pp. 181–203, m. 18, unison passage for Oboe d'Amore I (with slide written out in ordinary notation) and Soprano Voice (with the same slide notated by a sign), showing slide taken in the regular manner on the beat:

Ex. 77

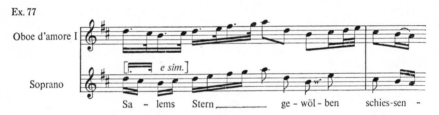

The speed of the slide depends chiefly on the context: quicker in allegro; slower in adagio. There is also a (standard) dotted variety (tending to be slow) and a considerable choice of other (not standard) rhythms.

6. TREMOLO AND VIBRATO

(a) The Italian vocal ornament known as *trillo* (especially in the early baroque period) is a tremolo-like pulsation (but *not* punctuation) on one note, with or without a gradual acceleration of the pulsation if time allows, but never precisely measured nor quite breaking the sound (beware of exaggeration).

(b) An instrumental tremolando, measured (and perhaps also unmeasured), is sometimes treated as an ornament, which may be notated by a continuous wavy line. I am indebted to Janet Beat for advice given privately on this subject. There is a clear example (measured eighth-notes) seen in Antonio Cesti's *Il Pomo d'Oro* (perf. Vienna,

1667), Act IV, Sc. 4 (DTÖ, IV, 2, Vienna, 1897, p. 135), and another in the famous frost scene of Henry Purcell's *King Arthur* (perf. London, 1691). The latter may possibly be meant for an unmeasured tremolo, which Christopher Simpson (*Division-Violist*, London, 1659, p. 10) called 'a Shake or Tremble with the Bow, like the Shaking-Stop of an Organ'. He did not much like it; but it would suit the frost scene well enough, including the voices. Nevertheless, a measured tremolo is also possible, since that appears to be the common significance of the sign, which is not at all rare in opera manuscripts (especially) of the late seventeenth and early eighteenth centuries; a row of dots may or may not appear with the wavy line, to suggest the measured subdivisions of a long note.

(c) Vibrato was customarily described as an ornament in baroque treatises; and there are even occasional signs for notating it (as in Marin Marais, *Pièces de viole*, Paris, 1697). But in practice, it only functions as an ornament when it is made both wide and prominent. What we should call a normal and moderate vibrato went on inconspicuously all the time in baroque singing (see Ch. IX, Sect. 6h) and string playing (see Ch. X, Sect. 8). What we should call an extreme and conspicuous vibrato was brought in deliberately for special effects of expression, in which form it was understandably classed among the ornaments.

7. TRILLS

(a) The trill is a more or less rapid and unmeasured alternation between a main note and an upper auxiliary a tone or a semitone above.

(b) When the trill has primarily a melodic function, it is begun optionally with its main note or its upper auxiliary (indifferent start). This was its behaviour in the sixteenth and the early seventeenth centuries.

When the trill has primarily a harmonic function, it is begun obligatorily with its upper auxiliary. This was its regular behaviour throughout the later baroque period and for some time afterwards (upper note start).

(c) When the trill is a cadential trill, its harmonic function is particularly prominent.

Innumerable baroque cadences appear in notation as plain dominant 5–3 to tonic 5–3. Here the trill, whether in any way notated or not, is in general an obligatory ornament on the dominant harmony: 'where for the most part it is very essential' (Pier Francesco Tosi, *Opinioni*, Bologna, 1723, trans. J. E. Galliard, London, 1742, p. 42, writing for singers), or 'indispensably necessary' (Joachim Quantz, *Essay*, Berlin, 1752, IX, i, writing for instrumentalists).

The harmonic function of the cadential trill is to introduce an unwritten modification into the dominant harmony. The upper auxiliary first strikes a 4 against the 5, resolving it on to the main note as 3; or a 6, resolving on to 5; or (with double trills in thirds or sixths) a 6–4, resolving on to a 5–3. The tonic 5–3 (or a delayed cadence) follows.

In each case, this forms a much more interesting progression than the written progression; and especially in the first case, which introduces an unwritten dissonance (the upper auxiliary) and its resolution (the main note). It is therefore the auxiliary, and not the main note, which must be heard as the accent of the trill, since it is the auxiliary which has to modify the harmony of the main note.

Hence the necessity for the upper-note on-the-beat, accented start.

Ex. 78. (a) Cadence notated as plain dominant 5–3 to tonic 5–3; (b) trill introducing dominant 5–4; (c) trill introducing dominant 6–3; (d) trill introducing dominant 6–4:

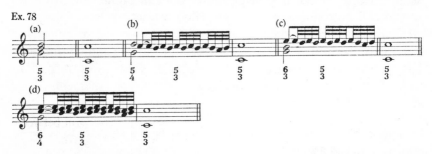

Ex. 78

(d) The upper-note start to baroque trills is described or illustrated with monotonous regularity from the middle of the seventeenth century onwards: for example in John Playford, *Introduction*, London, 1654, eds. from 1560 onwards; Jean Henri d'Anglebert, *Pièces de clavecin*, Paris, 1689; Georg Muffat, *Florilegium primum*, Augsburg, 1695; Henry Purcell, posthumous *Lessons*, London, 1696; Jacques Martin Hotteterre, *Principes de la flute traversiere*, Paris, 1707, pp. 11 ff.; François Couperin, *Pièces de clavecin*, Paris, 1713; Pier Francesco Tosi, *Opinioni de' cantori antichi e moderni*, Bologna, 1723, p. 42; Jean-Philippe Rameau, *Pièces de clavecin*, Paris, 1724; Gottlieb (Theophil) Muffat, *Componimenti*, Augsburg, [? 1735]; Joachim Quantz, *Essay*, Berlin, 1752; C. P. E. Bach, *Essay*, Berlin, 1753; Friedrich Wilhelm Marpurg, *Anleitung zum Clavierspielen*, Berlin, 1755, 2nd ed., Berlin, 1765, I, ix, 7, p. 55; Giuseppe Tartini, *Traité des agrémens*, [before 1756], ed. Erwin R. Jacobi, Celle and New York, 1961; Leopold Mozart, *Violinschule*, Augsburg, 1756; Daniel Gottlob Türk, *Klavierschule*, Leipzig and Halle, 1789; and very many others. It was, in short, a commonplace of the era.

(e) So habitual was the upper-note trill that it persisted long after the harmonic necessity for it had declined or disappeared. Thus Beethoven, on the last page of his autograph of the C major Piano Sonata, Op. 53 (Waldstein), where he shows the execution of certain of his trills, notates them with an upper-note start in exactly the old baroque manner. Johann Nepomuk Hummel began arguing strongly for lower-note trills in his *Anweisung zum Piano-Forte-Spiel*, Vienna, 1828; thereafter, evidence for either start is found throughout the nineteenth century.

(f) There were no standard exceptions, throughout the middle and late baroque periods, to the upper-note start of regular trills (for compound ornaments, see Sect. 10 below); not even when this means repeating, on the start of the trill, the same note as has been heard immediately before it.

(84) Friedrich Wilhelm Marpurg, *Anleitung zum Clavierspielen*, Berlin, 1755, French ed. as *Principes du clavecin*, Berlin, 1756, 2nd ed. Berlin, 1765, I, ix, 7, p. 55, and annotation on p. 56:

'A trill, wherever it may stand, must begin with its auxiliary note . . . If the upper note with which a trill ought to begin, immediately precedes the note to be trilled, it has either to be renewed by an ordinary attack, or has, before one starts trilling, to be connected, without a new attack, by means of a tie, to the previous note.'

Ex. 79. C. P. E. Bach, *Essay*, Berlin, 1753, II, ii, 9, an upper auxiliary of trill notated here (though not ordinarily notated) in order to show the necessity for starting the trill with it even if the note before is at the same pitch; (a) my approximate interpretation according to the first alternative given by Marpurg at (84) above; (b) my approximate interpretation according to the second alternative given by Marpurg at (84) above:

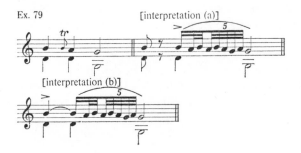

Ex. 79   [interpretation (a)]

[interpretation (b)]

French influence (above all in ornaments) on German music in general and the Berlin school in particular was at its greatest before and around the mid-eighteenth century. Marpurg's statement at (84) above, supported as it is by so much other unequivocal evidence, may be regarded as summing up the regular and international practice of the main baroque period.

A particularly unequivocal English statement comes in a set of 'Rules for Gracing' written, in a seventeenth-century hand, on the reverse of p. 67 in a copy of Christopher Simpson's *Division-Violist* (London, 1659) now at the Royal College of Music, London:

(84a) English anon., later 17th-cent.:

'Prepare all long shakes [trills]. . . . The Note before a Close is to be Shaked. . . . All shakes are taken from the note above.'

For a much fuller discussion of the evidence and reasons for taking later baroque trills on the beat and from the upper-note, see my *Interpretation of Early Music*, New Version, where the most recent work on this and allied topics is extensively considered.

(g) The first note of an upper-note trill, because of its appoggiatura-like quality, always and necessarily takes the beat; and always with some degree of stress.

It is impossible to overemphasize the importance of thus stressing the *top* notes of the trill, not the bottom notes. If the top note start is not given the accent, very firmy, and very accurately *on the beat*, it might as well not be there. Throughout the entire trill, the accentuation has to be this way up: top notes and not bottom notes getting the sense of accent. A top-note start, unaccented and just before the beat, so that the stress comes not on the auxiliary but on the main note, defeats its own purpose, and though it is a mistake very commonly heard today, it is still a mistake: just as much so as a main-note start. The top note is the important note: think of it as an appoggiatura to which the repercussions on the main note are merely the unimportant resolution.

(85) Joachim Quantz, *Essay*, Berlin, 1752, IX, 7–8:

'Each trill starts with the appoggiatura [i.e. the upper auxiliary] . . . often as quick as the other notes which form the trill. However this appoggiatura, whether long or short, ought always be be attacked. . .'

(h) The first note of an upper-note trill may be prolonged a little (very common), a moderate amount (still more common), or very much (common only in slow movements).

(86) Jacques Martin Hotteterre, *Principes de la flute traversiere*, Paris, 1707, pp. 11ff.

'The sound above [i.e. the auxiliary, may be so long as] about half the duration of the [main] note, especially in grave movements.'

(87) Pier Francesco Tosi, *Opinioni*, Bologna, 1723, transl. J. E. Galliard, London, 1742, p. 48:

'The Shake [i.e. trill], to be beautiful, requires preparation [by pro-longing its upper-note start], though on some Occasions, Time or Taste will not permit it. But on final Cadences it [the preparation] is always necessary.'

(i) So close is the relationship between the trill and the long appoggia-tura that a trill is quite frequently notated by an appoggiatura written as a small note.

Ex. 80. George Frideric Handel, Sonata in C major for Viola da Gamba and Harpsichord (Handel's own realization), (a) 1st mov., m.2, trill shown in harpsichord by appoggiatura sign; (b) m.4, matching trill in gamba shown by trill sign; (c) end, trills in tenths between harpsichord and gamba, notated differently but intended identically:

(j) The speed and number of repercussions in a trill are variable and unmeasured.

A trill was often written out in early baroque music, and occasionally afterwards, as measured repercussions: these, however, are in general not meant literally (and sometimes they do not even add up literally).

Measured repercussions do not constitute a trill, but a fragment of free ornamentation such as may often be found notated in sixteenth-century treatises and music (whence the trill seems to have evolved historically). These measured repercussions may be taken slurred or

199

unslurred; but whenever the repercussions are taken unmeasured, and therefore treated as a trill, they are from their very nature *to be taken slurred*. Thus we find, for example, the table of ornaments in Christopher Simpson's *Division-Violist* (London, 1659, p. 12 of 2nd ed. of 1665) showing slurs over the (conventionally and approximately notated) trills though in the actual music later in the book similar slurs are not notated, being taken for granted there and elsewhere as sufficiently obvious to good performers; so is the unmeasured interpretation of the measured repercussions similarly notated.

(88) Girolamo Frescobaldi, *Toccate*, Rome, 1615–16, Preface, 8:

'You must not divide the [written-out] trill exactly note for note, but only try to make it rapid.'

(89) Johann Andreas Herbst, *Musica practica*, Nuremberg, 1643, 2nd ed. as *Musica moderna prattica*, Frankfurt, 1653, p. 59:

'You beat as many [repercussions] in the trill as you desire.'

Ex. 81. Biagio Marini, 'Sonata per l'organo e Violino ò Cornetto', in his *Sonate, Symphonie, Canzoni . . .* Op. 8, Venice, 1629, trill written out in measured notes but intended to be taken in the ordinary way with unmeasured repercussion, as is confirmed in this case by the indication *groppo* (trill):

(90) François Couperin, *L'Art de toucher le clavecin*, Paris, 1716, ed. of 1717, p. 23:

'Although the trills are marked as regular in the table of ornaments in my first book, they are nevertheless to begin more slowly than they finish.' [A minority opinion.]

(91) Joachim Quantz, *Essay*, Berlin, 1752, IX, 2–5:

'There is no need to make all trills with the same speed . . . In sad pieces the trills are made more slowly; but in gay pieces they ought to be made more quickly . . . you must not fall into any excess . . . for trills to be perfectly beautiful, they must be made . . . of a regular speed and one kept to the same rapidity.' [The majority opinion.]

In short: the speed and regularity of a trill depend on taste and context.

(k) There were two standard endings, one of which is to be supplied on all regular baroque trills, whether or not any indication, misleading or otherwise, appears in the notation: (i) a little note of anticipation; (ii) a turned ending (by lower auxiliary, a tone or a semitone below the main note).

(92) Bénigne de Bacilly, *L'art de bien chanter*, Paris, 1668, p. 164:

'The ending . . . is a join made between the trill and the note on which it is desired to arrive, by means of another note touched very delicately . . . [p. 183: even] though the composer has not marked [it] on paper . . . otherwise the trill will be maimed, and will not be completed.'

The little *note of anticipation* thus inserted or modified can be either detached or slurred, according to taste and context.

Ex. 82. (a) Note of anticipation not indicated; (b) note of antici-pation misleadingly indicated; (c) approximate detached inter-pretation; (d) approximate slurred interpretation.

Ex. 82

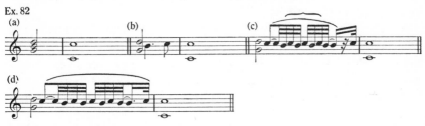

(93) Joachim Quantz, *Essay*, Berlin, 1752, IX, 7:

'The end of each trill consists of two little notes, which follow the note of the trill and are made at the same speed . . . sometimes these little notes are written . . . [otherwise] the ending must be understood.'

The *turned ending* thus inserted or modified is slurred to the trill, and becomes part of it, without the slightest separation. C. P. E. Bach (*Essay*, Berlin, 1753, II, iii, 13) confirms that it 'must be played as quickly as the trill itself, whether notated thus, or otherwise, or not at all'.

Ex. 83. (a) turned ending not indicated; (b) turned ending mis-leadingly indicated, but strongly implying a trill; (c) turned ending approximately indicated, and still more strongly implying a trill; (d) interpretation in all these cases:

Ex. 83

The choice of ending, if not indicated, is at the performer's option; but one or the other is *obligatory* on full trills. This is a most important and often neglected point. Notated or not, an ending must be performed.

(l) But on half-trills, no ending is required or possible.

The half-trill (*Pralltriller*) consists of two repercussions: i.e. four notes. The last of the four is the main note, and is held on plain.

More repercussions can occur if time allows, but not so many as to prevent the main note from sounding clearly at the end.

The half-trill, like the full trill, is an on-the-beat ornament, starting with the upper auxiliary, which is accented, and which if time allows may be more or less prolonged.

But above a certain speed, the four notes have a natural tendency, for lack of time, to become three; i.e. the half-trill (*Pralltriller*) is turned into an inverted mordent (*Schneller*). This is still an on-the-beat ornament, but starting with the main note. At the speeds involved, however, there can be little accent and no prolongation. (For the inverted mordent, see Sect. 8b below.)

At speed, it is often very difficult to bring half-trills (*Pralltriller*) or even inverted mordents (*Schneller*) accurately on their beats, without any unintentional anticipation; but anticipation, however slight, necessarily weakens the effect, and can always be avoided with sufficiently sharp and exact listening.

Ex. 84. (a) C. P. E. Bach, *Essay*, Berlin, 1753, II, iii, 30, 'the half or bouncing trill (*halbe oder Prall-Triller*)', as shown in his Table IV, Figure XLV; (b) context turning *Pralltriller* into *Schneller* ('jerky one') at speed, Table IV, Figure XLVIII; (c) i.e. to be interpreted, if at speed; (d) to be interpreted, if not at speed:

Ex. 84

(m) Continuous trills on long or very long notes are for colouring or sustaining the tone. They do not need to start (though in baroque music they regularly do) on the upper auxiliary; nor need this be (though it may be) accented or prolonged. The start is, however, on the beat. The speed will be more or less (though it need not be absolutely) constant. There is no necessity (though there may be a desirability) for an ending; but if made, it will be a turned ending (as usual, at the same speed as the trill, and joined to it without separation or delay).

(n) Continued series of trills on a succession of short notes are for brilliance only. They are taken on the beat, starting with the upper auxiliary, but are very brief and rapid, and require no ending. They can best be viewed as a species of half-trills compelled by their speed to occupy almost the whole of the short notes on which they stand.

8. MORDENTS

(a) The mordent is a rapid and unmeasured alternation between a main note and a lower auxiliary a tone or a semitone below. This is the regular (lower) mordent of the main baroque period.

(b) There is also an inverted (upper) mordent, alternating with an upper auxiliary a tone or a semitone above: this was common in the renaissance and early baroque periods, was out of fashion in the main baroque period, and began coming back by way of the *Pralltriller* curtailed to a *Schneller* (see Sect. 7 (1) above) about the middle of the eighteenth century.

(c) The standard mordent (Ital. *mordente*, biting) has primarily a rhythmic function and is for this reason an on-the-beat ornament, starting, more or less accented, on the main note.

(d) The standard mordent consists of one repercussion: i.e. three notes.

More repercussions can occur if time allows; but the longer a mordent, the less it keeps its rhythmic function, and the more its function becomes merely that of colouring or sustaining the tone.

The longer mordents tend to be slower, and may (though they do not need to) have their first (main) note more or less prolonged.

(e) The mordent may be taken either diatonically or chromatically.

(94) C. P. E. Bach, *Essay*, Berlin, 1753, II, v, 11:

'With regard to accidentals [the mordent] adapts itself to its [tonal] context in the same way as the trill. [Nevertheless,] its brilliance is frequently enhanced by [chromatically] raising its lower [auxiliary] note.'

(f) No baroque mordent anticipates the beat (see Sect. 1(b) (xi) above). Sometimes, at speed, it is (as with half-trills) quite hard to prevent this; but the effect is always musically stronger with the correct, on-the-beat, execution.

(g) Mordents can be used with great effect in very numerous situations where the lightest touch of ornamentation is desired, and anything longer or heavier might be too much. But notice:

(95) C. P. E. Bach, *Essay*, Berlin, 1753, II, v. 4–14:

'The mordent is particularly effective in an ascent by step or by leap . . . never on descending steps of a second . . . [14:] the opposite of the half-trill . . . [which is] used on a step only in descent . . . [10] the mordent is of all ornaments the most freely introduced by the performer into the bass, especially on notes at the highest point of a phrase.'

Ex. 85. C. P. E. Bach, *Essay*, Berlin, 1753, II, v, 11, (a) chromatic mordents, the D sharp shown (for demonstration only) above the mordent sign; (b) my approximate interpretation:

9. TURNS AND OTHER CHANGING OR PASSING NOTES

(a) The turn is a circling around a main note by upper and lower auxiliary notes a tone or a semitone away. It is, in short, an ornament comprised of changing notes.

(b) The turn may be (i) accented, as an on-the-beat ornament, with a function equally melodic and harmonic; or (ii) unaccented, as a between-beat ornament, with a melodic function.

(c) The standard (upper) turn begins with the upper auxiliary, passes through the main note, touches the lower auxiliary and returns to the main note.

The inverted (lower) turn begins with the lower auxiliary, passes through the main note, touches the upper auxiliary, and returns to the main note.

(d) The unaccented turn is commoner than the accented turn; and the standard turn is commoner than the inverted turn.

(e) The rhythm of the turn is most commonly equal; but it also occurs in a variety of unequal rhythms, including triplet rhythms and dotted rhythms.

But quick turns are ordinarily taken in an equal rhythm, so as to avoid a jerky effect.

(f) There is an irregular, but not uncommon five-note turn starting on the main note, then behaving like a standard (upper) turn; it can occur accented or unaccented, but has in either form a melodic function.

Ex. 86. (a) J. S. Bach, *Clavier-Büchlein vor Wilhelm Friedemann Bach*, 1720, accented upper turn in equal rhythm; (b) C. P. E. Bach, *Essay*, Berlin, 1753, ed. of 1787, II, iv, 24, unaccented upper turn in unequal rhythm:

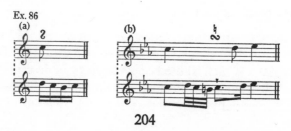

(g) A simpler ornament, comprising a changing note, is the springer: an upper auxiliary rises from and returns to, or crosses, its main note; or a lower auxiliary falls from and returns to, or crosses, its main note.

The springer (a melodic, unaccented, between-beat ornament), is graceful at almost any speed, and in both sharp and lilting rhythms. It appears in most descriptions and tables of ornaments throughout the baroque period.

Ex. 87. (a) John Playford, *Introduction*, London, 1654, eds. of 1660 on, table of ornaments, upper springer; (b) F. W. Marpurg, *Anleitung*, Berlin, 1755, Table IV, upper and lower springers.

(h) A note of anticipation (used as a melodic, unaccented, between-beat ornament related to the springer) is likewise graceful at most speeds, and in both sharp and lilting rhythms; it likewise commonly appears.

Ex. 88. Notes of anticipation, (a) John Playford, same table; (b) F. W. Marpurg, same table.

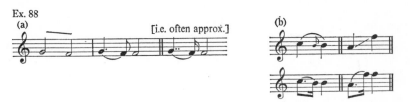

(i) Various other changing notes or passing notes were sometimes described or illustrated as specific ornaments, but belong more properly with free ornamentation.

10. COMPOUND ORNAMENTS

(a) Two or more ornaments might be habitually linked, the result being identifiable, and most clearly described, as a compound ornament. Behaviour follows usually what would occur separately.

(b) The long appoggiatura from below was habitually, when time allowed, finished off with a standard mordent (especially in France). The appoggiatura prepares the mordent, pushing it to a variable extent *past* its beat.

(c) An ascending slide was commonly used to introduce a trill (ascending trill). An accented upper turn was likewise commonly used to introduce a trill (descending trill).

Ex. 89. J. S. Bach, *Clavier-Büchlein vor Wilhelm Friedemann Bach,* 1720, ascending and descending trills:

Ex. 89

Doppelt Cadence   Idem   Doppelt Cadence   Idem
                             und Mordant

(d) A combination of unaccented upper turn and regular cadential trill is sometimes described as a double cadence. It is quite remarkably useful in the simple but versatile version shown in Ex. 90 (the rhythm may be varied a little to suit different speeds and moods).

Ex. 90. (a) Cadential formula commonly inviting (b) turn and trill, sometimes described as double cadence:

Ex. 90

POSTSCRIPT

(83a) Vincenzo Manfredini, *Regole armoniche*, 2nd ed., Venice, 1797, p. 65:

'If the player is not strictly obliged to execute an appoggiatura which is not indicated by the composer, it is not the same for the singer, who (especially in recitative) seeing two notes equal in value, and in sound [i.e. notated pitch], the first of them, especially when it is placed in a *tempo forte*, he must consider it as an upper appoggiatura, that is execute it a tone or a half-tone higher, according to the nature of the scale in which are written the aforesaid two notes.'

CHAPTER SEVENTEEN

Accompaniment

1. THE WIDE VARIETY OF BAROQUE ACCOMPANIMENT

(a) The accompaniments found in baroque music range through:

  (i) none;
  (ii) optional;
  (iii) unfigured bass parts;
  (iv) more or less figured bass parts;
  (v) fragments, or longer portions, of written-out realization;
  (vi) fully written-out realizations;
  (vii) written-out obbligato parts.

(b) Some baroque compositions are intended to be without accompaniment. No bass, therefore, is provided; and an indication such as *senza basso*, without bass, may appear.

(c) In other baroque compositions, both vocal and instrumental, the music is complete in itself but may be given an optional accompaniment. Madrigals, motets, part-songs, consorts for viols or recorders etc. usually permit, though they do not necessarily require, accompaniment on lute, harp, chamber organ, harpsichord etc. A bass part above which to make one may be but is not often provided.

The harmonic accompaniment here should double some or all of the existing parts, or at least give some sketchy outline of them, often with additional figuration to suit the instrument employed.

Madrigals, motets etc. may also be doubled by melodic instruments, with or without a harmonic accompaniment in addition.

(d) When an unfigured bass part is provided, the normal intention is that a harmonic accompaniment shall be provided above it: i.e. it is merely a figured bass without the figures.

If the solo to be accompanied is shown above the bass, a competent accompanist will not be inconvenienced by the lack of figures. If nothing but the bass line is shown, he will look at the music first when possible (and perhaps write in a few figures for himself); otherwise, he will just do his best with what he has in front of him.

(e) A bass part with a more or less adequate supply of figures to indicate the required harmonies is the standard baroque provision for accompaniment.

Less adequate figures are much commoner than more adequate; but experience enables a good accompanist to handle all ordinary situations.

(f) A considerable number of baroque manuscripts, though still a very small minority, show fragmentary jottings of ideas for realizing the bass: mostly little imitations or counter-melodies or figurations which work in well, and which can often be carried on throughout the piece or the passage. It seems that some accompanist, or even the composer, having thought of something felicitous, wanted to make sure of remembering it again next time, and scribbled it in. Having reminded himself of it in this scrappy way, he could carry the idea through readily enough in the usual more or less improvised fashion. We can do the same.

We also find longer portions of realization similarly written out: for example, ritornellos between the vocal passages of solo cantatas, made of material which may or may not be borrowed from the vocal melody, and which may or may not carry on or be suitable for carrying on as accompaniment when the voice enters again.

(g) Such written-out realizations occasionally extend through the entire piece, providing it with a completed accompaniment, and giving us a still more useful model on which to produce our own realizations in similar pieces.

We have written-out realizations from two main sources. One is treatises on accompaniment, where they serve for purposes of instruction, and for this reason may mislead us by being simpler than what we have cause to think usually happened in ordinary practice (for example, Georg Philipp Telemann's disappointing *Singe-, Spiel- und Generalbass-Übungen* [Hamburg, 1733–4], which is not only dull but surprisingly awkward in some of its progressions: an unusual feature at the time). The other is manuscripts used in ordinary practice, and reflecting that practice in a much more direct though less systematic manner.

An occasional realization survives which is a student's exercise, such as Heinrich Nikolaus Gerber's accompaniment for an Albinoni sonata with corrections by his teacher, J. S. Bach; here, too, we may find, for obvious pedagogic reasons, a much simpler and academically purer accompaniment than under the more adventurous conditions of ordinary practice.

(h) As such fully written-out realizations grow in elaboration and in richly independent interest, they merge into obbligato accompaniments, provided by the composer as integral components of his music, and not much subject to optional variation by the performer.

The accompaniment written out by Handel in his C major Gamba

Sonata is in some passages a typical though very excellent realization, and in other passages an independent obbligato (to which, however, some additional filling-out of chords is in places desirable).

The harpsichord parts of J. S. Bach's violin sonatas and gamba sonatas are typical obbligatos, but nevertheless include brief passages of figured bass which the performer must realize on his own initiative.

(i) There is no absolute difference of kind between a written-out realization and an obbligato accompaniment. There is only a relative difference of degree. Every realization requires some degree of independent completeness in its own right. Every obbligato remains in some degree a realization of the bass line on which all ordinary baroque compositions stand.

From the simplest of basses to the most elaborate of obbligatos, there is a continuous transition, at no point broken by any sharp line of distinction which the baroque musicians would have recognized. To us, it may pose a variety of problems. To them, it was all accompaniment.

(j) We too, therefore, must learn to take all varieties of accompaniment in our stride.

Whether we improvise, whether we prepare, whether we memorize, or whether we write out, and in whatever proportions, there is only one general principle: to fit the manner of our accompaniment to the matter of the composition.

We must be able to range from almost entirely chordal accompaniments relieved only by a few passing notes for keeping the voice-leading melodious and graceful, on the one hand, to genuinely contrapuntal accompaniments balancing the soloists in the most independent spirit, on the other hand.

The greater part of our work will lie somewhere between these two extremes; but any degree of simplicity or elaboration which suits the passage in question is possible. It is all accompaniment.

2. IMPROVISATION THE BEST REALIZATION

(a) A few modern editors are now publishing very fine realizations; but it must be admitted that the great majority still range from indifferent to bad, and advanced performers will not very often want to use them as they stand.

(b) Those accompaniments which date from a generation or two ago are likely to be thick, pianistic, and weighted down by perpetual doubling of the solo line or lines, at the unison or (not quite so bad) at the octave below, together with much doubling of the bass in octaves. If such an unsuitably opaque piano part has to be used, it should be thinned out in performance.

(c) In reaction against that, we began to get correct and suitable parts which are nevertheless not very elegant, and mostly not interesting at all. But they can readily be made interesting in performance by adding more figuration and melody: especially unaccented and accented passing notes.

A dull accompaniment leaves the accompanist rather bored, and the audience with him. At the very least, it is a missed opportunity; for an interesting accompaniment, provided it does not get in the way, can give the whole performance such a splendid lift.

(d) The latest reaction is towards interesting accompaniments which do sometimes tend to get in the way.

We have no longer to lament a shortage of talented accompanists capable of more or less improvising their realizations, and thus giving them an impetus and excitement which the best of written-out accompaniments cannot quite capture. We do quite often have to lament that this fine talent is running away with itself in distracting excess of imagination. This, however, will no doubt settle down. The important thing is to have the imagination. After that, the thing to learn is that only musical material very closely drawn from the given parts is likely to sound *relevant* to the music. What does not sound relevant, sounds distracting; and what sounds distracting, is bad accompaniment no matter how talented.

3. THE HARMONY OF THE ACCOMPANIMENT

(a) In theory, figured bass (thorough-bass, general bass, continuo accompaniment) is a shorthand system for indicating the main harmonies in which an accompanist can elaborate his own more or less improvised realization.

In practice, the figures are very often missing, and nearly always (with the partial exception of eighteenth-century Germany) grossly incomplete, as well as liable to numerous errors.

(96) Michel de Saint-Lambert, *Nouveau traité de l'accompagnement*, Paris, 1707, VI, p. 71:

'You can sometimes change the chords marked on the notes, when you judge that others will suit better.

'On a bass note of substantial duration, one can put in two or three different chords one after the other, although the text only asks for one, provided that one senses that these chords go with the melodic part.

'On the other hand one can avoid sounding all the intervals marked in the text, when one finds that the notes are too heavily loaded.'

(97) C. P. E. Bach, *Essay*, Berlin, 1753, Foreword:

'The harpsichordist ... must have at his command a thorough knowledge of continuo bass, which he must perform with judgement, often departing from the written text.'

(b) The bass itself may be modified by the performer to make a better accompaniment.

(98) Michel de Saint-Lambert, *Traité*, Paris, 1707, p. 120:

'[If the bass has too many notes] the accompanist . . . can content himself with playing the first note of each bar, leaving the bass viol or violoncello to play all the notes.

[p. 121]: 'On the other hand if the Bass has too few notes . . . he may add other notes by way of pleasing figuration, provided he is sure that this will not interfere with the melody.'

(99) Johann David Heinichen, *General-Bass*, Dresden, 1728, p. 377:

'Rapid repeated notes [in the bass can be reduced to] slower notes . . . the playing of the rapid notes is left to the other accompanying bass [melodic] instruments.'

(100) C. P. E. Bach, *Essay*, II, Berlin, 1762, Introd., 27:

'When the continuo is not doubled by other instruments, and the nature of the piece permits it, the accompanist may make improvised modifications in the bass line.'

(c) A special case of adding to the written bass is making the lead (back or on) so often desirable at repeats and new sections.

Ex. 91. (a) Jean-Baptiste Lully, *Cadmus et Hermione*, in the collected edition by Henry Prunières, Paris, 1930–9, Vol. I, p. 39, lead in bass notated in the printed ed. of 1674 but not in the MS score; (b) Marin Marais, *Alcione*, Paris, 1706, lead in bass notated (with under-dotting for convenience) in the printed short score, Paris, Bibl. Nat. Vm.² 204, p. 11, with the instruction 'Dernière Notte pour la Basse Continuo', but not in the MS full score, Vm.² 205, prepared for the revival of 1741, p. 10; (c) Jean-Philippe Rameau, *Hippolyte et Aricie*, Paris, [n.d.], 1st perf. 1733, pp. xx–xxi, bass as printed, (d) as written over in ink:

Ex. 91

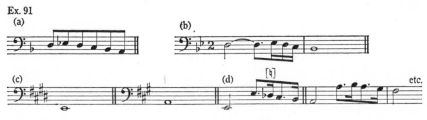

A similar lead back or lead on may also be made very valuably by the performer above the notated bass, without altering it.

Ex. 92. Arcangelo Corelli, Trio Sonata Op. II, No. 1, Corrente, section joins as realized by Robert Donington:

(d) The harmonies, though not usually the bass, may require a departure from the written text (i.e. the figures) to accommodate a harmonic ornament in a solo part.

When, for example, a soloist introduces, into a 5–3 harmony, a long appoggiatura, or the prolonged upper-note start of a trill, on the 4, the accompanist can, according to his judgement of the circumstances:

(i) play a bare fifth, leaving the soloist to complete the harmony (sometimes the best course);

(ii) double the ornament (nearly always the worst course with trills, and not always good with appoggiaturas);

(iii) play the 5–3 harmony as written, allowing the 3 to clash unashamedly against the soloist's 4 (good with trills chiefly when they are fairly short, but surprisingly often the best course with long appoggiaturas);

(iv) play a 5–4 resolving to a 5–3 in equal rhythm, i.e. giving half the bass note to the 5–4 and half to the 5–3 (nearly always the best course with the longer trills).

In justification of (iii), notice that Lorenzo Penna (*Li Primi Albori musicali*, Bologna, 1672, III, 14) states that 'the discords can be accompanied (if so desired) by the consonances of the note written'. Nearly a century later, C. P. E. Bach no longer sanctions in words this once common sounding of the discord against its own note of resolution; but it occurs among his own examples of accompanied ornaments, and was in fact freely practised in this context, where (helped, of course, by the difference of timbre) it often sounds extremely well.

212

Short appoggiaturas, not being harmonic ornaments, need no accommodation from the accompaniment. Nor do very short trills, for the same reason.

(e) The accompanist himself may introduce, into the bass or into the upper parts, not only melodic and rhythmic but harmonic ornaments; and not only unaccented passing notes (valuable for improving the melodic contours and voice-leading) but accented passing notes (further valuable for enriching the harmony).

(101) Michel de Saint-Lambert, *Traité*, Paris, 1707, Ch. IX, Sect. 15, p. 132:

'One can on the organ, as well as on the harpsichord, make from time to time certain trills or other ornaments, in the bass as well as in the other parts.'

(102) Johann David Heinichen, *General-Bass*, Dresden, 1728, I, ii, p. 521:

'The art of a properly embellished continuo [includes] sometimes introducing an ornament in all the parts (particularly the outside part of the right hand, which is the most conspicuous).'

Ex. 93. Francesco Geminiani, *The Art of Accompaniament*, London, [1755], II, Ex. xi, realization (Geminiani's) enriched by accented passing notes and appoggiaturas:

Ex. 93

But notice particularly well:

(103) C. P. E. Bach, *Essay*, II, Berlin, 1762, XXXII, 12:

'In the use of these harmonic refinements, great care must be taken to avoid interfering with or covering up the solo part.'

(f) Passing notes in the bass itself, on the other hand, need careful attention for an opposite reason: they must not be given separate harmonies, but allowed to pass under the existing harmony. The same is true of some notes which are not strictly passing notes (since they do not pass, i.e. move by step, but are taken or left by leap), but which are treated for harmony purposes as if they were passing notes (since they are not given separate harmonies).

It is not always easy to distinguish passing notes from harmony notes in the bass; but it is chiefly a matter of responding to the harmonic pulse. If this feels decidedly like two in a bar (for example, of whole-note duration), then there are likely to be two changes of harmony (at half-note intervals) with shorter notes in the bass (quarter notes or shorter) treated as passing notes. But if the feeling is decidedly four in a bar, quarter notes are likely to be harmony notes, and eighth or shorter notes are likely to be passing notes.

So also with triple pulses, simple and compound: one pulse in a bar mainly needs one harmony, or sometimes two; more pulses, more harmonies. Thus bass notes corresponding with pulses are likely to be harmony notes; bass notes of shorter duration are likely to be passing notes. But exceptions abound.   ·

Accented (as well as unaccented) passing notes are frequently encountered in the bass. These accented passing notes are ordinarily figured, if at all, for the dissonant harmony they are intended to produce. Occasionally, and rather disconcertingly, they are figured for the consonant harmony on which they are about to resolve; but the intention is the same. So it is if the figuring merely continues over from their preceding chord of preparation.

Dashes may, in eighteenth-century theory, show the prolongation of the harmony from any cause; but they are rare in practice.

One safe and good compromise may be to play in tenths with the bass: often a very excellent effect. When in doubt, an accompanist may prefer to treat a bass note as passing, since this will at worst do less harm than a fresh harmony, if wrong.

4. HOW FULL AN ACCOMPANIMENT

(a) There are passages where the harpsichord drops out, leaving the unharmonized bass line to a melodic instrument.

The instruction *senza cembalo*, without harpsichord, may be used to indicate this. The performer may himself decide upon it; but nearly always, the harpsichord support is liable to be quite badly missed. It is an effect to be used, in practice, very seldom.

(b) The harpsichordist may play only the bass line, unharmonized.

The instruction *tasto solo* (one key only), or *tasto*, or *t.s.*, may indicate this; but the performer may use it rather more often on his own initiative than the *senza cembalo*. It is one of the two best accompaniments for the opening of a more or less fugal passage; as further entries appear, the harpsichord can double these too, until most or all are in, when the harmonized accompaniment proceeds as usual.

The alternative (often still better) is to remain silent until the bass enters, and then to come in with a fully harmonized accompaniment of the usual kind.

The instruction *all' unisono*, or *unisoni*, rather illogically indicates doubling in as many octaves as desired, but without harmonization.

(104) C. P. E. Bach, *Essay*, II, Berlin, 1762, XXII, 3:

'Some composers do not always indicate their desire for an *all' unisono* accompaniment when writing out the bass. Figures are sometimes found over the bass where none are intended to be played.

[XXIV, 4:] 'It is not easy to figure pedal points, and they are therefore generally handled *tasto solo*. Those who do figure them must put up with their being performed *tasto solo* just the same.'

However, pedal points are often on simple harmonies, which only appear difficult because figured complexly over the static pedal bass; it is often good to play these harmonies (whether figured or not) as simple chords against the given upper parts.

(c) To thin out or to thicken up the accompaniment varies both the volume and the texture, and is one of the chief recourses of dynamic expression on the harpsichord (especially a simple harpsichord with no stops to subtract or add).

(105) C. P. E. Bach, *Essay*, II, Berlin, 1762, Introd., 24:

'Consistent four-part writing, or more, is used in music which is thickly composed, or is in the learned style with counterpoint, imitations and so forth . . .

[26:] 'Accompaniments in three or fewer parts are used in lightly-composed music . . .

[XXIX, 10] 'Distinguish the most important notes by reinforcing their chords, perhaps in both hands [i.e. by adding more notes].

[XXIX, 7] 'Merely doubling the bass [at the octave] has also a very penetrating effect [especially useful] when there is an entry in a fugue, or any imitation which needs bringing out.

[XXXII, 6] 'One of the main refinements of accompaniment is parallel movement in thirds [including tenths] with the bass [usually confining oneself to] three-part writing, and indeed in most cases two-part writing . . .

[8:] 'Sometimes sixths may be mixed in [and sometimes] sustained notes.'

A mainly two-part accompaniment can be excellent, and so can a mainly three-part accompaniment, in suitable movements. At the opposite extreme, for the greatest sonority, comes the filled-in accompaniment (or *vollstimmig*, full-voiced). This is already mentioned, as 'playing full, as much as one can', in an anonymous Italian manuscript treatise (Rome, Biblioteca Corsiniana, MS. Musica R1, 'Regole per accompagnar sopra la parte', *c*. 1700, f. 65 v); if it was a new fashion, as the author implies by writing 'nowadays', it soon became accepted practice (and indeed it was certainly not altogether a novelty).

(106) Johann David Heinichen, *General-Bass*, Dresden, 1728, Part I, Ch. II, Sect. 30, p. 131:

'[Sometimes] accompany in as many parts with the left hand as with the right . . .

[Footnote:] 'On such instruments as harpsichords, the fuller the accompaniment in either hand, the more satisfying the result [of the filled-in accompaniment]. With organs, however, especially in lightly-composed music, it is as well not to get too fascinated by an over-full accompaniment in the left hand.'

(d) Organ sounds sustain, and one has to be a little careful of too much sonority; but to keep a sufficient sonority going on the harpsichord, there have to be plenty of notes, plentifully distributed. The following examples of good harpsichord adaptation are excellent models.

Ex. 94 (i) and (ii). Johann David Heinichen, *General-Bass*, Dresden, 1728, (i) Pt. I, Ch. VI, Sect. 39 and (ii) Pt. I, Ch. VI, Sect. 31ff. figurations giving a good sonority on the harpsichord:

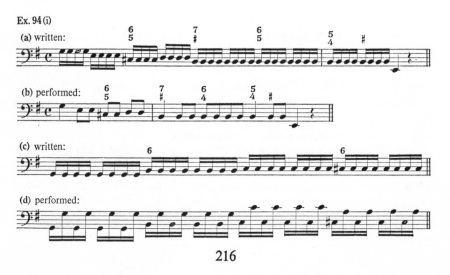

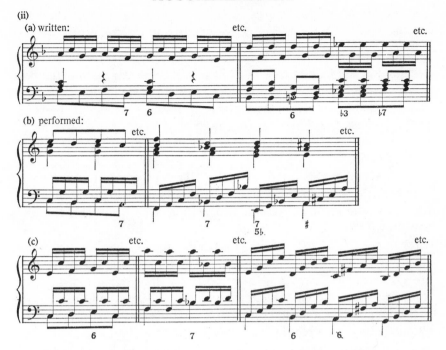

5. HOW CORRECT AN ACCOMPANIMENT

(a) How correct an accompaniment should be depends on circumstances, and to some extent on taste.

(107) Lorenzo Penna, *Li Primi Albori musicali*, Bologna, 1672, III, i, rule 10:

'[Forbidden consecutives] are to be avoided whether occurring by step or by leap; which rule is mainly applicable to the outside parts.'

(108) Michel de Saint-Lambert, *Traité*, Paris, 1707, Ch. VIII, p. 125:

'[Forbidden consecutives are harmless] when you are accompanying a big musical ensemble ... But when you are accompanying a single melody, you cannot attach too much importance to correctness ... for then everything shows.

[Ch. V., p. 65, gives a useful working rule for avoiding unintentional consecutives:] 'The hands should [where appropriate] always move in opposite directions.'

(109) Georg Philipp Telemann, *Generalbass-Übungen* [Hamburg 1733–35], No. 23:

'If the player were only guided by the figures, not having the score, he would play [occasional forbidden consecutives with the solo part], without being blameworthy.

[I, ii, 9:] 'I say: prepare [your discords] so long as you can prepare, and resolve so long as you can resolve . . . and for the rest leave the responsibility with the author of the figures and the composer.'

Do what an experienced accompanist might be expected to do, with nothing but the figured bass in front of him: that is generally the best way out of any continuo perplexities. The paper faults and the actual clashes which may result nearly always sound excellent in practice, partly because the difference of timbre ameliorates them, and partly because natural clashes usually come off better than over-clever ways of evading them.

(b) Remember this important rule: when, of two notes moving in parallel fifths, one is an accented passing note resolving by step before the other note has changed, the progression is correct. (This can also happen with long appoggiaturas.)

(c) In the filled-in (full-voiced) accompaniment, the only important rules (both given by Heinichen, *loc. cit.*, 32ff., and Ch. III, 54, p. 202) are (i) to avoid incorrect progressions between the extreme outside parts; (ii) to keep the two hands close together so as to avoid conspicuous incorrectness between their inside parts (and also so as to avoid thick chords in too low a register); and (iii) to keep the right hand as correct as possible in its progressions, while allowing the left hand either to double them, or to move freely.

6. HOW WIDELY SPACED AN ACCOMPANIMENT

(a) It came, in strict eighteenth-century theory, to be thought correct to play the bass with the left hand, and the remaining three parts of a consistent four-part accompaniment in the right hand; but even in theory we have already seen all manner of exceptions, and the practice was obviously very free indeed. We may content ourselves with Heinichen's revealing statement (Pt. I, Ch. II, Sect. 30): 'this [strict] kind is nowadays the most general and fundamental accompaniment, which every beginner is taught'. But not which every expert always practises.

(b) It is, among many other varieties of texture, perfectly correct to have two parts (of a more or less four-part realization) going on in either hand. This can be described as the extended accompaniment.

(110) C. P. E. Bach, *Essay*, II, 1762, XXXII, 10:

'An extended accompaniment . . . [i.e.] extended harmony can sometimes be very pleasing in contrast to close harmony.'

(c) It is sometimes effective to carry the accompaniment above the solo; but not very often for long at a time.

(111) Joachim Quantz, *Essay*, Berlin, 1752, XVIII, vi, 21:

'It has long been a well-established rule, that in playing continuo, the hands should not move too far apart from one another, and consequently that one should not play too high with the right hand.'

Exceptions were recognized. But there is a considerable danger of obscuring or detracting from the solo melody, if the accompaniment goes very high for more than an occasional note or two. Only when the solo itself lies low (e.g. on bass instruments or low voices) can the accompaniment comfortably go over the solo for any length of time.

(d) Smoothness is often the most important virtue of an accompaniment; and this tends to preclude high passages, since it precludes wide leaps.

(112) Michel de Saint-Lambert, *Traité*, Paris, 1707, Ch. III, p. 19:

'When once you have placed the hand on the keyboard . . . you must take all the subsequent chords in the nearest possible place.

[Ch. V, Sect. 21, p. 36:] 'see if any notes of the chord one is leaving can be used in the chord which one is approaching; when that can be done, one should not change these notes.'

(113) C. P. E. Bach, *Essay*, II, Berlin, 1762, Introd., 25:

'I shall treat of good construction and the smooth progression of the harmonies . . . avoiding unnecessary leaps and clumsy part-writing.

[XXIX, 3:] 'A noble simplicity in the calm accompaniment . . .

[14] 'Notes which are already part of the previous chord and can be carried into the next are sustained; for this method, together with flowing progressions well laid out, gives the part a singing quality.'

Accompanists whose style is full of scale-passages going off like rockets into the upper skies, or who have a general craving for heights and for leaps, can learn a really valuable lesson here. Smoothness is the basis of most good baroque accompaniment.

(e) Nevertheless, C. P. E. Bach (*Essay*, Berlin, 1753, Introd., 9, footnote) calls it 'quite proper and desirable for the accompanist to repeat [i.e. restrike] chords', to keep the beat clear; he might also have added, to keep the sound going on the harpsichord, as Heinrich Albert (*Arias*, II, Königsberg, 1640, preface) explained when on plucked instruments he wanted 'both the suspensions and the consonances often repeated and struck'.

(114) Penna, *Li Primi Albori musicali*, Bologna, 1672, Ch. XX, rule 19:

'Take care to arpeggiate the chords so as not to leave empty spaces [i.e. silences] on the [plucked keyboard] instrument.'

(115) Michel de Saint-Lambert, *Traité*, Paris, 1707, Ch. IX, Sect. 14, p. 132:

'On the organ one does not repeat chords, and one uses scarcely any arpeggiation: on the contrary one ties the sounds a great deal.'

7. HOW INDEPENDENT AN ACCOMPANIMENT

(a) Merely doubling the solo parts in unison is thoroughly unsatisfactory as a general texture, though it may be acceptable and even desirable briefly and occasionally.

Some doubling an octave below, in the middle of the accompaniment, is acceptable if not done too continuously; but in so far as it can be avoided without excessive cleverness or artificiality, that is likely to be better still.

(116) Andreas Werckmeister, *Anmerckungen*, Aschersleben [1698], ed. of 1715, Sect. 69:

'One must avoid continuous movement in octaves with the singers and instrumentalists.'

(117) Francesco Gasparini, *L'Armonico Pratico*, Venice, 1708, Ch. X:

'One must never accompany note for note as in the voice part or any other top part.'

(b) The very least degree of independence which is desirable in an accompaniment comprises chords connected by such excellent voice-leading (helped on with a few unaccented passing or changing notes) that the parts (and especially the top part) are agreeably melodious.

This is a very noticeable feature even of the simplest of our surviving baroque specimens. It requires considerable skill, particularly when more or less improvised; but it makes a very great difference to the total effect.

Ex. 95. (a) Johann Caspar Heck, *The Art of Playing the Harpsichord*, London [1770], 'The Art of Playing Thorough Bass', p. 94, Lesson I, specimen realization in simple style for Arcangelo Corelli, Trio Sonata Op. 2, Rome, 1685, No. 3, first movt., Allemanda Presto [ma non troppo!]; (a) mm. 1–3; (b) mm. 20–26: suggestion for slightly more elaborate realization by Robert Donington:

Ex. 95

(a) Presto [=Allegro non troppo]

Even in so simple a form, the accompaniment ought to sound like a piece of music complete in itself: unpretentious, but enjoyable. If it is not, it can give little or no pleasure to the accompanist, who cannot then be expected to play it very well; and it can provide no proper balance of musical interest with the solo part, which is to that extent left unsupported.

When Ernst L. Gerber (*Historisch-biographisches Lexicon*, I, Leipzig, 1790, entry on his father, Heinrich Nicol. Gerber) related of the style taught to his father by J. S. Bach that 'this accompaniment was already so beautiful in itself that no principal voice could add anything to the pleasure which I felt from it', we may allow a certain amount for filial exaggeration. But that an accompaniment should be beautiful in itself, and that it should sound complete in itself: these are undoubtedly valid principles of baroque realization, however complex or however simple.

The accompaniment, then, must at the very least be able to stand up musically in its own right, while at the same time blending suitably with the solo part.

(c) There is one working rule here which *sometimes* serves remarkably well: try keeping the rhythm of the accompaniment for the most part homophonically with the bass, i.e. just body out the bass in harmony.

This will not serve except in rather simple passages, moving at a certain speed, and usually with a certain lightness; but in such passages, it may sometimes serve much better than a more sophisticated part cutting across the rhythm of the bass.

(d) On the other hand, it is often possible and desirable to carry the independence of the accompaniment considerably beyond the minimum requirements of good voice-leading, and to develop a freely contrapuntal texture, with a good deal of loose imitation.

This must be managed so naturally and so inconspicuously that there is no distraction from the superior interest of the solo part. But the baroque age was, after all, an age when contrapuntal thinking did come

221

naturally to well-trained musicians. We find such a free and easy counter-point hinted at in many surviving fragments of baroque realization, and worked out in a few partial or complete examples, such as the following.

Ex. 96. Alessandro Scarlatti, cantata, 'Da sventura a sventura', first section, opening and closing measures, with freely contrapuntal realization (found in Naples, Conservatorio, MS 34.5.2, ff. 2–6, v. and other MSS), probably by the composer and certainly contemporary:

Ex. 96

ma-tu – ra.

(e) There are sometimes opportunities, without distracting from the given parts, to bring in more definite points of imitation: i.e. to make the counterpoint momentarily fugal.

Ex. 97. Johann David Heinichen, *General-Bass*, Dresden, 1728, I, VI, 40, point of imitation as it can be introduced into the accompaniment by the performer:

Ex.97

Tu

sei la speranza [no more words given]

imitation in the right hand

(f) In yet other passages, neither a chordal nor a contrapuntal accompaniment is desirable, but simply an idiomatic use of the harpsichord.

Here the method is to think of a good pattern of figuration, nicely fitted both to the solo part and for good harpsichord sonority; and having found it, to stay with it. One of the best all-purpose resources is broken chords: i.e. in some simple but measured rhythm, as opposed to unmeasured (and sometimes quite complicated) arpeggiation. The pattern in which the chords are broken, for example, in the first prelude of J. S. Bach's Forty-Eight makes one excellent model (as Gounod discovered!) for such broken-chord accompaniments; and so does the way in which the same pattern is more or less maintained throughout.

Of course, the harpsichordist must hold down the notes of each harmony to keep up the sonority. A few non-harmony notes may be brought in for interest and variety: see Ex. 98 below.

On the other hand, to keep on changing the figuration or the texture without musical justification is bad composing and worse accompanying, especially in baroque music where strong contrasts mostly happen not within movements but between movements.

The following Ex. 98 may be compared with Handel's realization of a similar slow movement at Ex. 63 in Ch. XV, Sect. 5(b) above.

Ex. 98. George Frideric Handel, Trio Sonata in G minor, Op. II No. 8, 3rd movt., Largo, realization with persistent figuration (essentially broken chords) by Robert Donington:

Ex. 98 Largo [ma non troppo lento, quasi andante]

ACCOMPANIMENT

(g) A bad fault in continuo realization may, in some cases, just be too many notes. For example:

(118) Johann Mattheson, *Organisten-Probe*, Hamburg, 1719, Mittel-Classe Prob-Stück 9, Erläuterungen, Sect. 1:

'There is seldom opportunity for ornamental and florid playing when the bass itself is purposely written in an ornamental and florid style. If, however, the bass is without particular embellishment [especially for an introduction, a ritornello, or a rest in the solo] these adornments, these figurations, these inventions, these embellishments find their proper, indeed one might almost say their necessary place.'

(119) Le Cerf de La Viéville, 'Comparaison', in Bonnet, *Histoire de la Musique*, Amsterdam, 1725, I, p. 297:

'A thorough-bass accompaniment unceasingly varied, this variation being often a kind of breaking of chords, and an arpeggiation ... [is often] good only for showing off the quickness of hand.'

(h) Not only too many notes, but any notes incongruous with the passage, will confuse and weaken its effect.

To invent phrases, figurations or counter-melodies which are either drawn from the existing solo and bass part, or in some more inconspicuous way are genuinely related to them; that is the hardest and most necessary skill.

Nothing is more distracting than to bring ideas into the accompaniment which, however attractive in themselves, do not add up with the main material of the piece. If they do not add up, they will certainly distract; and this is against the very function of good accompaniment.

(120) C. P. E. Bach, *Essay*, II, Berlin, 1762, XXIX, 3:

'[Particularly good opportunities for elaboration by the accompanist occur] when the solo part is resting or is performing plain notes.

[XXXII, 11:] 'But his inventiveness must be in sympathy with the feeling and substance of the music.

[XXXII, 3:] 'The accompanist [shows good judgement if he] can discriminate, and therefore realize his part to suit the character of a piece, the number of parts, the remaining performers and especially the soloist, the instruments and voices concerned, the auditorium and the audience ... He uses every refinement of execution and realization—provided it is in keeping with the emotional requirements of the music. But in using such refinements he takes the greatest care that they shall not interfere with anyone ... he never forgets that he is an accompanist, and not a soloist.'

(i) It really is something of a temptation to show off brilliantly but

226

unsuitably when accompanying; and the restraint and good judgement advocated by C. P. E. Bach and others need to be taken very much to heart.

Nevertheless, the elaborate accompaniment can add wonderfully to the music if it is done with just the right kind of imagination, and just the right sense of when and where and how much. The following well-known tributes both refer to J. S. Bach.

(121) Lorenz Mizler, *Musikalische Bibliothek*, Leipzig, I, 4, 1738, p. 48:

'Whoever wishes to form a real conception of refinement in continuo, and of what good accompaniment means, has only to put himself to the trouble of hearing our Capellmeister Bach here, who performs any continuo to a solo so that one imagines that it is a concerted piece, and as if the melody which he plays in the right hand had been composed beforehand.'

(122) Johann Friedrich Daube, *General-Bass*, Leipzig, 1756, XI, xii, footnote:

'The admirable Bach commanded [the elaborate style of] accompaniment in the highest measure; when he was the accompanist, the solo was bound to shine. He gave it life, where it had none, by his abundantly skilled accompaniment. He knew how to imitate it so cunningly in either right or left hand, and again how to introduce so unexpected a counter-melody, that the hearer would have sworn that it had all been composed in that manner with the greatest care. At the same time, the regular [chordal] accompaniment was very little cut down. All in all, his accompanying was always like a concerted part worked out most elaborately, [including] the bass, [yet] without interference to the solo part.'

8. WHAT INSTRUMENTS OF ACCOMPANIMENT

(a) The instruments used for accompanying solos and other chamber music of the early baroque period were quite various. They included harpsichord, chamber organ, lute, lyra da gamba (*lirone*), and guitar. If there was a favourite, it was probably, for vocal music, that large variety of lute with long bass strings known as the *chitarrone* (arch-lute); or for lighter vocal pieces, sometimes the guitar.

For two or three singers accompanied by organ or lute, Praetorius (*Syntagma*, III, Wolfenbüttel, 1618, Ch. VI, Sect. on Organ, App.) calls it 'very good, and indeed almost essential, to have this same general bass played in addition by some bass instrument, such as a bassoon, a dolcian, a trombone, or best of all on a violone' (meaning either bass viol–i.e. gamba–or cello; but not, in this context, double-bass viol).

But the doubling of the continuo with a melodic bass instrument does

227

not seem to have been, as it became in the later baroque period, a standard practice.

(b) The continuo instruments in an early baroque orchestra were not only varied but numerous. Their parts were more or less improvised, but sufficiently preconcerted at rehearsal, in Agazzari's vivid description (*Del sonare sopra'l basso*, Siena, 1607, p. 9), 'not to get in each other's way [but] wait for their own good time [to make ornamental passages] and not be like the sparrows, all playing at once, and each trying to make the greatest noise'.

Providing the continuo parts, and indeed some of the melodic parts, for an early baroque orchestra (especially in opera), is an enterprise in combined musicology and composition with which we are making considerable progress; but it can never be easy.

(c) The standard eighteenth-century accompaniment in chamber music had clearly come to be harpsichord (or chamber organ, or sometimes still lute) with a melodic instrument (cello, gamba, or sometimes bassoon) doubling the bass line.

No doubt the custom became gradually established in the later seventeenth century, as bass parts grew to be more frequently of a strongly melodic character. Pictures confirm this, showing a long-sighted cellist or gambist peering over the shoulder of a harpsichordist, and sometimes, in rather larger groups, a doubly long-sighted double-bass player peering over the shoulders of both.

Further confirmation is occasionally found in separate copies of the bass part, as in the four published parts (the two bass parts being very slightly different) for both Purcell's sets of trio sonatas (London, 1683 and 1697).

Dr. Burney (*History*, IV, London, 1789, p. 169) was told by Geminiani of the impression made when '*Franceschilli*, a celebrated performer on the violoncello at the beginning of this [eighteenth] century, accompanied one of [Alessandro Scarlatti's] cantatas so admirably, while Scarlatti was at the harpsichord . . .'

Jean-Baptiste Morin (*Cantates françoises*, Paris, 1706, Preface) asked for 'a harpsichord and bass viol' (gamba) to accompany his solo cantatas, in a way which shows that he regards this as the most ordinary of expectations. Couperin wrote in the 'Avertissement' to his *Leçons de Ténèbres* (Paris, 1714) that 'if one can join a Bass Viol or a Bass Violin to the accompaniment of the Organ or the Harpsichord, that will be good'.

Brossard's *Dictionaire de musique* (Paris, 1703, entry 'Basso-Continuo') mentions the makeshift of playing 'simply and without figures on the *Bass Viol* or the *Bass Violin* [or] the *Bassoon*, the *Serpent, etc.*'; and Roger North (autobiographical sketch, London, British Museum, Add.

MS 32, 506, c. 1695, quoted by John Wilson, *Roger North on Music*, London, 1959, p. 26) describes filling out harmonies when accompanying only on his gamba, singing the same bass part the while. David Kellner, in his very popular *Unterricht im General-Bass* (Hamburg, 1732, p. 1) mentions the gamba as an (apparently self-sufficient) instrument of accompaniment. C. P. E. Bach (*Essay*, II, Berlin, 1762, Introd., 8) excuses this only if 'done from necessity, for lack of a good keyboard player'.

Much more common, and effective, is a keyboard instrument without doubling by a melodic bass instrument. But even this, though always correct, is not completely satisfactory except for accompanying a rather quiet solo (for recorder, soft voice, etc.); and C. P. E. Bach (*loc. cit.*, sect. 9), states plainly that 'the most complete accompaniment, and the one to which no possible exception can be taken, is a keyboard instrument in combination with the violoncello'.

The gamba was a preferred alternative to the cello in England till around 1700 at the earliest, and for another half-century in France. It was acceptable anywhere; and Burney (*Present State of Music in Germany*, London, 1773, I, p. 139) still mentions the Elector of Bavaria playing a trio sonata bass part 'on his *Viol da gamba*, charmingly'.

The inclusion of a melodic bass instrument has the great advantage of bringing out the beauty of the bass as an independent melody balancing the melody of the solo part or parts. This balance is so characteristic of most baroque musical structure that we should certainly retain it whenever possible and appropriate.

A full accompaniment on a chamber organ, or a light accompaniment on a larger organ, can make a smoothly beautiful alternative to the sharper sounds of a harpsichord or a lute, in appropriate music. It is still usually preferable, though less obviously so, to include a cello or a gamba for melodic doubling of the bass.

There is, however, no doubt that, for the main baroque period, harpsichord with cello or gamba makes up the standard combination, and the most generally satisfactory in solos and small ensembles.

For rather larger ensembles, a modern double-bass, or a double-bass viol (a little silkier), can properly be added at the octave below if a deeper sonority is desired. Even in the smallest chamber groups, a double-bass was commonly added, and can sound extremely beautiful. There are contemporary pictures showing this.

(d) The continuo section in an orchestra of the main baroque period sometimes (especially in opera, and perhaps more than elsewhere in French opera) remained varied and numerous, with harpsichords and lutes prominent.

The introductions, ritornelli, choruses and dances in opera, and the

tuttis in concertos, are to be accompanied by all the continuo instruments, supporting much or all of the full orchestra; solos, small ensembles and concertino passages are to be accompanied either by
selected continuo instruments (with or without selected orchestral
instruments), or by one harpsichord (and melodic bass) alone.

Late in the baroque period, a more standardized continuo became
customary (except in France, where the organization of the operatic
orchestra into *grand choeur* [i.e. *ripieno*] and *petit choeur* [i.e. *concertino*]
persisted longer on the seventeenth-century pattern).

This more standardized continuo consisted, in a large orchestra, of two
harpsichords: one, with cello (and usually double-bass), supporting solo
singers or a small concertino group (perhaps two violins besides this continuo); the other, with cellos, bassoons and double-basses, belonging with
the *ripieno* and supporting the full orchestra. Though not standard, one or
more theorboes (moderately large lutes) were very common in addition.

In a still larger orchestra, a larger than standard continuo was quite
usual. The following instruments appear, though not continuously, in
Vivaldi's oratorio *Juditha* (perf. Venice, 1716; list given and discussed by
Walter Kolneder, *Antonio Vivaldi*, Wiesbaden, 1965, pp. 240ff.): two
recorders; two oboes; (?) shawm; two clarinets; (by inference) at least
two bassoons (probably more); two trumpets with drums; (?) three
assorted viols; the usual strings consisting of first and second violins,
violas, cellos and double-basses; the whole supported by one mandoline,
four theorboes, two harpsichords and an organ.

There was a natural disposition to employ an organ in music for
church or other sacred performance; but very numerous payments and
other records prove the regular presence of a harpsichord in addition,
and in particular, the harpsichord was often although not always preferred for accompanying recitative, sacred as well as secular.

Winton Dean (in his important book, *Handel's Dramatic Oratorios
and Masques*, London, 1959–see his Ch. 6 throughout, and especially
pp. 109ff.) describes all Handel's oratorios as requiring 'at least two
continuo keyboard instruments', and the Concerti Grossi (Op. 6) likewise, while two harpsichords as well as two organs are needed for
Deborah; probably these, and also a harp, a theorbo and a glockenspiel
for *Saul*; two harpsichords and one or two organs for the revived *Esther*;
two harpsichords and one organ for *Solomon*.

In a small orchestra, one harpsichord suffices for keyboard continuo;
but this at least has always to be present. Both the sonority and the
articulation are more crucially affected by the presence of the harpsichord in a baroque orchestra than is sometimes thought; for even when
it is not much heard in itself, it is heard as brightening the sound and
giving it a keener edge.

ACCOMPANIMENT

9. ACCOMPANYING RECITATIVE

(a) Accompanying recitative is an art in itself, and is subject to special considerations of its own.

The first of these special considerations is that recitative, being primarily declamation, has a speech-like flexibility of rhythm (see Ch. XVIII, Sect. 7 below). It is the words which suggest the rhythm for the music, and not the music which sets the rhythm for the words.

(123) Sébastien de Brossard, *Dictionaire de Musique*, Paris, 1703, entry 'Largo':

'[In recitative] we often do not make the beats very equal, because this is a kind of *declamation* where the Actor ought to follow the movement of the passion . . . rather than that of an equal and regulated measure.'

(b) From this first consideration, a second follows: that the accompanist must keep himself entirely free to follow the momentary (though it is to be hoped by no means arbitrary) fluctuations of the singer's tempo. Dry recitative should never be conducted.

(124) John Hoyle, *Dictionary of Music*, London, 1770, entry 'Recitativo':

'Notwithstanding this sort of composition is noted in true time, the performer is at liberty to alter the Bars, or Measure, according as his subject requires; hence the Thorough Bass is to observe and follow the singer, and not the person that beats time.'

(c) From that second consideration, a third follows: that the accompanist should on no account bring in any phrases of an ornamental or melodic character which, because they would have to be performed with some regularity of rhythm, more or less in measure, would impede the more or less unmeasured flexibility of the singer's rhythm.

(125) C. P. E. Bach, *Essay*, II, Berlin, 1762, XXXVIII, 5:

'[Bring in] no ornaments or [melodic] elaborations when accompanying recitatives.'

(d) The only exceptions to this more or less unmeasured flexibility of rhythm are 'accompanied' recitatives, usually requiring a well-marked rhythm (but certainly no melodic elaboration) from the accompanist.

(126) C. P. E. Bach, *Essay*, II, Berlin, 1762, XXXVIII, 2:

'Some recitatives, in which the bass, and possibly other instruments as well [i.e. in "accompanied" recitative], perform a well-defined melodic line or continuous progression which does not share in the singer's pauses, are to be taken in strict time so as to keep them in order.'

231

'The remainder [i.e. recitatives other than the "accompanied"] are declaimed according to their content, now slow, now fast, without regard to the measure, even though they are written with bars. In both cases, above all the latter, an accompanist ... must listen constantly to the soloist, and when there is dramatic action, watch him too, so as to be always punctual with his accompaniment.'

(e) Nevertheless, while the accompanist must follow the singer of recitative in every fluctuation (even in every arbitrary and ill-judged fluctuation) of tempo and rhythm, he has still the responsibility of giving the singer a firmly rhythmical impetus into each subsequent phrase: sometimes delaying spaciously; sometimes pressing on.

(127) C. P. E. Bach, *Essay*, II, Berlin, 1762, XXXVIII, 3:

'When the declamation is rapid, the chords must be ready in the instant, particularly at pauses in the solo part where the chord precedes a subsequent entry. When the chord ends, the next one must be played promptly. In this way the singer will not be held back in his expression or in the rapid delivery needed for it; for he will always be warned in good time of the progression and nature of the harmony.'

(f) The recitative so far considered is Italianate of the later baroque period.

Early baroque Italian recitative, together with all baroque French or French-influenced recitative (e.g. in England prior to the eighteenth century) has a much more lyrical and melodious character, nearer to arioso, and therefore needing to be matched by a somewhat greater regularity in the rhythm of the declamation, and a somewhat smoother continuity in the accompaniment, although it is still the words which influence the finer points of musical rhythm, and far greater flexibility is required than in the airs and the choruses.

(g) But in any baroque style of recitative, we may have:

(i) *action recitative*, for getting through as many words as possible in the shortest time; or

(ii) *expressive recitative*, for extracting the greatest possible emotion out of the words.

We should adapt the speed and character of the accompaniment accordingly.

(h) A fourth consideration is the necessity of giving the singer plenty of sonorous support from the accompaniment.

To give sonorous support from a harpsichord, without imposing any restraint upon the rhythmic flexibility of the singer, only one recourse will serve: arpeggiation; and in almost all circumstances, plenty of it.

From this in turn it follows that there must be plenty of notes in most of the chords to be arpeggiated. Sparse harmonies are usually quite inadequate for accompanying recitative at the harpsichord.

(128) Nicolo Pasquali, *Thorough-Bass Made Easy*, Edinburgh, 1757, p. 47:

'[The art of accompanying recitative on the harpsichord] consists in filling up the harmony as much as possible; and therefore the left hand strikes the chords in it as well as the right.

'Care must be taken not to strike abruptly, but in the harpeggio way ... for common speech a quick harpeggio; for the tender a slow one; and, for any thing of passion, where anger, surprise, *etc.*, is expressed, little or no harpeggio, but rather dry strokes, playing with both hands almost at once.

'The abrupt way is also used at a *punctum* or full stop, where the sense is at an end.'

The reader is asked to turn back to Ex. 71 in Ch. XVI, Sect. 4(d) for a specimen of Pasquali's attempts at suggesting approximately in notation his recommended arpeggiation for a passage of expressive recitative. *All arpeggiation should start on the beat.*

(h) The degree and manner of arpeggiation are variable factors.

(129) Michel de Saint-Lambert, *Traité*, Paris, 1707, Ch. IX, p. 131:

'When accompanying a long recitative, it is sometimes good to dwell for a long time on one chord, when the bass allows, and to let many notes be sung by the voice [in effect] without harpsichord accompaniment, then strike again a second chord, and next stop again, and thus only make an accompaniment at long intervals, assuming that as I have said the bass only has long notes, which is normally the case in recitative.

'At other times, after striking a full chord on which you dwell for a long time, you strike one note again here and there, but with such good management that it seems as if the harpsichord had done it by itself, without the consent of the accompanist.

'At other times again, doubling the intervals, you strike all the notes again one after the other, producing from the harpsichord a crackling almost like musketry fire; but having made this agreeable display for three or four bars, you stop quite short on some big harmonious chord (that is to say, without a dissonance) as though to recover from the effort of making so much noise.'

(130) Francesco Gasparini, *L'Armonico pratico al cimbalo*, Venice, 1708, ed. of 1754, p. 74:

'[In accompanying recitative] one must spread the chords ... but not continuously. For when the Harmony of the note has been heard, one must hold on to the keys, and allow the Singer to satisfy himself and sing as he pleases, and according to the expressiveness of the words; and not annoy him or disturb him with a continuous arpeggio or runs of passages up and down, as some do.'

(131) C. P. E. Bach, *Essay*, II, Berlin, 1762, XXXVIII, 4:

'The rapidity with which a chord is arpeggiated depends on the speed and character of the recitative. The slower and more expressive the recitative, the slower the arpeggiation.

[XXXVIII, 3:] 'Arpeggiation is to be avoided in rapid declamation, especially when there are frequent changes of harmony [where] it might very easily throw accompanist, singer and audience into confusion.

[7:] 'When a singer departs from the written notes, it is better to play repetitions of a full chord rather than single notes. The right harmony is the main factor in recitative; singers should not be expected to sing nothing but the written notes, especially in passages carelessly composed. It is sufficient if they keep their declamation within the right harmony.

[8:] 'When completing the arpeggiation of an introductory chord it is as well to reach the top of the arpeggio with the note on which the singer is to begin.'

(i) It will be appreciated from the above evidence that a continuous rumbling of arpeggiation in which all sense of measure disappears can be just as undesirable as a prim succession of unarpeggiated chords in which the measure is too strictly maintained. Too much arpeggiation confuses the progressions; too little arpeggiation gives insufficiently sonorous support. To match the piece, the hall, the singer and the tempo with just the right degree and manner of arpeggiation requires considerable discernment.

10. INSTRUMENTS FOR ACCOMPANYING RECITATIVE

(a) The lute, including the theorbo (large) and the archlute or *chitarrone* (largest), has its own idioms, among them a sketchy but sonorous arpeggiation, alternating with rapidly spread chords, which is very suitable for supporting flexible recitative.

In the early baroque *stile recitativo*, a melodic instrument doubling the bass line was not generally felt to be necessary, although it might occur. Long bass notes on a plucked instrument can always be repeated as required.

In both the Italian and the French recitative of the main baroque period, a melodic bass instrument was generally felt to be desirable, although not absolutely necessary. It enhances the continuity, increases the singer's assurance and fills out the general sonority, especially when the bass notes are very long.

(b) When an organ is used, there is no necessity for a melodic bass instrument simply in order to sustain the bass line, since the organ can do this for itself. Nevertheless, doubling with a melodic bass instrument was generally felt to be desirable in order to bring out the somewhat (if only slightly) melodic character of the bass line, in its function as the complement or balance of the solo part.

There are, however, other differences in the manner or realization which the sustained tone of the organ makes desirable.

(132) Johann David Heinichen, *Anweisung*, Hamburg, 1711, p. 226:

'In church recitatives [accompanied by the organ] the hands are quickly taken up again after striking a fresh chord . . . [at] the judgement and pleasure of the accompanist.' [But this seemingly implies that the bass is held on the pedals.]

(133) Georg Joachim Joseph Hahn, *General-Bass-Schüler*, Augsburg, 1751, p. 57:

'On organs [the chords in recitative] are struck simultaneously, and after they are struck the right hand is lifted and rests till the fresh chord' [the left hand (or the pedal-board) holding on the bass].

(134) C. P. E. Bach, *Essay*, II, Berlin, 1762, XXXVIII, 5:

'In a recitative with sustaining accompanying [orchestral] instruments one keeps staying on the organ simply with the bass note on the pedals, while one lifts up the harmonies quickly after striking them with the hands.'

The last quotation (134) refers to *recitativo accompagnato* ('accompanied' recitative), where the same rule evidently applies as in *recitativo secco* ('dry' recitative). This point is confirmed by Johann Samuel Petri (*Anleitung*, Lauban, 1767, 2nd ed., Leipzig, 1782, p. 13), where he says that 'the notes must be taken off short' by the organist, in an accompanied passage of vocal music. But the bass holds on. (So *may* the chords, or some of them; too much taking up of the chords can sound intolerably dry.)

(c) The organ, therefore, is a standard instrument for the accompaniment of recitative in church music; but no more so (and perhaps less so) than the harpsichord.

It was quite customary to pay special fees for bringing in a harpsichord, or for tuning it (examples in Thomas Culley, 'A Documentary History of the Liturgical Music at the German College in Rome, 1573–1674', unpublished Ph.D. dissertation, Harvard University, 1965, for the Roman church of S. Apollinare; in Oscar Mischiati, 'Per la storia dell' Oratorio a Bologna: Tre inventari del 1620, 1622 e 1682', *Collectanea historiae musicae*, III, Florence, 1963, pp. 131–70; and for the great church of San Petronio at Bologna, in a remarkably fine article by Anne Schnoebelen, 'Performance Practices at San Petronio in the Baroque', *Acta Musicologica*, XLI, 1969, i–ii, pp. 37–55).

Arthur Mendel's careful article 'On the Keyboard Accompaniments to Bach's Leipzig Church Music' (*Musical Quarterly*, XXXVI, July, 1950, pp. 339–62) mentions that a harpsichord stood in the choir-gallery of the Thomas-Kirche during Bach's tenure there: for rehearsal only, in his considered opinion; but if so, the case would seem (from prior, contemporary and subsequent evidence) to have been somewhat exceptional.

The following recommendation calls for a harpsichord to be used for (though not necessarily for all) recitatives and arias in church.

(135) C. P. E. Bach, *Essay*, II, Berlin, 1762, Introd., 3:

'The organ is indispensable in church music on account of the fugues, loud choruses, and more generally, on account of the binding effect. It adds to the grandness and it preserves order.

[4:] 'But whenever recitatives and arias are used in church . . . there must be a harpsichord.'

(d) For the interchangeability of organ and harpsichord in suitable music see (among much other evidence) Couperin's mention (already cited in Sect. 8(c) above) of organ or harpsichord as alternative instruments of accompaniment in his *Leçons de Ténèbres* (Paris, 1714).

The following warning comes from a not very good source, but it may sometimes be significant.

(136) [Peter Prelleur], *Modern Musick-Master*, London, 1730, ed. of 1731, in 'A Dictionary':

'Organo, signifies properly an Organ, but when it is written over any piece of Musick, then it signifies the Thorough Bass.'

11. HANDEL AS ACCOMPANIST

(a) The following is a report by Sir George Macfarren (*Proceedings* of the Musical Association, XII, 1885–86, pp. 39ff.) of what Sir George Smart told him he had been told when turning pages for Joah Bates, who as a boy had heard performances under Handel's own direction. It is a third-hand account: the echo of an echo; but nevertheless, the facts as stated are straightforward, by no means unexpected, and very probably true.

(137) Sir George Macfarren, *Proceedings* of the [now Royal] Musical Association, XII, 1885–86, pp. 39ff:

[p. 40:] 'He [Handel] had, by the side of the organ in the Hanover Square rooms, a harpsichord. In choruses he played on the organ; in most of the songs and in all the recitatives he played on the harpsichord. In some few instances, which seemed to be of a special and exceptional character, he used the organ in the songs.

'The organ part was not merely the duplication of the voices, but when the music was not in florid counterpoint it would be the amplification of the harmony. The harpsichord part of the songs was contrapuntal. It was not merely the filling up of the harmony, but improvisation in the case of Handel, and the carefully considered production, in the case of Bates, of an interesting florid contrapuntal part.

'It had always been the custom, in Handel's time, to accompany recitatives on the harpsichord, strengthened by a single violoncello and double-bass player of the bass part only, and this accompaniment for recitative was made interesting by the "sprinkling"–I remember Sir George Smart using that word particularly–of harmony, or spreading it in arpeggio across a large part of the compass of the instrument, and so confirming the voice with the note which was to be prominent in the suceeding phrase; never being struck together with the voice, [but] succeeding vocal closes, and anticipating the frontal notes of new phrases.

'It had always been the custom to accompany in the opera, as much as in the oratorio, recitative in this manner . . .'

(b) The phrase 'succeeding vocal closes' (i.e. succeeding to, following after) refers to the convention of accompaniment already mentioned (Ch. XVI, Sect. 4(h) above) in connection with obligatory appoggiaturas on closes in recitative. This convention is discussed in the following section.

12. THE DELAYED CADENCE IN RECITATIVE

(a) At a vocal close of the type described in Ch. XVI, Sect. 4(h) above, the accompaniment (whether in 'dry' recitative or in 'accompanied' recitative) is normally intended to remain on the dominant 6–4 harmony which carries both the singer's appoggiatura, and its resolution a fourth below.

Alternatively, the accompaniment may rest at this point.

After the singer has disposed comfortably both of his appoggiatura and of its resolution, the accompanist (or the conductor) pauses just long enough for the sound to clear, and for a momentary tension to build up. Then he releases the tension, and completes the cadence, by bringing in boldly and spaciously the dominant 5–3 and the tonic 5–3.

(b) Nevertheless, there are exceptions. Sir Jack Westrup first drew very scholarly attention ('The Cadence in Baroque Recitative', *Natalicia Musicologica Knud Jeppesen*, Copenhagen, 1962, pp. 243–52) to evidence suggesting that in opera, the accompaniment might often break in upon the vocal close for the sake of greater speed and dramatic excitement, without letting the singer first finish in the normal way; and this may result in superimposing the tonic harmony on top of the dominant harmony. This bold suggestion works remarkably well in almost all operatic cadences where it is dramatically convincing for the accompanist thus to stumble across the singer's declamation in the stir and hurry of the action.

An article by Sven Hostrup Hansell ('The Cadence in 18th-Century Recitative', *Musical Quarterly*, LIV, 2 April, 1968, pp. 228–48) appears to confuse evidence about the normal behaviour of the dissonant acciaccatura (for which see Ch. XVI, Sect. 5(a) above) with evidence about harmonic progressions (quite a different matter). But Winton Dean has confirmed this very important discovery conclusively, and clarified it further, in an article 'The Performance of Recitative in Late Baroque Opera', (*Music and Letters*, Jan. 1978).

(c) The standard convention was observed, as outlined at (a) above, even when the notation obscures it, in any situation other than opera.

(138) J. A. Scheibe in F. W. Marpurg's *Kritische Briefe*, Berlin, for 1760–2, letter 109, p. 352:

'Some composers are in the habit of anticipating [i.e. in their notation] the penultimate [bass] note of the cadence, without inserting [the necessary] rest.'

Ex. 99. J. A. Scheibe, *loc. cit.*, (a) and (b) illustrations to the above statement; (c) could be correctly notated thus; (d) or perhaps better, thus:

Ex. 99

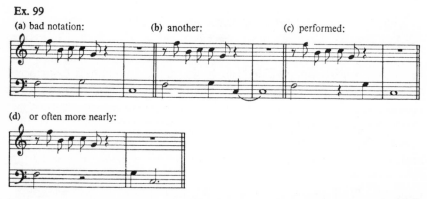

(a) bad notation: (b) another: (c) performed:

(d) or often more nearly:

Indeed, so rhythmically free is recitative in the proper manner of its performance, and so little can it be bounded by written measure, that

238

there is no way of notating this particular cadential convention quite satisfactorily. That is presumably why it is so commonly misnotated in the confident expectation that any well-trained performer would know what to do with it.

When a rest is inserted into the notation, as Scheibe seems to have thought it should preferably be, the effect could often be a single disconcerting measure of five quarter notes. There is even a late manuscript of Alessandro Scarlatti's cantata 'E penar deggio ancora' (Dresden, Sächsische Landesbibliothek, MS. Mus. 1/3/13, ? early 19th cent.) which rather bemusedly puts five beats into the accompaniment, though not into the voice part, of two such measures; and which, in two other such measures, without adding a fifth beat in the accompaniment, attempts to suggest it by distorting the vertical alignment.

(d) We have, therefore, to accept as standard this convention by which, except in late baroque opera, the vocal close is allowed to finish impressively before the accompanist, having left an appreciable moment of stolen time, completes the cadence. Moreover, the operatic exception apparently died out when *opera seria* did, and does not seem to apply, for example, to the less formal operas of Mozart and his contemporaries. Later still, the entire convention became lost to memory.

(139) Joseph Haydn, letter to an Austrian monastery (probably Zwettl, according to H. C. Robbins Landon, who translates the letter, and ascribes it to 1768, in his *Collected Correspondence and London Notebooks of Joseph Haydn*, London, 1959, pp. 9–11):

'In the accompanied recitatives, you must observe that the accompaniment should not enter until the singer has quite finished his text, even though the score often shows the contrary ... but I leave this to the harpsichord player [who would be very familiar with the convention], and all the others must follow him.'

(140) Sir George Macfarren, Preface (April, 1873) to the Novello edition of Handel's *Belshazzar*, London, [n.d.], p. v:

'As the now obsolete plan, of writing the two final chords under the voice notes which are intended to precede them, is not clearly understood by all musicians, the arrangement of notes and rests is so disposed in this pianoforte part as to show where the accompaniment is to follow the voice.'

PART FOUR

THE EXPRESSION

CHAPTER EIGHTEEN

Tempo

1. MUSICIANSHIP THE NECESSARY JUDGE OF TEMPO

(a) Probably the most important and difficult element in expression is tempo.

(b) Very little assistance can be had on tempo either from notation or from contemporary evidence. This is partly because there is seldom one right tempo in the absolute. Good tempo is relative.

In the same music, resonant acoustics or large forces may require a slower tempo than dry acoustics or small forces. An interpretation making for the most brilliance may require a faster tempo than an interpretation making for the most expressiveness. 'Taste', wrote Anton Bemetzrieder (*Leçons de clavecin*, Paris, 1771, p. 68) 'is the true metronome.'

(c) Tempo is a function of interpretation, and can only be right or wrong for a given interpretation. That interpretation, indeed, can be better or worse; but there is usually a considerable margin for individuality within the boundaries of the style.

2. TIME-WORDS VAGUE AND MISLEADING

(a) Time-words often suggest the mood from which the tempo follows, rather than the tempo itself: allegro (cheerful); andante (fluently); adagio (gently); largo (broad); grave (heavy). So vague are they, even when directly indicative of speed, as presto (quick) or lento (slow), that different contemporary listings place them in different orders of speed.

(b) Thus Purcell (*Sonatas of III Parts*, London, 1683, Preface) calls largo 'a middle movement', quicker than adagio and grave; Brossard (*Dictionaire de musique*, Paris, 1703) has largo slower than adagio, and that slower than lento; Leopold Mozart (*Violinschule*, Augsburg, 1756, I, iii, 27) has grave slower than largo and that slower than adagio; yet Jean-Baptiste Cartier again has largo slower than adagio, but that slower than grave. Brossard (*op. cit.*) defines assai as 'according to some, much; and according to others [not] carried to excess'.

243

(c) Similar inconsistencies run through the rest of the available evidence. 'Time', concluded Alexander Malcolm (*Treatise of Musick*, Edinburgh, 1721, p. 394) 'is a various and undetermined thing'; [p. 395] 'indeed they leave it altogether to Practice to determine the precise Quantity'.

(d) Original time-words often need an editorial qualification (e.g. [*ma non troppo*]) or alternative (e.g. *Presto* [allegro] or *Adagio* [andante]) to help the modern performer. Metronome markings suggest too much exactness, and are best avoided.

(e) Reducing note-values by half or a quarter is sometimes helpful (especially in changes to triple time), but can itself be misleading, and should only be done where the desirability of it is extremely obvious.

3. TIME-SIGNATURES IN CHAOTIC CONFUSION

(a) Time-signatures are no more explicitly or reliably informative than time-words.

(b) The proportional system of mensural notation, a confused legacy from which still lingered through the baroque period, was supposed to show relative tempos, not absolute tempos. The unit by which it was regulated was a hand-beat (tactus), itself always of moderate tempo but adaptable to the actual music. The system, never very systematic, was already under scathing attack by the great Zarlino (*Le Istitutioni armoniche*, Venice, 1558, ed. of 1562, p. 278); again, among others, by Pierre Maillart (*Les Tons*, Tournai, 1610, p. 349); and more conclusively than ever by the learned and much respected Athanasius Kircher (*Musurgia*, Rome, 1650, p. 676), who dismissed it as 'this most confused subject' (*hanc confusissimam materiam*), and 'this utter muddle' (*tota haec farrago*).

(c) In particular, little reliance can be placed on the distinction between plain C and stroked ¢, which Thomas Morley (*Plaine and Easie Introduction*, London, 1597, p. 9) already noticed being used by composers indiscriminately; which Pierre Maillart (*loc. cit.*) called 'superfluous and useless'; which Johann David Heinichen (*General-Bass*, Dresden, 1728, Part I, Ch. IV, Sect. 48, p. 348) also described as 'used without discrimination, sometimes for a naturally rapid piece and sometimes for a slow one'; which Kircher (*loc. cit.*) likewise called 'superfluous; indeed I have found that a majority of the most excellent musicians and the most expert in theory of the present time [i.e. c. 1650] have deliberately omitted them, and taken them for one and the same sign (*pro unico signo*)'.

Less learned writers kept repeating the conventional (but unreal) theory that the stroked ¢ doubles the time of the plain C; or (more realistically but still quite undependably) that the time indicated is somewhat faster.

But different manuscripts or prints of the same movement often appear with C or ¢ indifferently, and certainly with no difference of intention. There is even a canon in J. S. Bach's Musical Offering (p. 23 in Hans T. David's edition) with two staves showing C and one showing ¢, no difference in tempo being intended or possible. The canon is by augmentation, and a theoretical difference of pulse may be intended here. But completely unintentional instances of the casual interchange of C and ¢ are common.

However, when a *change* from C to ¢ occurs in course of a movement, some undetermined increase in tempo is almost certainly intended. A good rule of thumb is go faster, but let the music itself determine how much faster.

There *may* also be some hint about the pulse, since ¢ is often, though not dependably, used to show an alla breve, with or without these words (or alla capella) appearing as a confirmation. The pulse should then be two half-notes in a 4–4 bar rather than four quarter-notes (or four half-notes in a 4–2 bar rather than eight quarter-notes). This may not only affect the conductor's beat but also the accompanist's view of which notes in the bass to treat as passing (instead of harmony) notes: see Ch. XVII, Sect. 3 (f) above.

A special case is French recitative, where changes of time-signature are very frequent indeed. These are intended to keep the pulse and accentuation exactly fitted to the words, the note-values remaining constant: i.e. *quarter note equals quarter note throughout* (see my *Interpretation of Early Music*, New Version, London, 1973).

(d) Numerical time-signatures appear to be more specific than the hieroglyphics so far mentioned (and very many others). But in practice they are not much more informative.

Their chief importance for the performer again arises when a *change* occurs in course of a movement.

The numbers remained supposedly proportional in early baroque music, gradually altering to their modern numerator-denominator significance during the seventeenth and early eighteenth centuries.

Thus for seventeenth-century music, the 'tripla' time-signature 3 or more properly 3_j or $\frac{3}{1}$ means (not three units each of a whole note, but) three units in the time of the previous one: i.e., in theory, three times as fast.

The 'sesquialtera' time-signature 3 or more properly $\frac{3}{2}$ means (not three units each of a half-note, but) three units in the time of the previous two: i.e., in theory, half as fast again.

But in practice, these numerical proportions are not at all to be relied upon. All that is probable is some undetermined increase of speed.

This probability is itself, however, very strong. The increase of speed

245

is, in fact, likely to be very much greater than a modern performer might expect, so that we may need to take a measure of three whole notes at a speed which we nowadays might expect to see notated as 3–4 or even as 3–8. (We can reduce these long note-values in a performing edition.)

A good working rule here is (i) try any triple-time movements, apparently notated slow, much quicker than they look; (ii) try any change to triple-time much quicker than it looks.

In the period of Monteverdi and Schütz, this rough rule will prevent many gross misjudgements of triple-time tempo (i.e. taking them far slower than they ought to be). The same warning remains applicable, though gradually less so, through the seventeenth century, and sometimes even into the eighteenth.

But by then our modern meaning of numerator-denominator (so many units of such and such a duration) had imperceptibly taken the numerical time-signatures over; and good modern musicianship can more readily assess their implications.

4. TEMPO JUDGED BY DANCING SPEEDS

(a) Dances have frequently only one tempo at which (with very narrow margins of variability) they can be danced successfully, or at all.

The pavan, for example, has a certain spacious gait, a steady four in a bar, which feels natural to a dancer and to a musician who has once learned the dance.

The galliard which follows, in the ball-room or the concert-room, has a triple-time version of the same steady pulse. In notation, it may look slower (being in triple time) than the pavan, but it is not; if it is played as slow as it looks, the dancer cannot keep his momentum or even his balance. In contemporary descriptions, it is called gay and lively, which it is; but from this most modern historians have assumed that it is faster than the pavan, which it is not; for if it is played faster, the dancer cannot fit in the many more or less intricate steps which distinguish it choreographically from the pavan. Despite the notation, and despite the descriptions, it has in effect the tempo of the pavan: the gayness is in steps and the dancing; the liveliness is in the lightness with which the steady pulse is taken.

Thus Thomas Morley (*Plaine and Easie Introduction*, London, 1597, ed. R. Alec Harman, London, 1952, pp. 296ff.) called 'a pavane, a kind of staid musicke, ordained for grave dauncing', and 'a Galliard ... a lighter and more stirring kinde of dauncing'. Thomas Mace (*Musick's Monument*, London, 1676, pp. 129ff.) wrote that 'Galliards ... are perform'd in a *Slow, and Large Triple-Time*.' Charles Masson (*Nouveau Traité ... de la musique*, Paris, 1694, 2nd ed., Paris, 1699, pp. 7ff.) wrote that 'Galliards [are taken] lightly'.

These characteristics remain to a great extent proper to the pavan and galliard even when composed with intricate figuration for performance on the lute or the harpsichord, rather than more simply on a small orchestra for actual dancing.

The volta is commonly notated in 6–4 with a rather slow pulse of two in a bar. The dance includes a rapid turn by each pair of dancers, during which the woman rises into the air with the perfectly timed assistance of the man's knee beneath her posterior and his hands round her waist. But this perfect timing, without which she cannot be got into the air at all, itself depends on a perfect tempo, with the least possible margin of error. Once having danced the volta yourself, you know the volta tempo for the rest of your life; and here, too, artistic examples by lute or harpsichord composers seem to retain the character and the tempo of the actual dance.

(b) But this correspondence between dancing tempo and performing tempo by no means always follows. When taking a hint on tempo from actual dancing speeds, we have to remember that as an art-form a dance may have grown a long way distant from the ball-room, and that quite a different tempo may then be required.

(c) A further precaution to be remembered is that the same dance (nominally) may have very different characteristics and tempos (actually) at different periods and places.

For example, there is a very rapid English saraband of the seventeenth century, a moderate Italian sarabanda, and a slow French sarabande (and getting slower, as is most familiar to us in J. S. Bach's highly artistic examples in the French style, with French titles to confirm it, as well as 'les agrémens pour la même sarabande' to help us ornament the repeats of two of them). There are differences here both of date and of nationality.

Thus, with equal truth though thinking of different versions, the editors (Phillips and others) of the *New World of Words* (London, 1658, entry 'Saraband') wrote 'Lesson or Air in Musick going with a quick time' (crossed out, and 'a slow time' written into a copy in the British Museum owned by Rd. Kendall in 1719); Thomas Mace (*loc. cit.*, 1676) wrote '*Serabands*, are of the *Shortest Triple-Time* ... *Toyish*, and *Light*'; James Talbot (unsorted manuscript notes, c. 1690, Oxford, Christ Church Lib., MS 1187) wrote (under French influence) 'Saraband a soft passionate Movement, always set in a slow Triple'; Charles Masson (*loc. cit.*, 1699) wrote 'the Sarabande [is taken] gravely'; and Quantz (*Essay*, Berlin, 1752, XVII, vii, 58) wrote 'the Saraband has the same tempo [as the Entrée, the Loure and the Courante, given at about 80 beats to the minute], but is played with a rather more flattering expression'.

Similarly with the minuet, called 'very quick and rapid' by Talbot (*loc. cit.*, c. 1690); 'quick' by Masson (*loc. cit.*, 1699); 'a very lively dance' by Brossard (*loc. cit.*, 1703); while Jean-Jacques Rousseau (both in the *Encyclopedia* of Diderot and d'Alembert, Paris, 1751–65, and in his own *Dictionnaire de Musique*, Paris, 1768, entry 'Minuet', cited here) wrote 'According to [Brossard] this dance is very gay and its movement is very quick. But on the contrary the character of the Menuet is grave and of a noble simplicity; the movement of it is rather moderate than quick ... in our balls ... It is another matter in the theatre.' Quantz (*loc. cit.*) adds interestingly that 'the Menuet is played in such a fashion that it almost carries or lifts the dancer up, and one marks the quarter notes with a somewhat heavy, yet short stroke of the bow. Count [about 80 to the minute] for two quarter notes.' This seems to be partly a difference of date, and partly of function.

Similarly with the allemand: '*Allmaines* ... very *Ayrey*, and *Lively*' (Mace, *loc. cit.*, 1676); 'Almain ... somewhat quicker and more Airy [than the pavan]' (Talbot, *loc. cit.*, c. 1690); 'Allemande grave' (Brossard, *op. cit.*, 3rd ed. [? 1707]; 'Allemanda ... is a serious and dignified movement and should be so performed' (Johann Gottfried Walther, *Musicalisches Lexicon*, Leipzig, 1732). This may be a difference both of date and nationality.

Similarly with the Italian coranto and the French courante, where the differences are of character and rhythm quite as much as of tempo, and are primarily by nationality: 'Corantoes ... Lively, Brisk and Cheerful' (Mace, *loc. cit.*, 1676); 'Courante [taken] gravely' (Masson, *loc. cit.*, 1699). (For the chaconne and the passacaille see Sect. 6(b) below.)

It is important to keep in mind this possibility of very different tempos for the same dance-form in different places, times and functions.

5. TEMPO JUDGED FROM THE CHARACTER OF THE MUSIC

(a) Within limits sometimes wider and sometimes narrower, the music itself will suggest its own tempo to a good and experienced musician.

(140a) Alexander Malcolm, *Treatise of Musick*, Edinburgh, 1721, p. 394:

'The true determination of [tempo] must be learnt by Experience from the Practice of Musicians.'

(141) Joachim Quantz, *Essay*, Berlin, 1752, XI, 15:

'There are indeed various degrees of liveliness and sadness ...

[XII, 2:] 'It is necessary [to take tempo] more from the content of the piece than from the [time] word ...

[11:] 'Whatever speed an Allegro demands, it ought never to depart from a controlled and reasonable movement.'

(142) C. P. E. Bach, *Essay*, Berlin, 1753, III, 10:

'The tempo of a piece . . . is derived from its general mood together with the fastest notes and passages which it includes. Proper attention to these considerations will prevent an allegro from being hurried and an adagio from being dragged.'

(143) Leopold Mozart, *Violinschule*, Augsburg, 1756, I, iii, 7:

'[Tempo] must be inferred from the music itself, and this is what infallibly shows the true quality of a musician.'

(b) By far the most important advice given above is not to take an allegro too quickly nor an adagio too slowly: see the last sentence of (141), and the last sentence of (142).

Over and over again in rehearsal, difficulties of phrasing, accentuation, bowing, articulation and even dynamics will not be solved until somebody suggests that these are not the real problems in the passage concerned. Tempo is the real problem.

Try steadying down the allegro to a more spacious tempo. Try moving the adagio along a little more. It is wonderful how other problems begin to fall into place and settle themselves, given more leisure to phrase the allegro interestingly, and given more momentum to keep the adagio alive and meaningful.

(c) To some extent, tempos on the fast side may be carried off by really dazzling brilliance; and tempos on the slow side may be carried off by really inspired intensity.

But mostly it is best in baroque music to take the fast movements slower than you think and the slow movements faster than you think.

6. VARIATIONS OF TEMPO

(a) Tempo never remains constant throughout any ordinary movement. It fluctuates in a degree which ranges from almost imperceptible to very conspicuous.

Baroque music shares to the full in this ordinary flexibility of tempo, and will tolerate no better than any other music the rigidity of a metronomic rendering.

(144) Girolamo Frescobaldi, *Toccate*, Rome, 1615–16, preface, 1:

'This kind of playing must not be subject to the beat [but taken] now slowly, now quickly, and even held in the air, to match the expressive effects. . . .

[5:] 'The cadences, although they may be written quickly, are properly to be very much drawn out; and in approaching the end of passages or cadences, one proceeds by drawing out the time more adagio.

[9:] 'When you find [rapid] passages and [also when you find] expressive effects, it will be desirable to play slowly . . . it is left to the good taste
and fine judgement of the performer to regulate the tempo . . .'

(145) Thomas Mace, *Musick's Monument*, London, 1676, p. 81:

'*Liberty* . . . to *Break Time*; *sometimes Faster*, and *sometimes Slower*
. . .'

[p. 130:] 'Some [sections] very Briskly, and *Couragiously*, and some
again *Gently, Lovingly, Tenderly*, and *Smoothly.*'

(146) Jean Rousseau, *Traité de la viole*, Paris, 1687, p. 60:

'Liberties [with the tempo] may be taken . . .
[p. 66:] 'There are people who imagine that imparting the movement
is to follow and keep time; but these are very different matters . . .'

(147) François Couperin, *L'art de toucher le clavecin*, Paris, 1716, ed. of
1717, p. 38:

'I find we confuse time, or measure, with what is called cadence or
movement. Measure defines the number and time-value of beats;
cadence [movement] is properly the spirit, the soul that must be added to
it.'

(148) Joachim Quantz, *Essay*, Berlin, 1752, XI, 13:

'The performance should be easy and flexible . . . without stiffness and
constraint.'

(b) Toccatas, chaconnes, passacailles, variations and occasionally
rondos etc. may require different tempos to suit the different characters
of successive sections (see quotations 144 and 145 above).

It is usually better, so far as possible, to restrict the number of different
tempos. A multiplicity of tempos merely sounds unclear and restless.
Two, or at most three, should suffice, suitably distributed. It is generally
desirable to return to the opening tempo for the last section or sections.

No tempo or other difference can be established in general between
chaconnes and passacailles. Contemporary instructions are inconsistent
and contradictory; and the two forms in practice are not always distinct.
We even find (Paris, Bibl. Nat. Rés Vm⁷. 675 f. 57v to 58) a piece headed
'Chaconne ou Passacaille de Mᵣ [Louis] Couperin'.

When changing tempo for a new section, it is often desirable to change
style and mood at the same time, thus emphasizing the contrast.

For example, in the long chaconne which forms Sonata VI of Purcell's
second set of trio sonatas (*Ten Sonatas in Four Parts*, London, 1697,
Sonatas VI and IX ed. Robert Donington and Walter Emery, Novello,
London, 1959, pp. 1–14), the original time-word 'Adagio' appears

(though not in all the parts) at the beginning. Our editorial time-words '[Andante con moto]' appear over alternating passages, with '[tempo I]' in between, and over the last passage of 36 bars. There are also editorial indications for certain allargandos and rallentandos.

These markings have all been tested in many performances of the music by the Donington Consort. To underline the contrast, we take the adagio sections very massively and expressively, and the andante sections very lightly and incisively. The effect is both more interesting and more natural than maintaining a solemn adagio throughout.

(c) Most slow movements, and some fast movements, require plenty of stretching wherever the melodic line can gain expressiveness by doing this, or some increased tension of the harmony needs a little additional breadth to make its proper effect (144, 146, 148). We sometimes call this *stolen* time (*tempo rubato*).

When such stretching comes at the ends of phrases, or of smaller units of the pattern, it is often desirable, in addition, to insert a moment of stolen time before picking up the tempo. It is then possible to 'place' the next phrase or unit rather more tellingly than if it comes with strict punctuality.

The number and the extent of such stretchings and placings will vary with the character of the music, and also with the temperament of the performer; but it is important to realize (and it is not always realized) that such flexibility of tempo is in no way outside the boundaries of baroque style. On the contrary, we need to make it very evident.

(d) For a so-called *tempo rubato* not disturbing the regularity of the beat, see Ch. XIX, Sect. 13 below.

(e) Stolen time, however, need not (and ordinarily should not) more than momentarily disturb the underlying regularity.

C. P. E. Bach (*Essay*, Berlin, 1753, III, 28, annotation to ed. of 1787) rightly wishes us, 'in spite of the beautiful details [of flexible tempo] to hold the tempo at the end of a piece just as it was at the start, which is a very difficult achievement'.

7. THE TIMING OF RECITATIVE

(a) We have again to remember the special considerations which arise in recitative: see Ch. XVII, Sect. 9, above, and especially quotations (123), (124) and (126).

Angelo Berardi (*Ragionamenti*, Bologna, 1681, p. 136), writing just as the arioso style of early Italian recitative was approaching the transition into the still more declamatory and often perfunctory style of eighteenth-century Italianate recitative, gave the remarkable description of 'the representative style' that it 'consists in this alone, that singing one speaks, and speaking one sings'. See also Postscript on p. 253.

The free yet balanced rhythms of declamatory speech are the start for all good performance of recitative. They are not, however, quite the casual rhythms of our ordinary conversation. They are much more the stylized rhythms of theatrical declamation, as it used to be cultivated in spoken plays. By far the best surviving example of it can be heard in the superbly traditional performances of the *Comédie Française*, whose every gesture and timing has been reputedly preserved from the very days of Molière and Corneille.

This declamatory tradition is in no way stilted. On the contrary, it is most artfully naturalistic. Much of it is extraordinarily swift; and all of it is highly dramatic. It is merely that nature herself could never have produced such perfect delivery, such impeccable enunciation, such eloquent gesture of speech and acting, such infallible timing of words and movement.

An opera singer who could absorb fully this art of the theatre that conceals art, and who could blend it with the vocal virtuosity of *bel canto*, would be an artist indeed. That is, after all, how Lully set about learning good declamation, at the classical French theatre, when he, an Italian born, was moulding the future of French opera.

(b) The timing or delivery of recitative needs to be more or less outside measure; yet with its own well-proportioned symmetry and balance. If it is merely arbitrary, it loses force and clarity; and incidently, it becomes almost impossible for the accompanists to know what the singer is doing with the rhythm, and to keep with him.

(c) In recitative, after drawing out some lingering phrase, or slowing down some cadential appoggiatura, it is often very effective to pick up again at particularly rapid speed, as if in haste and agitation. Conversely, when a vocal entry is to be thus accelerated for dramatic impetus, it is usually best also to bring it somewhat late: the lateness prepares very effectively for the acceleration, and a sense of overall balance and proportion is retained. We may perhaps think of this as *borrowed* time.

8. RALLENTANDOS

(a) *Passing* rallentandos are a more or less slight yielding of the tempo, in acknowledgement of some hint of relaxation in the melody or of broadening in the harmony. They will hardly be noticed by the audience, but they prevent the performance from feeling rigid, and are as important in baroque music as anywhere else (144, 146, 148). It is seldom desirable to mark them into the parts; the ordinary give and take of sensitive ensemble playing should take care of them in course of rehearsal.

The tempo will usually be picked up promptly, with little or no delay for 'placing' unless the *phrasing* requires it.

(b) *Cadential* rallentandos are a more or less substantial stretching of the tempo, in acknowledgement of a cadential tendency or an actual cadence, to over-ride which as if it did not exist will always give a feeling of ruthlessness even if the audience does not notice why (see especially [5] at 144).

Many midway cadences and most concluding cadences need very decided rallentandos, which it is commonly desirable to mark quite accurately into the parts, before or during rehearsal.

The picking up of the tempo may often be delayed by a long enough 'placing' to sound like a new start, rather than tumbling into the new phrase with literal punctuality.

(c) Indications for rallentandos are very rare in baroque music, though not unknown.

(d) Slight or substantial, gradual or abrupt: the placing, the amount and the tapering of baroque rallentandos must be judged from the music, and particularly from when the harmony begins to feel cadential.

Too little sounds unfeeling; too much sounds shapeless; too late and too abrupt (a common fault) is like a driver who has suddenly realized that he had better put the brakes on hard.

Just right does not sound noticeable at all, but like all good expression, merely natural. The primary consideration is not to disturb, but to bring out, the overall proportionableness of the line.

(e) Adagio or grave over the last few bars of a movement is frequently not so much for a meno mosso (slower tempo) as for a molto rallentando or an allargando (more than usually pronounced drawing out of the tempo). J. S. Bach's C minor organ fugue (B.G. 38, p. 105) ends with an Adagio section bearing the word adagio again over the last half-bar, perhaps in effect a più rallentando.

POSTSCRIPT

Confirmation of the speech-like flexibility of recitative from later in the baroque period can be found in Johann Mattheson's *Der vollkommene Capellmeister*, Hamburg, 1739, Ch. 13, Sect 21, p. 213:

[Recitative] 'has freedom, in that it governs itself very much according to ordinary speech . . . . Recitative indeed has a beat; but it does not use it; that is the singer does not need to bind himself to it.'

CHAPTER NINETEEN

Rhythm

1. CONVENTIONS OF RHYTHMIC ALTERATION

(a) Just as a number of small, specific ornaments took shape within an old and general tradition of free ornamentation, so certain specific conventions of rhythmic alteration took shape within an old and general tradition of rhythmic flexibility.

(b) Both free ornamentation and specific ornaments, on the one hand, and both rhythmic flexibility and rhythmic conventions, on the other hand, are aspects of the same broad principle by which the baroque performer was expected to improve the expressiveness of the music, and adapt it to his own personality, in course of performing it.

(c) The specific conventions of rhythmic alteration which, before and still more during the baroque period, grew out of the general liberty to modify the rhythm, have chiefly to do with *pairing* notes into units of a beat or less.

(i) Groups of two notes, notated equally, may be paired in a variety of unequal rhythms. This is the problem of *inequality*.

(ii) Groups of two notes, notated unequally by dotting, may also be paired in a variety of unequal rhythms. This is the problem of *dotting*.

(iii) Groups of two notes, notated either equally, or unequally by dotting, may be adapted to the rhythm of triplets notated against them; or three notes notated in triplet rhythm may be adapted to the rhythm of duplets notated against them. This is the problem of *triplets*.

To a very considerable extent, these three problems of rhythm overlap. Nevertheless, it is clearer to keep them so far as possible distinct.

(d) A *general* flexibility of rhythm is desirable in any baroque music; but the *specific* conventions of rhythmic alteration are restricted to quite limited situations, outside which they produce very unmusical results. A detailed study of their boundaries and behaviour is therefore needed.

(e) Before starting on this detailed study, we may recall yet again that most fundamental of principles for good baroque interpretation: keeping in being a continuously proportionable and well moulded line.

254

The conventional modifications of rhythm here to be described can add to the vitality or the grace of the interpretation very valuably, when used with good judgement and good imagination in the right amounts and the right places. They can be very harmful in the wrong amounts and the wrong places. There is a very real danger in being too calculating (it might almost be said, too correct) over any small point of detail. It is the large effect which counts: in a word, the line. Details which contribute to the line are valuable; details which upset the line are harmful. That is the fundamental principle in question here.

It is particularly desirable to use good judgement in making the conventional alterations of rhythm here to be described. Too little is altogether better than too much; but better still is a good and reasonable amount.

The main varieties can be described as follows.

2. INEQUALITY

(a) Inequality is the unequal performance of notes notated equally.

(b) Contemporary instructions for performing inequality survive from before, during and after the baroque period, *and are of all nationalities.* They are consistent on the whole, but not in detail, especially in so far as they rely upon differences in time-signatures which we have already found the learned Kircher calling 'this utter muddle' in 1650 (see Ch. XVIII, Sect. 3, above); and of which Étiénne Loulié, himself a leading French authority on inequality, wrote (*Elements ou principes de musique*, Paris, 1696, p. 69) that 'the practice of them is not very certain, some use them in one way, some in another'.

(c) The following small but characteristic selection from the available evidence will be followed by a concise summary of the working rules, and by musical examples.

(148a) Loys Bourgeois, *Le droit chemin de musique*, Geneva, 1550, x:

'Sing [quarter notes] as if two by two, remaining longer on the first, than on the second.'

(148b) Fray Tomás de Santa Maria, *Arte de tañer fantasia*, Valladolid, 1565, '7th condition':

'The method to be observed in playing quarter notes is to linger on the first, to hurry on the second, to linger again on the third, and to hurry on the fourth [etc., as if notated with dotted quarter notes and eighth notes, though] care must be taken that the hurried quarter notes should not be too hurried, but only slightly so . . .

'[With eighth notes either] linger on the first eighth notes and hurry on the second [etc., or] hurry on the first eighth note, linger on the second [etc.] . . .'

255

(148c) Girolamo Frescobaldi, *Toccate*, Rome, 1615–16, preface, 7:

'[Make the second of each pair of] sixteenth notes somewhat dotted . . .' [N.B. the flexibility implied by 'somewhat dotted'.]

(148d) Giovanni Domenico Puliaschi, *Musiche varie a una voce*, Rome, 1618, 'L'autore a i lettori', last page:

'[Perform] now by dotting the first note, now the second, as the passage requires.'

(148e) Anonymous English MS c. 1660–70, 'Miss Mary Burwell's Instruction Book for the Lute', ed. Thurston Dart, *Galpin Society Journal*, XI, 1958, pp. 3–62, see pp. 46–7:

'The humour and fine air of a lesson . . . by stealing half a note from one note and bestowing it upon the next note.'

(148f) Bénigne de Bacilly, *Remarques curieuses sur l'art de bien chanter*, Paris, 1668, p. 232:

'Of two notes one is commonly dotted [but] it has been thought best not to notate them for fear of their being performed by jerks.'

(148g) Roger North, unsorted notes, c. 1690, etc., selections ed. John Wilson, *Roger North on Music*, London, 1959, p. 223:

'In short notes [the dot] gives a life and spirit to the stroke, and a good hand will often for that end use it, tho' not expres't [in the notation].'

(148h) Alessandro Scarlatti, *Pirro e Demetrio*, perf. Naples, 1694, Act. II, Sc. 15, under equally notated eighth notes in largo, apparently in order to prevent an inequality which might otherwise have been expected to be introduced in performance:

'One plays in equal time.'

(149) Georg Muffat, *Florilegium* I, Augsburg, 1695, preface:

'Several eighth notes continued in succession [in ¢ time] cannot be alternately dotted [as they can in C time] for elegance in performance.'

(150) Étienne Loulié, *Elements ou principes de musique*, Paris, 1696, Amsterdam ed. of 1698, p. 38:

'In each measure but especially triple measure, the half-beats are performed in two different ways, although they are notated in the same way.

'1. They are sometimes made equally [e.g.] in melodies of which the sounds move by leap, *and in all kinds of foreign music where you never dot them except where marked.*

'2. Sometimes the first half-beats are made a little long [e.g.] in melodies of which the sounds move stepwise . . .

'[Or] the first half-beat is made much longer than the second, but the first half-beat ought [in that case to be notated dotted].'

John Byrt (private communication, and see his letter to the *Journal of the American Musicological Society*, XX, 3, Fall, 1967) has pointed out that only inequality of eighth notes may be meant in the statement italicized by Loulié at (150) above, and also by Couperin at (153) below, as it is explicitly by Corrette at (155). That would still not make Loulié's statement, or Couperin's, true of baroque music as a whole: see especially (148h), (149) and (154) above and below. But, for example, the sort of Italian bass-part, striding along in equal eighth notes, of which Corelli and others were so fond, most certainly ought not to be made unequal; and in this connection the following is interesting.

(151) Sébastien de Brossard, *Dictionaire de musique*, Paris, 1703, entry on the Italian term 'Andante':

'Andante . . . means above all for Basso-Continuos, that all the notes must be made equal, and the sounds well separated.'

(152) Michel de Montéclair, *Nouvelle méthode pour apprendre la musique*, Paris, 1709, p. 15:

'It is very hard to give general principles as to the equality or inequality of notes, because it is the style of the pieces to be sung which decides it [but broadly] the notes of which four go to the beat are intended to be uneven, the first a little longer than the second.'

(153) François Couperin, *L'Art de toucher le clavecin*, Paris, 1716, ed. of 1717, p. 38:

'We write otherwise than we perform . . . the Italians on the contrary write their music in the true values which they have conceived for it. For example, we dot several eighth notes [continuing] in succession by step: and yet we notate them equal.'

The second sentence at (153) above, concerning Italian notation, is contradicted by the weight of international evidence (some of it quoted above and below in this section); and it appears to be either thoughtlessly exaggerated or incompletely expressed. See comment under (150) above.

(154) Pier Francesco Tosi, *Opinioni de' cantori antichi, e moderni*, Bologna, 1723, p. 114 (my transl., but see also the English transl. and annotations by J. E. Galliard, as *Observations on the Florid Song*, London, 1742, pp. 178-9, with a music example added; and the German transl. and annotations by J. F. Agricola, as *Anleitung zur Singekunst*, Berlin, 1757, p. 234):

'When over the equal movement of a Bass, which proceeds slowly from eighth note to eighth note, a Singer [proceeds] almost always by step with inequality of motion . . .' [Itself an Italian comment on (150), (151), and (153) above.]

(155) Michel Corrette, *Methode pour . . . la flute traversiere*, Paris and Lyons, [c. 1740], p. 4:

'The four-time C or ₵ is much used in Italian music . . . It is necessary to dot the sixteenth notes two by two.

'[Of French 2 time] the Italians never use it. The eighth notes must be made unequal two by two, that is to say make the first long and the second short . . .

'The $\frac{2}{4}$ or $\frac{2}{8}$ is the 2-time of the Italians . . . the eighth notes must be performed equal, and the sixteenth notes made unequal . . .

'The $\frac{12}{8}$ is found in Italian, German, French and English music . . . the eighth notes must be performed equal and the sixteenth notes made unequal . . .'

[*Methode . . . pour . . . le violoncelle*, Paris, 1741, pp. 4ff.]: 'The eighth notes are performed equally in Italian music as for instance in the Courante of Corelli's Sonata Op. 5 No. 7. But in French music the second eighth note in each beat is performed more quickly.' [Notice the attention given to Italian inequality: see comment under (150) above.]

(156) Joachim Quantz, *Essay*, Berlin, 1752, XI, 12 (my transl. based both on the German and on the French texts, same place and date, equally authorized by Quantz, and slightly though not substantially different here):

'It is necessary in pieces of a moderate speed and even in Adagio for the quickest notes to be played with a certain inequality, even though they appear at sight to be of the same value; so that at each figure the accented notes, namely the first, third, fifth and seventh, must be pressed upon more than those which pass, namely the second, fourth, sixth and eighth, though they must not be sustained so long as if they were dotted . . .

'This no longer occurs, however, so soon as these notes are found mixed with figures of notes yet quicker or half as short in the same time; for then these latter must be played [with] the first and the third of the four notes a little pressed upon, and their tone made a little louder than that of the second and fourth notes.

'But we except from this rule in the first place quick passages, in a very quick movement, where the time does not permit of playing them unequally, and where we can thus only use length and strength on the first of the four . . . [there are also unslurred staccato passages, where] inequality has no place . . . [nor has inequality any place with] notes on which there are dashes or dots . . . [nor with] several notes at the same pitch, or when there is a slur over more notes than two . . . [nor with] eighth notes in Gigues. All these notes ought to be rendered equally, the one no longer than the other.' [Particular attention is recommended to these limitations on inequality.]

[XVII, ii, 16:] 'If in a slow allabreve or in normal common time there is a sixteenth-note rest on the accented beat followed by dotted notes, you must take the rest as if it had a dot attached to it, or [another] rest of half its value, and as if the note after it [though notated as a sixteenth note] were a thirty-second note.'

(157) François Bédos de Celles, *L'art du facteur d'orgues*, [Paris], 1766–78 p. 600:

'In lively melodies [inequality] should be more marked than in melodies which are gracious and of a tender expression.'

(158) Marie-Dominique-Joseph Engramelle, *La Tonotechnie*, Paris, 1775, p. 230:

'Inequalities . . . in many places vary in the same piece . . . it is left to fine taste . . . a little more or less inequality substantially changes the expression of a piece.' [This variability helps with many problems.]

3. VARIETIES OF INEQUALITY

(a) Inequality, of all varieties described as such by baroque writers, is essentially a way of emphasizing the pairing of notes already disposed to be taken by pairs: 'two by two' (148a, 155).

(b) Inequality can be performed in a considerable variety of rhythms, as:

(i) triplet rhythm or smoother, which we may call *lilting* inequality;

(ii) dotted rhythm or sharper, which we may call *vigorous* inequality.

(See 148a, 148b, 148f, 148g, 149, 150, 152, 156, 157, 158.)

(c) Inequality can be performed in a choice of two directions, as:

(i) most commonly, by lengthening the first note and shortening the second, which we may call *standard* inequality;

(ii) most strikingly, by shortening the first note and lengthening the second, which we may call *reversed* inequality.

(See 148a, 148b, 148c, 148d, 150, 152, 155, 156.)

4. CONDITIONS FOR INEQUALITY

(a) For *lilting* inequality, notes should:

(i) fall naturally into pairs;

(ii) be mainly stepwise;

(iii) be the shortest occurring in substantial numbers within the passage;

(iv) be neither very fast nor very slow;

259

(v) be not longer than one pair to a beat;

(vi) be of graceful rather than energetic character;

(vii) form melodic figures rather than integral turns of melody.

(b) For *vigorous* inequality, notes should:

(i) fall naturally into pairs;

(ii) be neither very fast nor very slow;

(iii) be not longer than one pair to a beat;

(iv) be of energetic rather than graceful character;

(v) form melodic or rhythmic figures rather than integral turns of melody.

(c) Slurs notated over pairs of notes are an encouragement to inequality. Slurs notated over more notes than two prevent pairing, and therefore preclude inequality. Staccato signs (dashes, wedges, dots) or instructions (détachez, notes martelées, mouvement décidé or marqué) discourage pairing, and preclude inequality. (See 148a, 151, 156.)

Lilting inequality, even if not slurred in the notation, should be slurred by pairs in performance. It is a way of giving a sighing effect, requiring some stress on the first note; some dying away on the second note; and some separation after each pair of notes. (See 148f, 156, above, and Ex. 113 below.)

Vigorous inequality need not be slurred either in the notation or in the performance. It is a way of getting dotted rhythms from equal notation. It requires no special stress on the first note nor dying away on the second note. If taken crisply, standard inequality requires a marked separation between each note of a pair, but none between each pair; reversed inequality requires a marked separation between each pair, but none between each note of a pair. (See Ex. 113 below.)

(d) The sighing effect of lilting inequality comes more naturally in steps than in leaps.

Predominantly stepwise passages are often eligible for lilting inequality. A few leaps can either be taken into the prevailing inequality as they come along, or allowed to stand equally in the midst of it.

Predominantly leapwise passages are never eligible for lilting inequality: leaps are for energy, lilting is for grace. But changing from inequality to equality, or the other way about, within the same piece where different passages suggest it, is perfectly possible, so long as too restless an alternation is not produced. (See 152, 154, 158.)

Predominantly leapwise passages are sometimes eligible for vigorous inequality, so long as too jerky an effect is not produced: but this jerkiness easily happens, and can be most unmusical. (See 148f, 149, 151, 156.)

When inequality is used in sequential passages, and in imitations, it is almost invariably desirable to maintain it throughout the matching phrases or entries, and more or less (though not rigorously) in the same rhythm.

(e) Inequality cannot occur between beats, but only within beats (see 150). This sets a lower limit to the speed of notes eligible for inequality.

But only the shortest (i.e. the fastest) notes occurring within the passage are eligible for inequality (see 156); and while for this purpose a small number of very short and fast notes can be ignored (and the next shortest notes taken unequally), a substantial number cannot be thus ignored. If they are too short and fast to be taken unequally themselves, their presence precludes inequality.

If, however, the shortest notes are few in number, yet not too short and fast to be taken unequally themselves, then instead of being ignored, they may occasionally be taken unequally as well as the next shortest notes.

(f) In any case, lilting inequality sounds graceful only at a moderate speed: if too slow, it sounds sluggish; if too fast, it sounds jerky.

Vigorous inequality can sound exhilarating at rather higher speeds, but not at much higher speeds, which make it too agitated for ordinary purposes. And if, for special purposes, this was wanted, the rhythm would probably be already notated unequally by dotting; as also if it were wanted at unusually slow speeds. (See 156.)

These facts set an upper limit to the speed of notes eligible for inequality, as well as confirming the lower limit.

Thus only notes of moderate speed are eligible for inequality.

(g) Lilting inequality is more for grace, and vigorous inequality is more for energy. An intermediate disposition is also possible. (See 148f, 148g, 149, 150, 152, 157, 158.)

But an extreme vigour, such as we shall meet under the problem of dotting in Sect. 6ff. below, is not compatible with inequality. This limitation excludes from inequality many martial and assertive allegros. Nor is inequality compatible with movements which are essentially solid and four-square.

Michel de Saint-Lambert (*Principes du clavecin*, Paris, 1702, p. 25) put it that certain notes are made unequal 'because the inequality gives them more grace', adding that 'taste judges of this as it does of tempo'.

Only movements of a somewhat flowing character are compatible with lilting inequality. Vigorous inequality, which can occur in energetic movements, is not what we most readily think of as inequality, having in effect (though not in cause) more to do with the problem of dotting.

(h) Inequality is a convention; and conventions only apply to relatively conventional situations.

We have to learn from experience how to distinguish an integral turn of the melody, often without any conventional implications, from a corner or a sequence which more or less reflects a stereotype, and which may therefore more or less imply a stereotyped convention.

Only notes forming melodic figures, rather than integral turns of melody, may be conventional invitations to inequality.

(i) Some passages which, otherwise, we might or might not have regarded as good places for inequality, may have it indicated by the instructions: inégales (unequal), notes inégales, etc.; also lourer (tie), couler (slur); pointer (dot), etc.

Other passages which we might or might not have regarded as good places for inequality may have it contra-indicated by the instructions: égales (equal), notes égales, etc.; or coups égaux (equal strokes), etc. See also under (c) above; and (148h), of which the Italian original reads: *si suona a tempo eguale* (one plays in equal time).

(j) Rhythms corresponding to inequality (standard or reverse, lilting or vigorous) may also be (approximately) notated by dotting.

When, however, dotted notes are notated in among other, equally notated notes, and these latter are given unnotated inequality in performance, then the notated dotted rhythms must necessarily be over-dotted for greater contrast. See Sect. 6 below.

(k) By analogy with standard inequality (both lilting and vigorous), we find:

(i) a pair consisting of an equally notated rest and note, unequalized in performance;

(ii) an initial up-beat, given the same delay and shortening as if it were the second note of a pair equally notated, but unequalized in performance.

(l) Statement (i) above may be expanded as follows.

When an equally notated rest and note either begin, or interrupt, a phrase or passage either notated unequally by dotting, or unequalized in performance, then this rest and note will already take part in the inequality: i.e. the rest will be lengthened, and the note will be delayed and shortened, in the same rhythm (whether lilting or vigorous) as the phrase or passage.

It is particularly common to see a phrase or a passage notated unequally by dotting everywhere except on pairs consisting of a rest and note. The intention is to pick up the dotted rhythm right from the opening pair, although it is not so notated; and to continue it through any other pairs consisting of a rest and a note, although they are not so notated.

We seem to observe a certain reluctance to dot rests, even in passages where notes are freely dotted. This inconsistency, however, is only in the notation, and not in the intention.

(See 156 above, end of quotation; and Ex. 111 (i) and 111 (ii) below.)

262

(m) Statement (ii) above may be expanded as follows.

Before sections, or repeats, of movements in dance forms, it is particularly common to see an initial up-beat note, the notated duration of which is longer than is intended in performance.

Usually it is best to perform this up-beat note as an *unmeasured* note of anticipation: i.e. late, short and light. (See Ex. 112 (i), (a)–(c), below.)

Sometimes it may be best to take this up-beat note as a *measured* note of anticipation: i.e. in the rhythm (whether lilting or vigorous) of the movement itself. (See Ex. 112 (ii) below.)

5. EXAMPLES OF INEQUALITY

(a) In most of the following examples, some inconsistency of *notation* between unison passages, between matching passages, or between the same passages notated differently in different sources, suggests a more or less consistent *expectation* of inequality.

It will again be noticed that all baroque periods and nationalities are well represented.

Ex. 100. Giulio Caccini, *Nuove Musiche*, Florence, 1602, preface, brief passages inviting inequality, with Caccini's recommendations for (a) standard, (b) reversed, (c) free rhythm:

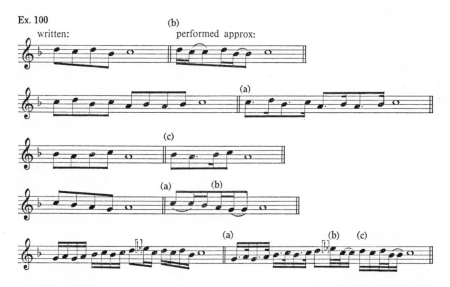

Ex. 101. Giovanni Battista Vulpio, cantata 'Dolce zampogna mia', mid-17th cent., Rome, Biblioteca Nazionale Centrale Vittorio Emanuale II, MS Musicale 162, ff. 109v–110r., many typical inconsistencies in the notation of the rhythm of matching passages requiring

consistency in performance (in the instance following, the fragment
of realization is original):

Ex. 101

Ex. 102. 'M.ʳ Hardel', harpsichord piece, later 17th cent., Paris,
Bibl. Nat., Rés. Vm⁷. 674, f. 38, 2nd pagn.), matching eighth notes
with inequality consistently notated in the right, inconsistently in the
left hand, but requiring similarly consistent inequality throughout:

Ex. 102

Ex. 103. Anonymous author of 'Miss Mary Burwell's Instruction
Book for the Lute', c. 1660–1670, ed. Thurston Dart, *Galpin Society
Journal*, XI, 1958, pp. 3–62, see pp. 46–7, 'demonstration for the
humouring of a lesson', (a) as notated, (b) as instructed to be performed (compare the lilting inequality in Purcell at Ex. 51 above):

Ex. 103

Ex. 104. Roger North, selected notes (c. 1690) ed. John Wilson,
Roger North on Music, London, 1959, p. 223, equal (plain), dotted
(vigorous) and triplet (lilting) rhythms as performer's options for
equally notated quarter notes (he writes 'it comes to the same account'
in the following):

Ex. 104

Ex. 105. Marin Marais, *Alcione*, perf. Paris, 1706, vigorous inequality, (a) printed short score, Paris [1706], p. 187, equal notation

('violons' and 'B.C.' shown here); (b) MS full score for revival of 1741, Paris, Bibl. Nat., Rés. Vm.[2] 205, p. 219, same passage notated dotted (as previously performed although not so notated); (c) the famous 'tempeste', Act IV, sc. iii, bass part as printed in 1706 (similar in 1741); (d) as printed for the revival of 1711; but (e) as altered in ink by (?) a contemporary conductor in the copy in the library of the Paris Opéra, A. 16, c; (f) the same copy, p. 42; as printed; (g) as altered in red crayon (many other similar cases can be found):

Ex. 105

Ex. 106. Alessandro Scarlatti, cantata, 'Alme, voi che provaste', lilting inequality, inconsistently notated, but consistently intended, (a) in Ann Arbor, Univ. of Michigan, Stellfeld MS 1283 (c. 1720), ff. 47–54r; (b) in Naples, Bibl. del Cons. di Mus. 'S. Pietro a Maiella', MS 34.5.4 (dated 1739), ff. 32r–37v; (c) in Florence, Baron Kraus Coll. (unnumbered, unfoliated, undated but rather late in the opinion of Edwin Hanley, who very kindly provided these examples) (see p. 266).

Ex. 107. Domenico Scarlatti (1685–1757), sonata in D major (K.490, L.206) has a dotted figure in m.3, frequently recurring, in m.10 and in m.12 notated equal but presumably to be performed dotted; similarly in the paired sonata in D major (K.491, L.164),

THE EXPRESSION

266

shown here (a) at m. 38, notated equal, (b) at m. 81, notated dotted,
both presumably meant consistently for vigorous inequality.

Ex. 107

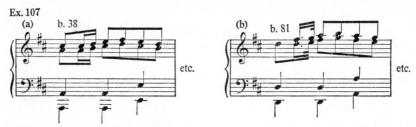

Ex. 108. George Frideric Handel, cantata 'Dolce pur d'amor
l'affanno', early 18th cent., facsimiles of autograph copies in different
keys, Cambridge, Fitzwilliam Museum, MS 30-H-2, reproduced by
kind permission of the Syndics of the Fitzwilliam Museum, (a) p. 11,
with lilting inequality notated quite inconsistently in both voice and
bass parts; (b) p. 9, with lilting inequality almost (but not quite)
consistently notated throughout (notice similar fragments of written-
out ornamentation in both copies, confirming that the performing
expectations were the same, and that the inconsistency of rhythm is
only notational and not intentional; also notice that the *eighth notes
are equal* and intended so; compare also Ex. 59 in Ch. XV, 3 above):

Ex. 108
(a)

(b)

Ex. 109. Jean-Philippe Rameau, (a) *Pièces de clavecin*, Paris, 1741, Musette in E major, eighth notes notated equally, but presenting a typical situation for lilting inequality, and confirmed as such by (b), unequally notated version of the same piece as the orchestral Entrée III, Scene 7 of *Les Fêtes d'Hébé*, perf. Paris, 1739 (also noteworthy are the written out upper-note preparation for the half-trill in the first full measure, and the treatment of the similarly notated ornament in m. 2 as a complete trill, a turned ending being therefore implied, and a sufficiently long upper note start being hinted in the notated appoggiatura; the appoggiaturas notated in m. 4 are on the beat, but are best taken short, and thus indistinguishable in effect from reversed inequality); and see Ex. 59 in Ch. XV, 3 above for continuation:

Ex. 109

Very similar inconsistencies of notation (though not of intention) in the dotting can be seen in Agostino Steffani's German-produced Italian

268

opera, *Tassilone* (perf. Düsseldorf, 1709), Act III, Sc. 6; Berlin score in DTB, XIII, 2, p. 159, Madrid score, DrM, VIII, p. 135); a wide search would probably turn them up everywhere in quantity.

Ex 110. J. S. Bach, 'Trauer-Ode, I' (1727; N.B.A., I, 38, pp. 186–187), mm. 17 ff., soprano solo notated equally, but shown to be intended in lilting inequality by the unison part for oboe d'amore notated unequally (notice that lilting inequality, rather than vigorous inequality, is suggested solely by the character of the music, since the dotted notation could serve as well for either):

(b) The extension of inequality to pairs consisting of an equally notated rest and note is of great practical importance. It is shown at Ex. 111 (i) and Ex. 111 (ii) (a)–(b) below.

The extension of inequality to what would be pairs of an equally notated rest and note, except that the rest is not usually notated at all (occasionally it is), though not of great practical importance, is a very agreeable and desirable refinement. It is shown at Ex. 112 (i) and Ex. 112 (ii) below.

Ex. 111 (i). Giacomo Carissimi, cantata, 'Nella più verde età dell' anno' (mid-17th cent.), Florence, Bibl. del Conservatorio di Musica 'Luigi Cherubini', MS 3808, ff. 71–74v (same rhythm notated also in Bologna, Civico Museo Bibliografico Musicale, MS X235, No. 2; and in Oxford, Christ Church Lib., Music MS 51, pp. 116–28), dotted rhythm established in voice part, and meant to be picked up, although not so notated, at the entry of the ritornello imitating it:

Ex. 111 (ii) (a) Jean-Baptiste Lully, *Amadis*, Paris, 1684, orchestral parts in Paris, Library of Opéra, Fonds La Salle, 37, ouverture, fugal section, m. 3, (a) entry as shown in both surviving copies of B.C.; (b) as shown in bassoon part, notated differently but requiring to be performed the same:

Ex. 111 (ii)

Ex. 112 (i). Henry Purcell, Fourth Suite for Harpsichord (late 17th cent.), Corant, three versions collated by Howard Ferguson, *Eight Suites* [by] *Henry Purcell*, London, 1964, and reproduced here by kind permission, (a) Paris, Bibl. Nat. MS Rés. 1186 bis, I; (b) Oxford, Christ Church Lib., MS 1177; (c) first ed. of 1696, showing initial note shortened approximately as would be normal in performance, though more usually shown as in (a) and (b); also showing, like (a), further inequality such as would be normal in performance, though more usually shown as at (b):

Ex. 112 (i)

Ex. 112 (ii). J. S. Bach, Partita I, Courante, initial up-beat note taken into the performed (unequal) rhythm of the movement itself, (a) as notated, (b) as it may be played:

Ex. 112 (ii)

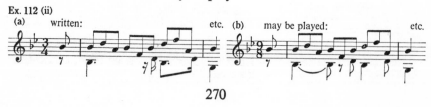

Ex. 113. *Approximate* rhythms and separations appropriate; (a) for standard lilting inequality; (b) for reversed lilting inequality; (c) for standard vigorous inequality; (d) for reversed vigorous inequality:

Ex. 113

6. DOTTING

(a) The dot (of augmentation) in baroque music lengthens the note after which it is placed by a variable amount.

(b) The variable duration of the baroque dot is, in its *general* aspect, implied by the rhythmic freedom exercised by baroque performers at all dates and places.

In its more *specific* aspects, the variable duration of the baroque dot is touched upon in the following brief but typical selection from contemporary descriptions.

(159) Michel L'Affilard, *Principes très-faciles pour bien apprendre la musique*, Paris, 1694, ed. of 1705, p. 30 (similar sentence in first ed.):

'To perform the dots in their [implied] value, it is necessary to hold on to the dotted quarter note, and pass quickly over the following eighth note.' [Compare 148c, 148f, 150 above.]

(160) Étienne Loulié, *Elements ou principes de musique*, Paris, 1696, p. 16:

'When the dot is within the same beat as the eighth note which precedes it, we must hold on in singing this eighth note a little longer [than it is notated], and pass quickly over the sixteenth note which follows it.'

(161) Jacques Martin Hotteterre, *Principes de la flute traversiere . . .*, Paris, 1707, p. 35:

'We sometimes put dots after the notes, which augments them by half of their value [but] in movements where the eighth notes are [performed as] unequal, the dot which is after the *quarter note* acts as an equivalent to the dotted eighth note [i.e. the dot becomes equivalent to a double dot]; in such manner that the eighth note which follows a dotted *quarter note* is always short [i.e. approximately a sixteenth note].'

(162) Johann Mattheson, *Kern melodischer Wissenschaft*, Hamburg, 1737, p. 47:

[For Entries and certain dances] 'the very dotted manner'.

(163) Joachim Quantz, *Essay*, Berlin, 1752, V, 21:

'With dotted eighth notes, sixteenth notes and thirty-second notes, the standard rule is altered, for the sake of the liveliness these notes must express ... whether in slow or quick tempo ... it is not possible to determine exactly the time of the short notes after the dot.' [But see Ex. 120 below.]

(164) C. P. E. Bach, *Essay*, Berlin, 1753, III, 23:

'The short notes following dotted notes are always performed shorter than their notation requires. [But compare:]

[II, 1762, XXIX, 15:] 'Since a proper accuracy is often lacking in the notation of dotted notes, a general rule of performance has become established which nevertheless shows many exceptions. According to this rule, the notes following the dot are to be performed with the greatest rapidity, and this is frequently the case. But sometimes notes in the remaining parts [determine the dotted lengths, or] a feeling of smoothness impells the performer to shorten the dotted note slightly.'

(165) Leopold Mozart, *Violinschule*, Augsburg, 1756, I, iii, 9:

'In slow pieces ... the dot has to be joined to its note with a diminuendo [and slurred to the short note following].

[10:] 'In fast pieces ... each note is detached from the other [of the pair].'

7. VARIETIES OF DOTTING

(a) The baroque dot may lengthen its note:

(i) by half as much again, which we may call *standard dotting*;

(ii) by less than half as much again, which we may call *under-dotting*;

(iii) by more than half as much again, which we may call *over-dotting*.

(See 159 to 164 above.)

(b) *Standard dotting* corresponds to our modern convention: it occurs very frequently in baroque music.

But this is not now, and never has been, as mathematical a convention in practice as in theory. It was and is the same as we can hear it on historical recordings going back to the late nineteenth century: an approximation subject to varying amounts of fluctuation for expressive reasons. Dots are often smoothed down a little for slow movements, and usually sharpened up a little, or more than a little, for quick movements: especially those of an energetic (and perhaps march-like) character.

(c) *Under-dotting* may:

(i) reduce (for expression) a passage, notated unequally by dotting, to the softened rhythms of lilting inequality (see Sect. 3 (b) above);

(ii) reduce (for synchronization) a passage, notated unequally by dotting, to fit with notated triplets (see Sect. 10 below);

(iii) reduce (for convenience) the notated duration of a dotted note, to allow more or slower notes after it than the beat could otherwise contain (see Ex. 117a below).

(d) Conversely, *over-dotting* may:

(i) point up (for expression) a passage, notated unequally by dotting, to the sharpest rhythms of vigorous inequality, or beyond (see Sect. 3 (b) above, also 159 to 164 above, and Sect. 8 below);

(ii) point up (for synchronization) a passage, notated unequally by dotting, to fit with the shortest notes after dotted notes of a lesser duration (see 164 above, also Ex. 115 and Sect. 8 below);

(iii) point up (for convenience) the notated duration of a dotted note, to allow fewer or quicker notes after it than the beat would otherwise require (see 164 above, Ex. 116, Ex. 117 (b) and Ex. 122 (b) below).

8. CONDITIONS FOR VARIABLE DOTTING

(a) For *under-dotting*, dotted notes should

(i) be moderately fast;

(ii) be not longer than one pair to a beat;

(iii) come in a passage of graceful rather than energetic character;

(iv) form melodic figures rather than integral turns of melody.

(b) For *over-dotting*, dotted notes should

(i) be moderately slow or moderately fast;

(ii) be not longer than one pair to two rather slow beats;

(iii) come in a passage of energetic rather than graceful character;

(iv) form melodic or rhythmic figures rather than integral turns of melody.

(c) Under-dotting for expression (i.e. when dotted notes are softened down) is musically identical with lilting inequality (i.e. when equal notes are sharpened up); and it requires the same kind of slurring and phrasing.

Much the most common is the standard direction, the first note of each pair being dotted. But the reverse direction, the second note of each pair being dotted, can also be performed in this softened-down rhythm, musically identical with reversed lilting inequality. The effect, however, is almost lethargic; and good opportunities for it are quite rare.

On the other hand, many good opportunities occur for under-dotting in the standard direction. When a long series of dotted notes is notated in a graceful piece moderate in speed, especially a vocal piece, over-dotting would be quite out of character, and even the standard dotted rhythm may be rather too energetic: it is therefore nearly always better to soften down the rhythm by expressive under-dotting.

273

The effect of this (like the effect of performing equal notes with lilting inequality) will be approximately a triplet rhythm. The long dotted passages in moderately fast triple time of which Purcell, for example, was so particularly fond, will flow with far more natural charm and expressiveness if performed under-dotted to about this extent (see Ex. 51 above).

(d) On the other hand, even moderately slow dotted notes will probably sound too dragging if performed under-dotted; and in any case, as with inequality, the beat is the limit (see Sect. 4(e) above, also 150 and 160 above). Only dotted notes which fall within one beat come under the conventions of under-dotting.

The beat sets the lower limit of speed. The upper limit is set by the feeble effect of under-dotting fast dotted notes of which the essential character is vigorous, and therefore disposed rather to over-dotting than under-dotting.

(e) Over-dotting for expression is, at the least, equivalent to very vigorous inequality; and at the most, is sharpened to a more pointed rhythm than can reasonably be achieved by the mere unequal performance of notes notated equally.

Both the standard direction (dotted note first) and the reversed direction (dotted note second) are equally eligible for over-dotting; though the standard direction is by far the most commonly encountered.

Slurring is possible, but not necessary, and as a whole not desirable (the most frequent exceptions are perhaps in reversed dotting; and necessarily for the voice whenever the notes are sung to one syllable).

On the contrary: the lengthened part of the dot (or even the whole of the dot) can usually best be performed as a rest (i.e. a silence of articulation).

(f) There is no necessity to restrict over-dotting to dotted rhythms falling within a single beat. But there is not much likelihood of more than two beats, in a moderately slow tempo, being involved.

The lower limit of speed is set by the slowest duration which can be sensed as a melodic or rhythmic figure, rather than as some integral turn of the melody (see Sect. 4(h) above).

The upper limit of speed is set by the agitated effect (or even the practical impossibility) of over-dotting very fast dotted notes, which already have, from their rapidity as notated, all the vigour they require.

Long dotted passages in moderate tempo, if vigorous rather than graceful in character, usually gain very greatly in effectiveness from being slightly (or if tempo and suitability permit, considerably) overdotted.

(g) Like other such conventions, variable dotting for expression is *specifically* indicated (by its suitability) only on melodic or rhythmic figures of more or less conventional character.

It may also occur on dotted notes which are not melodic or rhythmic figures, but integral turns of melody, shaped individually rather than conventionally (see Sect. 4(h) above). These and similar nuances, however, are to be decided purely on the merits of the phrase itself, as part of the *general* freedom of the baroque performer.

9. EXAMPLES OF VARIABLE DOTTING

Ex. 114. George Frideric Handel, Passacaille from harpsichord suite in G minor, (a) opening best performed more-or-less in notated rhythm; (b) continuation as it may be notated in a modern edition so as to suggest over-dotting to the performer without imposing it upon him, and without concealing the original; (c) as it may thus be performed:

Ex. 115. Joachim Quantz, *Essay*, Berlin, 1752, Tab. II, Fig. 7, f, g, over-dotting for synchronization:

Ex. 116. François Couperin; (a) L'Apothéose de Corelli, movt. 6 and (b) XIV Concert, prelude, m. 1, over-dotting for convenience (and at (a) one beam too many to emphasize the great, though unmeasured, velocity):

Ex. 117. Other variable dottings for convenience; (a) under-dotting; (b) over-dotting:

10. TRIPLETS

(a) In baroque music (other than certain rather late baroque music in the galant style) triplet rhythms against duplet or quadruplet rhythms were as a whole not favoured.

(166) Giannantonio Banner, *Compendio musico*, II, Padua, 1745, p. 111:

'Observe in composing, never to put three Notes against two, this being one of the most prohibited musical situations.'

(b) It was most common to avoid two against three by assimilating duple to triple rhythm.

(167) C. P. E. Bach, *Essay*, Berlin, 1753, III, 27:

'Now that triplets have come increasingly into use in common or $\frac{4}{4}$ time, as well as in $\frac{2}{4}$ and $\frac{3}{4}$, many pieces have made their appearance which could with greater convenience be notated in $\frac{12}{8}$, $\frac{9}{8}$ or $\frac{6}{8}$.'

Ex. 118. C. P. E. Bach, *loc. cit.*, correct performance shown, by the vertical alignment, (a) of notes notated unequally by dotting, and (b) of notes notated equally; but in performance, (a) compressed by under-dotting, and (b) expanded by inequality, to fit the rhythm of the notated triplets:

Quantz (*Essay*, Berlin, 1752, V, 22) preferred, in situations as at Ex. 118(a) above, not to under-dot, but to over-dot, thereby bringing the little note not with, but decidedly after, the last note of the triplet. Either

C. P. E. Bach's recommendation or Quantz' recommendation is in most situations correct; the choice should therefore be made, by the performer, on his own judgement of which best suits the particular passage in question. (Merely standard dotted rhythm will sound feeble in such a situation, and is not to be recommended.)

Ex. 119. Arcangelo Corelli, Op. V, No. 3, Rome, 1700, Allegro, simultaneous time-signatures, (a) correctly used as a legacy of proportional notation; (b) degenerating into incorrect but convenient notation which would (see 167 above) be better and more correctly notated as at (c):

Ex. 120. George Frideric Handel, Recorder Sonata No. 4 in A minor, Larghetto, (a) as originally notated with typical baroque casualness; (b) as intended to be performed with over-dotting for assimilation to triplet rhythm (treble, m. 1) and for expression (treble, m. 6); with under-dotting for assimilation to triplet rhythm (bass, m. 1 and m. 5); and with inequality for assimilation to triplet rhythm (bass, m. 6); the whole being (see 167 above) better notated (and here shown) in $\frac{9}{8}$ time:

(c) It was also possible (see Michael Collins, 'The Performance of Triplets in the 17th and 18th Centuries', *Journal of the American Musicological Society*, XIX, 3, Fall, 1966, pp. 281–328, in a brilliant though probably over-stated argument) to avoid two against three by assimilating triple to duple rhythm.

This can be done by replacing e.g., a triplet of three eighth notes by a duplet: (i) of one eighth note and two sixteenth notes; or (ii) of two sixteenth notes and one eighth note.

But I do not now believe, as I at first did (see my *Interpretation of Early Music*, London, 1963, 2nd ed., 1965, p. 403), that this is a good solution for the 'Tempo di Gavotta' in J. S. Bach's E Minor Partita for harpsichord. Much more probably, the notated groups of two sixteenth notes and one eighth note are intended to represent a written-out slide, unmeasured and quick; the groups of four sixteenth notes are intended as unmeasured runs; and the rhythm throughout is that of the notated triplets, performed as written.

The assimilation of triplet to duple rhythm was almost certainly very much less common than the assimilation of duplet to triplet rhythm.

(d) In galant music, two against three, and three against four, became fashionable, the intention being as notated.

Ex. 121. Georg Philipp Telemann, Gamba Sonata in A minor, (a) second movement, notated rhythm of three against four between bass and solo; (b) last movement, notated rhythm of two against three: both intended to be performed as notated:

Ex. 121

11. FRENCH OVERTURE STYLE

(a) The French overture itself, as a musical form, came, ironically enough, from Italy, as did Lully, who did most to establish it by his own operas, whence it spread internationally. For Lully did not invent the form, with its familiar slow introduction, quick continuation in lightly fugal imitation, and optional slow conclusion. He modelled it, like most else in his operas, on the prevailing Italian opera of the mid-seventeenth century, examples of which by Cavalli and by Luigi Rossi were performed in Paris during his most impressionable years.

(b) The slow introduction to a French overture has a remarkable style of its own. The underlying pulse is majestic, even massive; the rapid figuration impose on it is, by contrast, vigorous in the extreme.

This combination of steady pulse with explosive energy depends upon altering (where necessary) the notated rhythms in performance, partly by over-dotting, and partly by other rhythmic sharpenings closely allied to over-dotting.

(c) The style of the French overture spread to or is shared by other movements of a similar character although not in overture form. The Entry is closest to the overture; but the influence of French overture style is felt much farther afield. There are even fugues in which the same vigour, imposed on the same steady pulse, requires the same over-dotting and general sharpening of the rhythm in performance: a good example is J. S. Bach's D major fugue from Book One of the Forty-Eight (see Ex. 123 below). For Entry, see (162) above.

(d) French overture style is a convenient modern term, but it is not historical and it is not exact.

English operas by Blow or Purcell, Italian operas by Agostino Steffani or Italianate operas by Handel, have overtures as French as Lully's; and perhaps all we are doing in talking about a French overture style is to focus our attention upon one particularly recognizable development of the general baroque principle of rhythmic sharpening.

Indeed, Quantz was content to refer to it, equally recognizably, just as 'the majestic style':

(168) Joachim Quantz, *Essay*, Berlin, 1752, XII, 24:

'The majestic (*prächtige*) style is as much introduced with long notes, among which the other parts make a quick motion, as [it is introduced] with dotted notes. The dotted notes must be pushed on sharply by the performer, and executed with vigour. The dot is held long, and the succeeding notes made very short.

[XVII, vii, 58]: 'in so far as three or more thirty-second notes follow a dot or a rest; such [notes], especially in slow pieces, are not always played according to their [notated] value, but at the very end of their allotted time, and at the greatest speed; as for example often happens in overtures, entries and furies. Nevertheless, each of these quick notes must be separately bowed; and few slurs occur.

[XVII, ii, 16]: 'When, after a long note and short rest, thirty-second notes follow . . . these last must always be played very quickly; this is so in adagio or allegro. Therefore one must wait till the very end of the time, with the quick notes, in order not to displace the balance of the measure.'

(169) C. P. E. Bach, *Essay*, Berlin, 1753, III, 23:

'Dots on long notes, likewise on short notes in slow time and also [occurring] singly are usually held on [as sound]. But when many come in succession, especially in quick tempo, they are often not held on [i.e. silences of articulation are inserted], notwithstanding that the notation requires it . . .

[Ed. of 1787:] 'On figures where four or more short notes follow the dot, these last [must] become sufficiently short on account of their numerousness.'

(170) J. A. P. Schultz, in J. G. Sulzer's *Allgemeine Theorie der Schönen Künste*, Leipzig, 1771 etc., entry 'Ouvertüre', quoted by Michael Collins, 'A Reconsideration of French Over-Dotting', *Music and Letters*, L, 1 Jan. 1969, pp. 111–23, see p. 120 (my transl.):

'In the previous century' [i.e. the 17th] 'one obtained the best overtures from France, where, as' [already] 'said, they first came into use. Next, they were also imitated elsewhere, particularly in Germany [among others by Handel and Telemann].

'In the first place [the overture] usually appears to be a piece of serious but fiery character in 4/4 time. The motion has something lofty, the paces are slow, but embellished with many small notes, [which must be] fierily executed . . .

'The principal notes are usually dotted, and in performance are held beyond their [notated] value. After these principal notes follow more or fewer smaller [notes], which must be played with the utmost rapidity and so far as possible, staccato, which indeed is not practicable when 10, 12 or more notes come in one quarter-note beat.'

Harold Watkins Shaw (*A Textual and Historical Companion to Handel's Messiah*, London, 1965) confirms the use of over-dotting in the (French) overture to *Messiah* by pointing out that the tradition persisted right through the nineteenth century in British performances. Giving as his reference W. G. Cusins, *Handel's Messiah*, London, 1874, pp. 21–3, Watkins Shaw writes: 'In 1874 (Sir) William Cusins asserted that the

Grave movement of the overture should be played as ♩ .. ♪, and added that Sterndale Bennett agreed with him.' Watkins Shaw further quotes William Crotch's organ arrangement (London, [pre-1819]) as actually printing such double-dotting in the overture and several other numbers. He also quotes Sir Charles Stanford (*Pages from an Unwritten Diary*, London, 1914, p. 43) as having heard during his boyhood, in Dublin, the overture double-dotted, and as having accepted this with approval as correct tradition. Which indeed it is.

12. FRENCH OVERTURE STYLE IN PRACTICE

(a) In an excellent article, Michael Collins ('A Reconsideration of French Over-Dotting', *Music and Letters*, L, 1 Jan. 1969, pp. 111–23), prints a number of musical examples from Lully onwards, which (i) illustrate situations implying rhythms to be thus sharpened in performance; (ii) show a tendency (no more) towards rather more accurate notation during the eighteenth century.

Since these rhythms are left to the performer to make as sharp as possible (see 168 and 170 above), we can never take the notation as more than approximately accurate. But Michael Collins prints a passage of this kind, for instance, occurring in Lully's *Amadis*, which in the original score (perf. and publ. Paris, 1684) shows sixteenth notes, but which as revised for subsequent revival (2nd ed., 1721, presumably as in the revival of 1718), shows thirty-second notes, the intention (and I agree with Collins) being the same (for another view, see Frederick Neumann, 'The Dotted Note and the So-called French Style', *Early Music*, V, 3, July 1977; also reply to this by David Fuller, *Early Music*, V, 4, Oct. 1977). See (168), (169) and especially (170) above.

(b) Of the following examples from J. S. Bach, the first is a French overture; the second is a fugue showing the general characteristics of French overture style.

Ex. 122. J. S. Bach, *ouverture* for harpsichord, (a) as first notated in C minor, autograph manuscript, Berlin, Deutsche Staatsbibliothek, P226, pp. 43ff., short notes shown as sixteenth notes; (b) as transposed by the composer for publication (Clavierübung, II, 1735) in B minor, short notes shown as thirty-second notes, i.e. approximately as they are meant to be performed in both versions alike:

Ex. 122
(a)   etc.

Ex. 123. J. S. Bach, Fugue in D major (*Das wohltempierte Clavier*, I, 1722); (a) as notated, with rhythms written in the frequent manner of French overture style; (b) as these rhythms may be interpreted by sharpening them in performance:

Ex. 123

13. TEMPO RUBATO IN THE BAROQUE SENSE

(a) A melody and its bass, notated in similar rhythms, may sometimes be performed, for a shorter or longer passage, in dissimilar rhythms, by syncopating or otherwise modifying the melody, while not modifying the bass.

This convention, which does not disturb the underlying measure, was called by some baroque and post-baroque authorities *tempo rubato*. It is only somewhat remotely connected with that freely expressive stretching of the rhythm, more or less disturbing the underlying measure, which we now call rubato, and for which see Ch. XVIII, Sect. 6, above.

CHAPTER TWENTY

Punctuation

1. PHRASING

(a) Good musicians have generally an excellent *sense* of where one phrase ends and another begins.

But it is of the utmost importance in baroque music to make the separation between phrases plainly *audible* to the listener, either:

(i) by a very appreciable silence taken out of the note before; or

(ii) by a more conspicuous silence not taken out of the note before, but inserted as stolen time.

Of these alternatives, (i) gives less separation, but sufficient for many (though not for all) phrasing within a larger unit such as a section; (ii) gives more separation, and is nearly always required between larger units such as sections.

Both methods are not only compatible with a well maintained and well moulded line, but are actually necessary to its proper shaping. As always, line comes first; but punctuation (which includes phrasing) is itself an element in line.

(b) In addition to such actual separation of phrases, other factors can contribute to good phrasing, such as:

(i) a certain stretching of the tempo, not amounting to a ritardando or rallentando;

(ii) a certain placing of the next phrase, not quite punctually, but after a very slight delay which may be (but is not necessarily) a silence of separation;

(iii) a certain moulding of the dynamics, whereby the sound may rise slightly to the peak of the phrase, and fall slightly to its conclusion;

(iv) after thus giving away the conclusion of the last phrase, a certain added intensity or significance at the opening of the next phrase.

(c) The pause sign ⌢ has its modern significance, and may in addition imply an ornamental cadenza.

The comma sign ' is occasionally found in French music (introduced, so he said, by Couperin) for a silence of separation between phrases.

283

(But it is also a common French sign for a trill, or less commonly, an appoggiatura.)

(d) Ordinarily, phrasing is left to the performer without assistance from the notation.

(171) Girolamo Frescobaldi, *Toccate*, Rome, 1615–16, preface, 4:

'. . . a pause prevents confusion between one phrase and another.'

(172) Thomas Mace, *Musick's Monument*, London, 1676, p. 109:

'. . . a kind of *Cessation, or standing still*, sometimes *Longer*, and sometimes *Shorter*, according to the *Nature*, or *Requiring* . . . of the *Musick*.'

(173) François Couperin, *Troisième Livre de Pièces*, Paris, 1722, preface:

'[The] almost imperceptible . . . silences [intended by the phrasing comma] should make themselves felt without altering the time.' [Interesting, but see (175) below.]

(174) Joachim Quantz, *Essay*, Berlin, 1752, VII, 4:

'The end of what goes before, and the start of what follows, should be' [Fr. version] 'well separated and distinguished one from the other.

[XI, 10]: 'Thoughts which should belong together must not be divided; just as on the contrary, those where a musical sense ends, and a new thought begins, without [notated] break or pause, must be divided; especially when . . . on the same note.'

(175) C. P. E. Bach, *Essay*, Berlin, 1753, III, 28:

'[Certain] notes as well as rests must sometimes as a result of the expression be allowed a longer value than the notation shows.'

2. ARTICULATION

(a) Within a phrase, all degrees of separation can occur, from none (legato) to very much (staccato).

Articulation, like phrasing, is of the highest importance in baroque music, and capable of the highest subtlety. Even within one passage, although the separation may be basically of one kind, the refinements can be varied from note to note: and no two notes running should necessarily be given quite the same degree or manner of separation.

As usual, the sense of line comes first; and good articulation, like good phrasing, is an element in good line.

(b) Notated slurs sometimes occur, but as hints rather than as instructions; and as a rule very incompletely and inconsistently. It is for the performers to work out good and consistent bowings, breathings, articulation syllables, fingerings etc.

Dots, dashes and wedges are staccato signs not distinct from one another until very late in the baroque period, when the dot tended (no more) to imply a lighter staccato.

A slur over notes bearing dots or dashes indicates spiccato or staccato, of various weights, taken in one bow.

(c) Normally, no indication for the articulation will be found in baroque music; but (then and earlier) it was expected from the performer in adequate variety.

(176) Diego Ortiz, *Trattado de glosas sobre clausulas*, Rome, 1553, f. 3r:

'When two or three quarter notes occur in one example, only the first is to be defined and the others passed over without a fresh stroke of the bow [i.e. slurred].' [An important hint for early string music.]

(177) John Playford, *A Breefe Introduction to the Skill of Musick*, London, 1654 and many eds., ed. of 1674, p. 36:

'[A slur] is, when two or more Notes are to be sung to one Syllable, or two Notes or more to be played with once drawing the Bow on the *Viol* or Violin.'

(178) Joachim Quantz, *Essay*, Berlin, 1752, XI, 10:

'One must be careful not to slur notes which ought to be detached; and not to detach [notes] which ought to be slurred.

[XVII, ii, 5:] 'When many figures of the same kind follow one another, and only the first of them is shown with bowing [marks], the remainder must be played in the same way, so long as no other kind of notes comes in.'

(179) C. P. E. Bach, *Essay*, Berlin, 1753, III, 5:

'In general, the liveliness of allegros is conveyed by detached notes, and the expressiveness of adagios by sustained, slurred notes ... even when not so marked.'

(180) F. W. Marpurg, *Anleitung zum Clavierspielen*, Berlin, 1755, 2nd ed. 1765, I, vii, 29:

'Opposed to legato as well as to staccato is the ordinary movement which consists in lifting the finger from the last key shortly before touching the next note.'

Our modern 'ordinary movement' is much nearer to legato; and it is worth remembering this baroque concept (for which there is further evidence) of an intermediate degree of articulation as the average condition: the starting-point, of course, for any amount of varied finesse between one note and another.

(d) The most varied and elaborate bow-strokes on string instruments, and tonguings on wind instruments, were taught and practised in virtuoso music. The old bows, and the old instruments, are capable of all effects of articulation, except for a certain massive weight which in any case is hardly compatible with a good style of baroque interpretation.

But in ordinary orchestral parts, and to a considerable extent in ordinary trio sonatas and other chamber music, fancy bowings or tonguings, or elaborately varied articulations of any kind, are quite out of context, and are to be avoided. Exceptions occur, for example more or less virtuoso passages in some trio sonatas by Handel and others; and any genuine opportunities for display and showmanship can unhesitatingly be exploited. But these are not in the usual character of chamber music.

Except in virtuoso solos or passages, slurs should in the main be brief (e.g. over two, three, four or six notes) and laid out very simply and symmetrically, not at all intricately or irregularly. Two slurred, two bowed is one of the most common and serviceable patterns; two by two will often be associated with inequality (see Ch. XIX, Sect. 2ff., above). The notes of triplets, if not all separately bowed, may go very well either with all three notes slurred, or two slurred and one bowed (in that order). Mixing different patterns, effective as it is in many virtuoso contexts, is hardly ever so good in orchestral and chamber parts as choosing a simple pattern and staying with it.

But within any chosen pattern of articulation, and still more so within the intermediate or 'ordinary' articulation recommended for average use by Marpurg at (180) above, there can be an unending play of slight variations in the intensity and duration of notes, identical in notation, but by no means identical in performance.

A very important use of this varied finesse of emphasis and articulation is for bass parts in allegro. They used quite recently to be played, and still are at times, with too unyielding and ponderous a legato; now, however, they are more generally played with too choppy and unvaried a staccato. What they need is Marpurg's 'ordinary movement', i.e. an intermediate articulation: not massive, but quite crisply into the string; yet with the imagination to nuance each note, a little more legato or staccato, and a little more stressed or relaxed, as the music requires, so that the bass part becomes not just a monotonous support for the harmony, but a melodic line in its own right. That is the prime necessity for good bass playing in baroque music. The principle of well maintained and well moulded line applies just as much to the bass as to any other part.

(e) In short, articulation in baroque music, most of all when its patterns are kept most classically simple and unpretentious, requires an

286

imaginative subtlety in making it continuously interesting by slight variations of intensity and separation.

3. UNDERLAY

(a) A problem related to both phrasing and articulation is the under-laying of the verbal text in vocal music.

Underlay affects the words, which cannot be well or clearly enunciated unless they fall in naturally with the movement of the melody; and the music, which cannot be effectively phrased and articulated unless it is closely accommodated to the stresses, durations and divisions of the syllables, the words and the sentences.

(b) Composers are primarily responsible for a good and suitable set-ting of the words to the music, both for sense and for scansion.

(180a) Thomas Morley, *Plaine and Easie Introduction to Practicall Musicke*, London, 1597, p. 178:

'We must also have a care so to apply the notes to the wordes, as in singing there be no barbarisme committed; that is, that we cause no sillable which is by nature short be expressed by manie notes or one long note nor no long sillable bee expresssed with a shorte note.'

(180b) Charles Butler, *Principles of Musik*, London, 1636, p. 97 (phonetic script transliterated):

'As the Ditty [poem] is distinguished with Points (Period, Colon, Semi-colon and Comma); so is the Harmony [music], answering unto it, with Pauses and Cadences.'

Butler was influenced by Morley, and Morley by Zarlino. Later writers, especially such as Scheibe in the mid-eighteenth century, elaborated similar doctrines to a considerable degree of detail; and good composers of the baroque period were at some pains to achieve a reasonable standard, at times a very high standard, of word-setting. Carissimi, for example, in the middle of the seventeenth century, maintained the greatest sensitivity in the matter; Handel, in the eigh-teenth, was less consistent, but never altogether negligent.

(c) But this varying degree of attention to the general suitability and detailed accuracy of the setting of the poet's words by the composer is only the first half of the problem. The second half arises from the extreme casualness, so typical of all baroque notation, with which the words are actually written down into the notation.

Whether in manuscript or in printed sources, very little attempt was made to place each syllable, or even each word, either carefully or similarly beneath the note or notes to which it should be sung. There is, therefore, no possibility, in many cases, of a modern editor being able to publish a definitive underlay. He can only, as with so many other details of baroque interpretation, publish a well-considered underlay.

For a solution of the underlay to be well-considered, it is desirable to compare all available sources of the work in question, and to pick up any clear hints where they are relatively (they are very seldom altogether) consistent. It is desirable to study as many examples as possible of original underlay which appears to be rather less casual, and rather more exact, than is usually the case, so as to cultivate a good eye for baroque tendencies. But it is above all desirable to remain quite open-minded, deciding each detail more by good scansion and good musicianship than by the placing of the words in the notation itself.

In doing this, the advice to composers quoted at (180a) and (180b) above should equally be regarded by editors and performers; and the general principles suggested there should be imaginatively extended and adapted to the case in hand.

In baroque practice, the detailed working out of the underlay was, in common with a great many other details of interpretation, regarded as falling less within the composer's than within the performers' responsibility. A modern editor will, no doubt, have done his best; but a modern performer who sees his way to improving upon the editor's underlay has every right and obligation to do so. An intelligent singer with an ear for poetry can often make many small changes for the better.

Good declamatory enunciation is the foundation of good underlay. The words must so fall under their notes that stresses and durations, together with dramatic pauses, breathing spaces and other desirable contributions to good phrasing and good articulation, arrange themselves as naturally and effectively as the case allows. It then only remains to make full use of these verbal opportunities to shape and pattern, with sufficient clarity, a good melodic line. Good verbal enunciation is a declamatory rather than a conversational art; for song is a stylized and not a naturalistic convention. The shaping and the patterning must be done with skill and judgement, but they must also be done decisively enough to be plainly perceptible to the audience. A pause should generally be a palpable pause, no mere imperceptible catching of the breath; for the secret of *cantilena* is that the line of the melody shall never flag unintentionally, yet shall always be broken meaningfully at the proper places.

(d) The following is one example of a baroque tendency in underlay which may guide performers in a great variety of similar instances.

Ex. 124. Antonio Cesti, *Il Pomo d'Oro*, (a) Act I, scene 3, in

Denkmäler der Tonkunst in Österreich, Jahrg. IV/2, Band 9, p. 12 (146) and (b), Act IV, scene 4, p. 136 (270), typical baroque underlay shown by slurs, where modern underlay would have been otherwise:

Ex. 124

(a) Se tua vi - sta— hog - gi mi be - a - [-to]

(b) ren - da il va - lo - re—

CHAPTER TWENTY-ONE

Dynamics

1. LOUDS AND SOFTS

(a) Words, abbreviations or signs for dynamic variation occur throughout the baroque period, and increasingly so during the latter part of it. But most of this extremely important element of expression was left, in the usual way, to the enterprise and good judgement of the performers.

(181) Domenico Mazzocchi, *Partitura de' madrigali a cinque voci*, Rome, 1638, preface:

'The other letters P, F, E, T, understood for Piano, Forte, Echo, and Trill, are certainly [ways of notating] common things, known to everyone.'

But notice well that, in French string music (especially for the viol), the letters 'P and T' are used for abbreviations for *poussé* (pushed, i.e. forward- or up-stroke of the bow) and *tiré* (pulled, i.e. backward- or down-stroke of the bow); and that the letter 'E' may be used as an abbreviation of *enflé* (swelled, i.e. with expressive crescendo).

(182) Christopher Simpson, *Division-Violist*, London, 1659, 2nd. ed. (as *Division-Viol*), 1665 and 1667, p. 10:

'We play Loud or Soft, according to our fancy, or the humour [mood] of the music.'

(183) Thomas Mace, *Musick's Monument*, London, 1676, p. 130:

'*Humour a Lesson* [composition], by Playing some *Sentences Loud*, and others again *Soft*, according as they best please your own *Fancy*.'

(184) Scipione Maffei, 'Nuova Invenzione d'un Gravecembalo', *Giornale dei Letterati d'Italia*, V, Venice, 1711, p. 144:

'[Good performers give] particular delight to their listeners [by] piano and forte.'

(185) Joachim Quantz, *Essay*, Berlin, 1752, XII, 23:

'The interchange of soft and loud' [Fr. version] 'gives much grace to the performance.'

(b) It is very important to work out a good scheme of louds and softs, even where (as is mostly the case) few or no dynamic markings appear in the original notation.

Failure to do this usually results in a very half-hearted and ineffectual performance. The baroque habit was, in the main, to do it in rehearsal. In the main for modern performers it is much better to have the chief dynamic contrasts (but not the smaller refinements) marked into the parts ahead of time, to make sure of them.

(c) On the organ, and on the harpsichord, the instrument itself, as made and used in the baroque age, is strongly disposed to 'terrace dynamics': whole passages on one level of volume (and colouring) followed by whole passages on another level.

Modern mechanisms can make it easy to depart from terrace dynamics, and to change volume and colouring frequently, and even gradually. But in the main, this is not only contrary to the nature of these instruments, but also contrary to the music so well composed for them.

It is therefore best, in the main, to arrange the dynamic contrasts on the organ or the harpsichord in blocks rather than in gradations.

(d) Other instruments are designed for, and meant to use, flexible dynamics.

However, many baroque allegros have a *structure* implying fairly level planes of volume. A loud opening, not marked, is to be assumed as obvious. After the first decided cadence (needing the first decided rallentando), a marked *piano* is occasionally notated, and frequently appropriate, as the music enters upon a more contemplative, modulating passage, in some ways resembling a sonata-form development. Try a real *sempre piano* until the opening material returns, and can be taken loud for a decisive contrast, all the more effective for having been purposely delayed. Another decided rallentando, followed by a momentary delay for 'placing', can point up the final return, usually best kept loud to the end.

But *within* these fairly level planes of volume, a constant play of light and shade can keep the dynamic texture alive with interest.

Slow movements usually lend themselves to a more complex and powerful interplay of dynamic variation.

2. CRESCENDOS AND DIMINUENDOS

(a) Not only blocks, but gradations of volume are sometimes notated, and are freely to be admitted, in baroque music.

291

(186) Giulio Caccini, *Nuove Musiche*, Florence, 1602, preface (tr. in Playford, *Introduction*, London, 1654, ed. of 1674, p. 40):

'In Encreasing and Abating the Voyce, and in Exclamations is the foundation of Passion.'

(186a) Wolfgang Michael Mylius, *Rudimenta Musices*, Gotha, 1686, p. 49:

'Yet it is to be observed that with both [*forte* and *piano*] one should not fall suddenly from *piano* into *forte* but gradually strengthen the voice, and then again let it drop, so that consequently, on those notes where such [effects] are needed' [N. B., not always] 'the *piano* [comes] before the *forte* [which comes] in the middle, and [the passage] must again be ended with *piano*.'

(187) Roger North, *Autobiography*, c. 1695 (ed. Jessopp, London, 1887, sect. 106):

'Learn to fill, and soften a sound, as shades in needlework, in sensation, so as to be like also a gust of wind, which begins with a soft air, and fills by degrees to a strength as makes all bend, and then softens away again into a temper [temperate strength], and so vanish.' [Compare the instructions in Matthew Locke's music for *The Tempest*, perf. London, 1675: 'lowder by degrees'; 'violent'; 'soft and slow by degrees'.]

(188) François Raguenet, *Paralele des italiens et des françois . . .*, Paris, 1702 (tr. ? Galliard, London, 1709, ed. O. Strunk, *Musical Quarterly*, XXXII, iii, July, 1946, pp. 411–36, see pp. 420 and 429):

'Swellings of prodigious length . . . in their tender airs [the Italians] soften the voice insensibly and at last let it die outright.'

(189) Joachim Quantz, *Essay*, Berlin, 1752, XI, 14:

'Light and shade must be continuously introduced . . . [by the] incessant interchange of loud and soft.'

(b) Our familiar horizontal hairpin (wedge-shaped) signs for crescendo and diminuendo became common from early in the eighteenth century. Sometimes the open end of the hairpin is found closed by a vertical line (giving a slender horizontal triangle): no difference is meant in the intention.

A series of markings such as pp, p, mf, f, ff or the reverse, or merely p and f or the reverse may, at any time during the baroque period, indicate crescendo or diminuendo (see 186a above).

3. THE OVERALL DYNAMICS AND THE FINE FLUCTUATIONS

(a) We may distinguish:

(i) An *overall scheme* of dynamic contrasts, both by blocks and by gradations;

(ii) a *continual fluctuation* of fine contrasts, both sudden and gradual.

(b) It is desirable, on the whole, to preconcert the overall scheme, but to feel one's way through the finer nuances. It is most often the harmony which is the best guide to the finer nuances whereas the melodic line is most often indicative on a rather larger scale. Rising dynamically to the peak of an ascending phrase, and falling away from it again as the melody descends, is one of the most natural of musical responses. This can often happen intuitively, within the yet larger planning (best pre-concerted) of loud and soft passages.

4. BALANCE

(a) Balance in concerted music is largely although not entirely a dynamic matter.

In fugues and other more or less imitative music, for example, there is a method of bringing out an entry by performing it with somewhat more emphasis, significance and intensity, and only a little more actual volume; and this is usually better than forcing the entry through with much more volume.

But then the other performers should be withdrawing a little into relative insignificance, in order to let the entry through. The more closely the entries follow upon one another, the more necessary it is for each performer to get out of the way of the next entry, so soon as he has made his own.

(190) Lodovico Zacconi, *Prattica di musica*, Venice, 1592, LXVI, p. 59:

'Entries should be emphasized a little so as to be instantly and clearly perceived by the hearer.'

(191) Joachim Quantz, *Essay*, Berlin, 1752, XII, 23:

'[Bring out the subject by] a distinctive manner of performance . . . as well as by loud and soft.'

(192) Charles Avison, *Essay on Musical Expression*, London, 1752, p. 128:

'When the inner Parts are intended as Accompanyments only, great Care should be taken to touch them in such a Manner, that they may never predominate, but be always subservient to the principal Per-former, who also should observe the same Method, whenever his Part becomes an Accompanyment; which generally happens in well-wrought Fugues and other full Pieces, where the Subject and Air are almost equally distributed . . .

'Every Performer [must therefore be] listening to the other Parts, without which he cannot do Justice to his own.'

(b) It is especially important to bring out the bass with a strength at least equal to the upper parts, and to make a real melodic line of it. The entire texture and polarity of most baroque music depends on this strength and melodiousness of the bottom line.

(193) [L'Abbé Marc-Antoine Laugier], *Apologie de la musique françoise*, [Paris], 1754, p. 69:

'Furnish all the parts sufficiently, to see that each makes its effect, that the chief parts, such as the treble and the bass, stand out to advantage ... One cannot too strongly recommend furnishing the basses beyond the rest; for they are the foundation of the harmony.'

5. ACCENTUATION

(a) Dynamic force enters into all actual accentuation; but other factors are also involved.

(b) On organ or harpsichord, dynamic accents can be simulated by taking a silence of articulation out of the end of the note before; and still more so, by slightly lengthening, in addition, the note on which the dynamic accent is to be simulated (this lengthening is sometimes described as an agogic accent).

(c) On instruments capable of dynamic accentuation, such a silence of articulation before the accent very greatly increases the effect of it; and an agogic accent can also be combined with a dynamic accent to increase its effect.

An agogic accent can be used without a dynamic accent; but this does not usually occur, on instruments capable of both.

(d) A dynamic accent can be produced by any instrument capable of direct control over volume; but there is sometimes a choice of methods.

For example, on bowed instruments, there can be dynamic accentuation:

(i) by the weight of the arm and the bow falling from the air (especially with violins or violas and almost as much with cellos, because of their overhand bowing, but rather less with viols, because of their underhand bowing), i.e. the *weight accent*;

(ii) by a rapid movement, usually with some added pressure, at the start of the bow, i.e. the *speed accent*;

(iii) by a rapid movement, with some increase of pressure, just after the start of the bow, i.e. the *sforzando*;

(iv) by a sharp pressure of the forefinger on the stick of the bow (with the violin family), or of the second finger on the inside of the hair (with the viol family), immediately released as the bow gets into motion, i.e. the *attack accent*.

Of these, (i) is seldom suited to baroque music, least of all when taken at the heel of the bow where the effect is strongest.

Both (ii) and (iii) are useful in baroque music, though care must be taken not to allow either of them, especially (iii), to become a habitual mannerisim, which can easily happen without the player even noticing that it is happening.

But the most frequently useful and versatile of string accents in baroque music is (iv), the attack accent, either with or without some degree of (ii) or (iii), and in any desired intensity from the slightest crispness to the sharpest. Unlike (i), (ii) and (iii), it is only possible to take (iv) on the string, and not from the air. But in any case, this is nearly always (apart from certain virtuosi passages) the best baroque technique.

(e) Considerable subtlety and judgement are needed both in the placing and in the management of baroque accents. They should commonly occur, without necessarily being conspicuous, on the note (which is often but not always the highest note) to which the phrase is moving.

(194) Francesco Geminiani, *Art of Playing on the Violin*, London, 1751, p. 9:

'If by your manner of bowing you lay a particular Stress on the Note at the Beginning of every Bar, so as to render it predominant over the rest, you alter and spoil the true Air of the Piece, and . . . there are very few Instances in which it is not very disagreeable.'

(195) Joachim Quantz, *Essay*, Berlin, 1752, XII, 19:

'When after quick notes there unexpectedly follows a long [note], which holds up the melody; one must mark the same with especial emphasis.'

(196) Leopold Mozart, *Violinschule*, Augsburg, 1756, XX, 13:

'In lively pieces the accent is generally taken on the highest note.'

These are, of course, the merest hints, and it is always for the performer to make up his mind which is the note to which the phrase is going. In most passages, whether fast or slow, that is the note which is most likely to require some degree of emphasis.

Another small but useful hint is that notes which are syncopated require to have their rhythmic displacement emphasized by a prior silence of articulation, taken out of the end of the note before; and (where possible) by receiving an accent. A shorter note following a syncopated note will be joined to it and lightened, almost like the resolution of an appoggiatura: 'with a diminution of volume', as Leopold Mozart explains (*loc. cit.*, 23).

6. THE HEMIOLA

(a) A much more important displacement of accentuation, commonly known as hemiola, or hemiolia, occurs when two measures of triple time are, in effect, thrown into one measure of twice the duration. The rhythmic and harmonic pulse is thereby carried up to the next higher level in the metrical hierarchy; and it is extremely important for the performer to recognize this fact, and to make it very audible in his accentuation

(b) The change of pulse which constitutes the hemiola is commonly though not always visible in the notation of the bass part (and sometimes of other parts), which may be tied across the middle bar-line: i.e. the bar-line of which the rhythmic effect is being suppressed. Occasionally, as at Ex. 125 (b) below, the bar-line is itself suppressed from the notation, and the presence of the hemiola is thereby made still more visible.

Visible or not, however, the hemiola makes its presence known by the shift of pulse, which can be heard in the harmony, and must then be made audible in the rhythm by the necessary change in the accentuation. The effect is of remarkable beauty and interest, in a good specimen; and it only needs to be well brought out in performance. To overlook a hemiola spoils the whole intention of the passage, but there is little danger of this, once the idiom is familiar. The change of accentuation then needs to be made striking enough for the audience to share vividly in the pleasure.

Ex. 125. Giacomo Carissimi, cantata 'Amor mio, che cosa è questa', Bologna, Lib. of Conserv., MS V289; (a) mm. 29–32, hemiola made visible by the bass part being tied across the (inoperative) bar-line in the middle; (b) matching passage on the same bass at mm. 69–71, hemiola made still more visible by suppressing the inoperative bar-line from the notation:

CHAPTER TWENTY-TWO

Then and Now

1. THE PLEASURE OF UNFAMILIARITY

(a) In all the general principles and varied details considered in this book, there is nothing which can guarantee a good sense of baroque style.

But if we find our performances hanging together with more inner consistency, at once compatible with the surviving evidence and convincing to our audiences, we may feel a reasonable confidence that we are moving in the right direction.

(b) Any absolute confidence in the authenticity of our performances can only be self-deluding, for we cannot ever be that sure of how it used to go. The most at which it is realistic to aim is substantial authenticity; and that is already a big change from our usual modern habits. Nor is this to everybody's liking. Why should it be so?

(c) It is unrealistic and unfriendly to brush aside the pleasure taken by so many people in deliberate modernizations such as Busoni's Bach, or Stokowski's Bach, or nowadays the new electronic Bach. These have not the enduring validity, shall we say, of Bach's Bach; but they may each have some passing interest for their own generation. There is no crime in that.

(d) Others of us like our baroque performances no more modernized than the altered circumstances of our times require. Even so, we cannot avoid an unknown quantity of inadvertent modernization; but we can at least reduce it to a minimum by taking notice of the available information, as sampled in this book.

(e) There can be numerous compromises in between, of which the test should be: do they actually do the job?

A compromise which cuts too much across the implications of the music does not really do the job, because we are not really going to get the experience, even if what we do get is enjoyable in a mixed kind of way. But if the compromise does not basically cut across the music, we may still get the experience, even if not quite in an acoustic embodiment which could have happened historically at the time. That may well be regarded by many people as artistically acceptable.

297

It rather depends on what we want from baroque music. If we want it more or less to meet our familiar expectations of a musical occurrence, we shall allow it, whether deliberately or inadvertently, to come out sounding not much different from our usual habits. But if we want it to expand our familiar expectations, giving us back something which delights and surprises us because we did not put it in ourselves, then we shall attempt to get further away from our usual habits, and nearer to the baroque habits in some such ways as are suggested in this present book.

The result of this attempt will not be an altogether familiar or modern experience. But paradoxically enough, that may be, if we can take it, the best way of making baroque music over into our modern experience.

The unfamiliarity itself contributes to the value of the experience. There is, I feel sure, a place for certain deliberate compromises, either to meet the practical circumstances, or to fall in with a personal preference provided that this does give a genuine experience of the music. But that means welcoming something unfamiliar and not wholly of our own age. It means aiming substantially even if not altogether literally at authentic performances. That is the intention of this present book.

2. THE PLEASURE OF NATURALNESS

(a) Nothing so confirms that we are getting substantially authentic performances as their sounding natural.

(b) Opinions may indeed differ as to what sounds natural; but we have begun to move on towards a broad agreement, at least among informed and musicianly opinions.

The reason for this is that between music and its stylish performance there is a recognizable affinity. Music does carry its own implications: flexible, and nowhere more so than in baroque music; but nevertheless contained within the natural boundaries of style.

(c) To recognize a long-neglected style may require some homework such as this book outlines; but the boundaries are where they always were. The implications of the music have not altered. Nor has our musicianship essentially altered.

There is no satisfaction quite like this satisfaction of feeling the music slip into place in its own natural interpretation.

(d) Conversely: if it sounds too unnatural to be true, it is not true; and if it sounds too unmusical to be good, it is not good.

Of course, we have to make experiments, and we have to allow time for getting used to them; but if we end up sounding rather too gimmicky and calculated, or rather too uninterestingly correct, then something has gone wrong with our scholarship, or our musicianship, or both in combination.

298

3. THE POINT OF AUTHENTICITY

(a) Authenticity is for getting a natural match between the music and its interpretation. It is not history for history's sake. It is history for the music's sake.

It can be very misleading to come at baroque music naïvely, without giving a thought to the necessary information. But it can be much more misleading to follow even true and authentic baroque instructions, without having assimilated them musically. This can readily happen, since they are often difficult to understand, as well as being, of course, not invariably true. When confronted with a musicological solution which does not carry conviction as a musical solution, we should perhaps just bear in mind that not all musicology is successful musicology, any more than all musicianship is good musicianship.

(b) Newcomers to the idea of authentic performances should be particularly careful not to make them sound too contrived and gimmicky. Simplest is often best, especially in simple music. Overdoing the conventional baroque liberties not only is, but always was a fault. The line comes first, and anything which disturbs a good sense of the line is quite certainly mistaken in performances of baroque music.

Too much of the fashionable inequality, over-dotting, free ornamentation and elaborate continuo realization can sound worse than too little.

Doing the right thing in the wrong place, again, can sound very wrong indeed. Moreover, the right notes, in the right place, may still have the wrong nuance. The most correct of upper-note trills or on-the-beat appoggiaturas will not sound like good musicianship until the subtle distribution of stress and rhythm is balanced in the proper proportions. There is no writing this down: it has to be learnt through hearing it and through musicianly intuition.

But one principle can always be relied upon. If it does not sound like good musicianship, it is not good musicianship. And if it is not good musicianship, it is certainly not good authenticity.

(c) Under-playing baroque music, on the other hand, is contrary both to its implications, and to the evidence of which we noticed a small but typical selection in Chapter II above.

For example, present-day performances on the viol are often insufficiently focused and robust, apparently from fear of making a gamba sound too much like a cello. But a properly fitted gamba, masterfully handled, will sound like the fine and highly individual string instrument it is, and much more truly a gamba than when its tone is not being firmly enough produced nor precisely enough controlled.

Scaled-down performances cannot be authentic performances. The

baroque age was an age of virtuoso performers and bravura performances. We cannot become authentic by falling short of their solid proficiency and abundant brilliance, nor by any lack of robust vitality.

The proficiency and the brilliance, the robustness and the vitality, are
part of the authenticity.

(d) Unless, therefore, our performances have that unmistakable
authority which comes from solid proficiency and good musicianship,
we are not matching up to the best of the baroque performers; and any
detailed authenticity which we may be achieving is of secondary importance.

The only authenticity of primary importance is the authenticity which,
without any fuss or need for explanation, gets straight across to the
audience.

Reading List

This is not a bibliography, but a brief list of writings, almost wholly in English or English translation, which performers and other readers might find it especially useful to follow up.

For a long but still Select Bibliography, see my *Interpretation of Early Music*, new version, 1973 (listed below).

For a very full but not selective list, see 'Bibliography of Performance Practices', listed below under Vinquist.

For works quoted in the text of this present book, look up under authors' names in my Index; sufficient bibliographical reference will be found at each quotation for purposes of identification.

In these quotations, translation (unless, on rare occasions, otherwise ascribed) is mine, literal closeness and not literary merit being the aim in view. In the case of Quantz' famous *Essay*, some sentences in my translation follow the French version (authorized by Quantz himself in his preface to it) rather than the German version (now much more readily available, since a facsimile edition is in print); in this, I am following the same policy as Edward R. Reilly, whose excellent English translation is listed below.

My wife Dr. Rose has worked ungrudgingly to improve the precision and accuracy of all bibliographical information here given, and vastly more so for my *Interpretation of Early Music*. My graduate assistant Sharon Kay Hoke at the University of Iowa helped with the proof-reading. Jerrold Moore, then at Yale, took me invaluably through many historical recordings there. Judith Osborne of Faber and Faber Ltd. earned my gratitude by making many meticulous corrections; as also did Terence Miller, in addition to preparing the index with most exceptional skill and thoroughness.

Arnold, Frank T. *The Art of Accompaniment from a Thorough-Bass as Practised in the XVIIth and XVIIIth Centuries*. London, 1931.
Paperback reprint in 2 vols. Introd. by Denis Stevens. New York, 1965.
(Indispensable for serious students of baroque accompaniment)

Babitz, Sol. 'Concerning the Length of Time that Every Note Must be Held', *Music Review* XXVIII (Feb. 1967) pp. 21–37.
(A good sample of this very eccentric writer's style)

Bach, Carl Philipp Emanuel. *Versuch über die wahre Art das Clavier zu spielen.* Berlin, 1753. Pt. II, Berlin, 1762.
Facsimile of Pts. I and II, ed. L. Hoffmann-Erbrecht. Leipzig, 1957. 2nd ed. 1969.
Trans. and ed. W. J. Mitchell. New York and London, 1949.
(Pt. I important in general; Pt. II mainly for accompaniment)

Bacilly, Bénigne de. *Remarques curieuses sur l'art de bien chanter.* Paris, 1668.
Trans. and ed. A. B. Caswell, as *A Commentary upon The Art of Proper Singing.* Brooklyn, N.Y., 1968.
(Has much of interest to serious students of baroque singing)

Bacon, Richard Mackenzie. *Elements of Vocal Science.* London [1824].
Ed. Edward Foreman. Champaign, Illinois, 1966.
(Genuine *bel canto*)

Boyden, David D. *The History of Violin Playing from Its Origins to 1761 and Its Relationship to the Violin and Violin Music.* London, 1965.
(Indispensable for serious students of baroque string playing)

Buelow, George J. *Thorough-Bass Accompaniment According to Johann David Heinichen.* Berkeley and Los Angeles, 1966.
(Important for accompanists of baroque music)

Collins, Michael. 'A Reconsideration of French Over-Dotting', *Music and Letters* L (Jan. 1969) pp. 111–23.
(A good sample of this interesting writer's contribution)

Couperin, François. *L'art de toucher le clavecin.* Paris, 1716. [Enlarged ed. Paris, 1717.]
Facsimile of 1717 ed. New York, 1969.
Ed. and German trans. by A. Linde, with English trans. by M. Roberts. Leipzig, 1933.
(Short but invaluable for harpsichordists)

Dart, R. Thurston. *The Interpretation of Music.* London, 1954. 4th ed. [same as the 1st ed. except for an updated bibliography and a few changes in minor details] London, 1967.
(Invaluable as a general introduction to baroque performance)

Dolmetsch, Arnold. *The Interpretation of the Music of the XVIIth and XVIIIth Centuries Revealed by Contemporary Evidence.* London [1915]. New ed. London [1944].

Paperback reprint of the 1946 [*sic*] ed. Introd. by R. Alec Harman. Seattle and London, 1969.
(A pioneering classic)

Donington, Robert. *The Interpretation of Early Music*. London, 1963; New York, 1964. 2nd ed. London, 1965; New York, 1966. [New Version, wholly revised and very much expanded, in preparation 1973.]
(Lengthy discussions based on extensive contemporary quotations: a work of reference to which serious students of baroque music may wish to proceed)

Donington, Robert. 'A Problem of Inequality', *Musical Quarterly* LIII (Oct. 1967) pp. 503–17.
(Baroque evidence and music examples, from several nations and periods, quoted and discussed)

Ferand, Ernest T. *Die Improvisation in Beispielen aus neun Jahrhunderten abendländischer Musik* (*Das Musikwerk*). Cologne, 1956. English ed. (*Anthology of Music*) Cologne, 1961.
(Indispensable for the serious student of baroque ornamentation [mainly music examples])

Gasparini, Francesco. *L'armonico pratico al cimbalo*. Venice, 1708. Facsimile. New York, 1967.
Trans. F. S. Stillings, ed. D. L. Burrows. New Haven, 1963.
(Brief but excellent, and invaluable for accompanists of baroque music)

Harich-Schneider, Eta. *The Harpsichord: An Introduction to Technique, Style and the Historical Sources*. Kassel and St. Louis, 1954.
(Useful. Her *Die Kunst des Cembalo-Spiels* (Kassel, 1939), which is not translated, is long and excellent)

Heinichen, Johann David. *Der General-Bass in der Composition*. Dresden, 1728.
Facsimile. Hildesheim and New York, 1969.
(Invaluable for the serious student of baroque accompaniment: see under Buelow, for a summary and partial translation)

Hotteterre le Romain [Jacques Martin.] *Principes de la flute traversiere, ou flute d'Allemagne; de la flute à bec, ou flute douce, et du haut-bois*. Paris, 1707.
Facsimile and German trans. of Amsterdam [1728] ed. by H. J. Hellwig. Kassel, 1941. 2nd ed. 1958.
English trans. (the best) by D. Lasocki. London, 1968.
English trans. by P. M. Douglas. New York, 1968.
(Indispensable for serious students of baroque woodwind)

303

Lockwood, Lewis. 'A Sample Problem of *Musica Ficta*: Willaert's *Pater Noster*', in *Studies in Music History: Essays for Oliver Strunk*, ed. H. Powers (Princeton, 1968), pp. 161–82.
(Pre-baroque, but just the right method of approach)

Mace, Thomas. *Musick's Monument*. London, 1676.
Facsimile. Paris, 1958.
Facsimile. New York, 1966.
(Indispensable for lutenists, valuable for viol players, and has much of general interest)

Mackerras, Charles. 'Sense about the Appoggiatura', *Opera* XIV (Oct. 1963) pp. 669–78.
(Just what its title says)

Mackerras, Charles. 'Editing Mozart's Operas', interview with Stanley Sadie, *Musical Times*, vol. 109 (Aug. 1968) pp. 722–3.
(Highly intelligent on both sides)

Mancini, Giambattista. *Pensieri, e riflessioni pratiche sopra il canto figurato*. Vienna, 1774.
Trans. and ed. E. Foreman. Champaign, Illinois, 1967.
(Important for *bel canto*)

Mozart, J. G. Leopold. *Versuch einer gründlichen Violinschule*. Augsburg, 1756.
Facsimile of 1st ed., ed. B. Paumgartner. Vienna, 1922.
Facsimile of 1st ed. Frankfurt am Main, 1956.
Facsmile of 3rd ed. (1787), ed. H. J. Moser. Leipzig, 1956.
Facsimile of 3rd ed., ed. H. J. Jung. Leipzig, 1968.
Trans. E. Knocker. London, 1948. 2nd ed., 1951.
(Valuable especially for virtuoso violin playing of the late baroque period)

Neumann, Frederick. *Baroque and Post-Baroque Ornamentation*, in preparation.
(An extremely long and thorough though in part, as I think, speculative study, which no student specializing in baroque ornamentation should neglect)

North, Roger. *Roger North on Music: Being a Selection from His Essays Written during the Years c. 1695–1728*, ed. John Wilson. London, 1959.
(Much scattered information on seventeenth-century English performance)

Purcell, Henry. Sonatas VI and IX from the *Ten Sonatas in Four Parts* (London, 1697), ed. Robert Donington and Walter Emery. London, 1959.

(Text securely established from the original sources, with full discussion and all significant variants given, by Walter Emery; performing version, with tempo and dynamic markings, ornamentation and ornaments, realization of the figured bass, etc., and brief performing hints, by Robert Donington.)

Quantz, Johann Joachim. *Versuch einer Anweisung die Flöte traversiere zu spielen*. Berlin, 1752. French ed.: *Essai d'une methode pour apprendre à jouer de la flute traversiere*. Berlin, 1752.
Facsimile of 3rd ed. (Breslau, 1789), ed. H.-P. Schmitz. Kassel, 1953.
Trans. and ed. E. R. Reilly, as *On Playing the Flute*. London, 1966.
(Invaluable general guide to performance in the age of Bach and Handel)

Schmitz, Hans-Peter. *Die Kunst der Verzierung im 18. Jahrhundert*. Kassel, 1955. 2nd ed., 1965.
(Indispensable for the serious student of baroque ornamentation [mainly music examples])

Schnoebelen, Anne. 'Performance Practices at San Petronio in the Baroque', *Acta Musicologica* XLI (1969) pp. 37–55.
(An excellent sample of valuable information skilfully extracted from archives)

Shaw, [H.] Watkins. *A Textual and Historical Companion to Handel's Messiah*. London, 1965.
(An admirable study, including brief but good sections on performance)

Simpson, Christopher. *The Division-Violist: or, an Introduction to the Playing upon a Ground*. London, 1659.
Facsimile of 2nd ed. (1665), ed. N. Dolmetsch. London, 1955.
(Indispensable to serious students of the gamba; also includes outstanding music)

Stevens, Denis, ed. *The Art of Ornamentation and Embellishment in the Renaissance and Baroque*. (Recording on) Vanguard Records. New York, 1967 (BGS 70697/8 stereo) and London (VSL 11044–5 stereo).
(Mainly excellent, but for further comments see Robert Donington, 'Ornamentation Galore', *Musical Times* CX (July 1969) pp. 738–9)

Strunk, Oliver. *Source Readings in Music History*. New York, 1950, London, 1952. Paperback reprint in 5 vols. New York, 1965.
(Invaluable to any reader of the present book)

READING LIST

Tobin, John. *Handel's Messiah*. London, 1969.
(Very detailed, and although not all acceptable, has much of great practical interest)

Tosi, Pier Francesco. *Opinioni de' cantori antichi, e moderni*. Bologna, 1723.
Trans. J. E. Galliard, as *Observations on the Florid Song*. London, 1742.
German trans. and additions by J. F. Agricola, as *Anleitung zur Singekunst*. Berlin, 1757.
Facsimile of Tosi, New York, 1968.
Facsimiles of Tosi and Agricola, ed. E. R. Jacobi. Celle, 1966.
Facsimile of Agricola, ed. K. Wichmann. Leipzig, 1966.
Reprint of Galliard trans., 2nd ed. (1743). London, 1926 and 1967.
Reprint of Galliard trans., 2nd ed. Preface by P. H. Lang. New York, 1968.
(Indispensable to serious students of baroque singing)

Vinquist, Mary and Neal Zaslaw, eds. *Performance Practice: A Bibliography*. New York, 1971.
(Mainly reliable and extremely useful)

Westrup, Jack. *Musical Interpretation*. London, 1971.
(Excellent introductory information and advice)

ADDITIONS

Harris, Simon. 'Lully, Corelli, Muffat and the Eighteenth-Century Orchestral String Body', *Music and Letters*, Vol. LIV No. 2, April 1973, pp. 197–202.

Mather, Betty Bang, *Interpretation of French Music from 1675 to 1775 for Woodwind and Other Performers* . . . . New York, 1973.

Neumann, Frederick, 'The Dotted Note and the So-called French Style', *Early Music*, V, 3, July 1977.

Answered by David Fuller, and by Robert Donington, in *Early Music*, V, 4, October 1977.

Index

Compiled by Terence A. Miller

Page numbers in italics indicate quotations, those in bold type denote more important references. Musical examples are shown within brackets.

Aaron, Pietro, on accidentals, *113*
Acciaccatura, **191–3**, 238
Accidentals, 14, 27, **113–59**; Aaron on, *113*; affected by context, *115–16*; Agazzari on, *148*; altering but not defining, (116–17); ambiguity, 113; augmented octave, (142); augmented second, (138), (141), 145, 149–50; in Bach, J. S., 114, (120), (121), 131, (131–2); bar-line effect, 25, 117, **132–3**; baroque signs for, **114–15**; Bathe on, *114*; in Beethoven, 133; Bianciardi on, *157*; in Blow, 132, 140, (141); Burney on, *141*; Butler on, (148); in Carissimi, *see* Carissimi, G., accidentals in; in Carleton, 142, (143); chord change influence on, 120, (121); chromatic sequence influence on, 120; consistency as guide to, **136–7**; in Coperario, (142); Curtis on, 124–5, (125); Delair on, *135*; diminished octave, (142); diminished third, (138); in Dowland, *see Lachrimae* (Dowland); Ebner on, *157*; in Ferrabosco, 116, (117); in figured bass, 115, (128), (134–5), 157; 'flat key', 116; flattening at peak of phrase, **152–5**; 'flatted notes', (116), (117); Geminiani on, *132*; in Giamberti, (137); in Handel, 114, 132; harmony indicative of, 129, (130), **140–4**; hexachordal system, **123–5**, 129–30, (130), 153; inconsistent, 114, **118–20**; improvisation of, 33; interpretation of, 30; in Jenkins, (122); key signatures and, **115**; in Kirnberger, (121); in Landi, (128); leading note, sharpening the, **147–149**; in Leclair, 116, (117); Locke on, *148*; in Lully, (155); in Mazzocchi, *117–118*, (118); medieval notation and, 114; melody indicative of, 129, (130), **138–40**; misplaced, (134); in Mondonville, (120); in Monteverdi, *see* Monteverdi, C., accidentals in; Morley on, *114, 147–8*; *musica ficta* inheritance, 113; new phrase effect on, 121–2, (122); Niedt on, *157*; in Palestrina, (125); Penna on, *157*; performer's responsibility for, **159**; in Peri, *118*, (118–19), (121), (126), (145); Phrygian cadence, 135, (144), (148); Picardy Third, (149), **157–9**; placing of, 115; precautionary, (121), (139), **144–7**,

(146), (154); problem of, **113–33**; prospective influence of, **117–25**, 126; in Purcell, 132, 140, 141, (153); in Rameau, 133, (152) *bis*; repeated notes influence on, (120); rest effect on, 120, (121), 122; retrospective influence, **125–32**, (137), (144), 145–7; in Rossi, (119); Salzilli on, *114*; 'sharp' key, 116; sharp sixth implied, **149–52**; 'sharped' notes, (116), (117); sharpening at trough of phrase, **155**; Simpson on, *115, 117*, 132; situations necessitating, 147; standard baroque notation, 116, (117); in Sweelink, (136); tablature as check on, **135–6**, 150, (151); in Treiber, 116, (117); tritones, avoiding undesired, **155–7**; Türk on, *133*; *Una nota super la Semper est canendum fa*, (153), (154); Vanneo on, *113–14*; in Viadana, (126), 146, (147); in Vivaldi, 114, (138), (140); Zarlino on, *114*
Accompaniment, **207–39**; Abert on, 219; adding to bass, 211; Agazzari on, *227*; *all' unisono*, 215; appoggiaturas in, 212–13, 218; Bach, C. P. E., on, *see* Bach, C. P. E., accompaniment; of Bach, J. S., 209, 223; bassoon, 227, 228, 230; broken chords, 223; Brossard on, *228*; Burney on, *228, 229*; carrying above solo, 218; cello, 228, 229, 230; in chamber music, 228; *chitarrone*, 227; chords execution of, 219; continuo, 44, 210–11, 218–19, 228, 229; contrapuntal, 221–4; of Corelli, (212); correctness, **217–18**; Couperin on, *228*; Daube on, *227*; Dean on, 230; dolcian, 227; Donington's realization, (212); double-bass, 229, 230; double-bass viol, 227, 229; doubling continuo, 227–8; dynamic expression, 215; extended, 218; figured bass, 33, 45, **208–9**, 210, 217; forbidden consecutives, 217; fullness of, **214–16**; full-voiced, 216, 218; gamba, 227, 228, 229; Geminiani on, *213*; Gerber on, *221*; Gerber's, 208; glockenspiel, 230; guitar, 96, 227; of Handel, 208–9, (224–5), 230; harmony of, **210–14**; harp, 90, 230; harpsichord, 209, 210–11, 214–17, 219, **227–30**; Heinichen on, *see* Heinichen, J. D.; imitation of solo part, (223); improvisation, 33, **209–10**; independence of, **220–7**; in-

307

Accompaniment—*contd.*
congruous notes in, 226; instruments of, **227–30**; Keller on, *229*; keyboard, 44, **227–30**; Kolneder on, 230; of Lully, (211); lyra da gamba, 227; lute, 96, 227, 228; mandoline, 230; of Marais, (211); Mattheson on, *226*; Mizler on, *227*; modifying the bass, 211; Morin on, *228*; North on, 228–9; obbligato, 208–9; octave doubling, 215; optional, 207; organ, 216, **227–30**; ornaments in, 212–213; over-elaborate, 219, 226; parallel fifths, 218; passing notes, 213–14; pedal points, 215; Penna on, *212, 217, 219*; Praetorius on, *227*; of Purcell, 228; Quantz on, *218*; of Rameau, (211); realizations, written-out, 208–9; of recitative, *see* Recitative, accompaniment of; relevancy of, 210; restraint in, 227; rhythm in, 221; of sacred music, 230; Saint-Lambert on, *210, 211, 213, 217, 219* (*bis*); of Scarlatti, A., (222–3); *senza cembalo*, 214; serpent, 228; smoothness, 219; spacing of, **218–19**; *tasto solo*, 214–15; Telemann on, *217*; of Telemann, 208; theorboes, 230; three-part, 216; trills in, 212; trombone, 227; two-part, 216; unfigured bass, 207; *unisoni*, 215; variety of, **207–9**; Viéville on, *226*; in Vivaldi, 230; voice-leading, 220, 221; Wilson on, *229*
Accurate organist, Der (Treiber), 116, (117)
Acoustics, **37–9**, 46, 51, 297
Acta Musicologica, 236
Adagio (*gently*), 243, 244, 250, 253
Ademollo, Alessandro, on *bel canto*, 55
Affilard, Michel L', on rhythm, *271*
Agazzari, Agostino: *Del sonare sopra 'l basso*: on accidentals, *148*; on accompaniment, *228*
Agricola, Johann F.: *Anleitung Zur Singkunst*, 304; on appoggiatura, (188); on *bel canto*, *56*; on rhythm, *257*
Agricola, Martin, on vibrato, 85
Albert, Heinrich, on accompaniment, *219*
Albini, Emma (*soprano*), 59, 64
Albinoni, Tommaso, 208
Alcione (Marais), (211)
All' unisoni (in unison), 215
Allargando (*becoming broader*), 251, 253
Allegro (*cheerful*), 243, 248–9
Allemande (*dance*), 248
Alto, male (*countertenor*), **71**, 72
Amadis (Lully), (155), (269–70), 281
American Musicological Society, Journal of: Byrt on rhythm, 257; Collins on triplets, 278
Amstad, Marietta, on *bel canto*, 69
Andante (*fluently*), 243
Ander Theil (Farina), 92
Anglebert, Jean H. d': *Pièces de clavecin*: on slide, (193), 194; on trill, 196
Anleitung zum Clavierspielen (Marpurg): on acciaccatura, *191*; on appoggiatura, *182, 184, 186*; on articulation, *285*, 286; on notes of anticipation, (205); on springer, (205); on trill, 196, 197
Anleitung zur Singekunst (Agricola), *56*, (188), *257–8*
Anthology of Music (*Das Musiwerk*), 164

Antonio, Don (*bass singer*), 55
Antonio Vivaldi (Kolneder), 230
Anweisung (Heinichen), *235*
Anweisung zum Piano-Forte-Spiel (Hummel), 194, 197
Apollo's Banquet, (153)
Apologie de la musique françoise (Laugier), 294
Apparatus Musico . . . (Muffat), 194
Appoggiatura, 23, **181–90**; in accompaniment, 212–13, 218, 237; Bach, C. P. E., on, *182*, (183), *184*, (185); in Bach, J. S., 181; cadential, 187–90; consecutive fifths and, 180, (183); consonant, 181; Couperin on, *181–2*, (183); in *da capo* vocals, 164; dissonant, 181, 184; editing, 27; Galliard on, *182*; Geminiani on, *184*; length of, 182, 184–5, 189; long, 160, 178, 181, 184–5; in Mahler, 181; Marpurg on, *182, 184*, 186, moderate, 184; with mordent, 181, 205; Mozart on, *186*; notated and un-notated, 189; obligatory, 186–7, 189; optional, 189; ornamental, 181; passing, **186**; Quantz on, *181, 182*, (183), *184, 185–6, 186*; in recitative, *see* Recitative, ornamentation in; Rousseau on, (186); short, 184–5; spontaneous interpretation of, 32; stress, degree of, 184, 189; structural, 181; with trill, 181, (200)
Arch-lute (*chittarone*), 95, 227, 234
Arditi, Luigi, 63, 64
Arias (Abert), *219*
Arias, ornamentation in, 160–1, 163–4
Arioso (*song-like*), 160–1
Armonico pratico . . . (Gasparini), 191
Arnold, Frank T.: *The Art of Accompaniment . . .*, 301
Arpeggiation on harpsichord, 107, 232–4
Art de bien chanter, L' (Bacilly), *170*
Art de toucher le Clavecin, L' (Couperin), 301; on appoggiatura, *181–2*; on feeling, 20, *108*; on harpsichord touch, *106*; on rhythm, *257*; on tempo, *250*; on trill, *200*
Art du facteur d'orgues, L' (Bédos de Celles), *259*
Art of Accompaniament (Geminiani), (213)
Art of Fugue (J. S. Bach), 131, (132)
Art of Playing the Violin, The (Geminiani): on accidentals, *132*; on appoggiatura, 184; on bow technique, *98*; on dynamics, *295*; on holding the violin, *82*; on string fingering, 84; on string vibrato, *86*
Art of Violin Playing, The (Flesch), *86*
Arte de tañer fantasia (Santa Maria), *255*
Arte del Violino, L' (Locatelli), 84
Arte Prattica e poëtica (Ebner), 157
Articulation, 23, **284–7**; Bach, C. P. E., on, *285*; for bass parts, 286; in *bel canto*, 67; bow technique, 81, 83, 284, 286; breath control and, 284; dashes, 285; dots, 285; in Handel, 286; legato, 284; markings for, 34; Marpurg on, *285*, 286; of oboe, 99; 'ordinary', 286; of organ, 109; Ortiz on, *285*; performer's responsibility for, 284; Playford on, *285*; Quantz on, *285*; of recorder, 98; separation, degrees of, 284; slurs, 284, 285, 286; spiccato, 285; staccato, 284, 285; syllables of, 284; tonguing, 285; triplets, 286; underlay

INDEX

and, 287, 288; wedges, 285; of wind instruments, 97
Authenticity, 48, **297–300**
Ave Maria (Gounod), 71
Ave Verum (Mozart), 74–5
Avison, Charles, on expression, *293*

Babitz, Sol., 80, 88, 92, 301
Bach, C. P. E.: on accompaniment, *see* Bach, C. P. E., on accompaniment; ... *Art das Clavier zu spielen*, 302; *Essay*, 1753, (*q.v.*); *Essay*, 1762, (*q.v.*); on harpsichord, 43
Bach, C. P. E., on accompaniment: fullness of, *215* (*bis*); use of gamba, *229*; harmony of, *213*; independence of, *226*; ornaments in, 212; spacing of, *218*, *219*
Bach, J. S., 69, 208, 221; acciaccatura in, (*192*); accidentals in, 114, (*120*), (*121*), 130, (*131–2*); accompaniment of, **209–210**; appoggiatura in, 181; Art of Fugue, 131, (*132*); *J. S. Bach* (Spitta), *75*; on *bel canto* choir, 75; *bel canto* technique. 53; Brandenburg Concerto, Fourth, 98; Brandenburg Concerto, Sixth, 95; broken chord accompaniments, 223; choruses, size of, 76; Chromatic Fantasy and Fugue, 108; *Clavier-Buchlein* . . ., (*204*); 'Coffee Cantata', (*120*); use of cornetto, 100; Couperin, admiration for, 108; electronic interpretation of, **48**, 297; figuration, 29; 'Forty-Eight', 223, 279; French Overture style, (*281–2*); gamba music, 95; harpsichord music, 107; use of horn, 100; manuscripts, 24; markings, 26–7; Mass in B minor, 76; modernizations of, 297; *Musical Offering*, (*121*), 245; Partita, (*131–2*), (*270*), 278; Prelude in G minor, 78, 87; rhythm in, (*269*), (*270*); his sarabande tempo, *247*; use of slide, (*194*); style in performance, 30; his tempo, 253; time-signatures in, 245; 'Trauer-Ode I', (*194*), (*269*); trio sonata in C major, 26; on turn, (*204*); unaccompanied music, 78, 84, 92–3
'Bach' bow, 81
Bacilly, Bénigne de: *L'art de bien chanter*, *170*; on ornamentation, *170*, *201*; *Remarques curieuses* . . ., *256*, 302; on rhythm, *256*; on trill, *201*
Bacon, Richard M.: *Elements of Vocal Science*, 302
Baltzar, Thomas (*violinist*), 83
Banner, Giannantonio, on rhythm, *276*
Barbiere di Siviglia (Rossini), 60 (*bis*)
Barchetta, La (Nardini), 61
Baroni, Adriana B. (*prima donna*), 55, 64
Bass, figured, *see* Figured bass
Bassoon, 37, 41–2, 227–8, 230
Batement (vibrato), 86
Bathe, William, on accidentals, *114*
Battistini, Mattia (*baritone*), 60, 64
Bayreuth opera house, 62
Beat, Janet, 194
Bédos de Celles, François, on rhythm, *259*
Beethoven, Ludwig van, 15, 30; Lener Quartet style, 87; Piano Sonata in C major, 197; his quartets, 79, 194; use of slide, 194; trill in, 197
Bel canto technique, (*see also* Voice production *and* Underlay), 14; accuracy of, 67; Ademollo on, *55*; age, effect of old, 58; Agricola on, *56*; articulation, 67; Bottrigari on, *55*; breath control in, 67–68; Burney on, *57*; cantilena, (*q.v.*); Castiglione on, *54*; Cavalieri on, *69*; choral training in, **74–6**; conductor's role, 70–1; decline of, **61–4**, 65; descriptions of, **53–8**; Donati on, *55–6*; Doni on, *69*; enunciation in, 68–9, 75; Eritreo on, *54*; Fontanelli on, *54*; forcing in, 67; Garcia M., influence on, 60–1; Giustiniani on, *55*; glissando, 60; Historical Sound Recordings Collection, 61; language effect, 75; Maffei on, *54*; main features of, **65–9**; Mancini on, *57–8*; Marpurg on, *56*; Monteverdi on, *55*; necessity for, **69–71**; Newcomb on, *54–5*; parlando, 60; phrasing, 67; placing of the voice, 66; *portamento*, 63, 67; Praetorius on, *68*; Puccini's influence, **61–2**, 64; Quantz on, *56*; Rameau on, *56–7*; similarity of all, **64–5**; Solerti on, *55*; Tosi on, *56*; vibrato, 59, 68, 75; *voce bianca* and, 70; Wagner's influence, **62–4**
Bell' Adriana . . ., La (Ademollo), 55
Bellini, Vincenzo: *Norma*, 59
Belshazzar (Handel), *239*
Bemetzrieder, Anton: *Leçons de clavecin*, 243
Berardi, Angelo: *Ragionamenti*, on recitative, *251*
Bernacchi, Antonio (*male soprano*), 56
Béthizy, Jean-Laurant de: *Exposition*, 99
Bianciardi, Francesco, on accidentals, *157*
Blow, John: accidentals in, 132, 140, (*141*); his operas, 279; *Venus and Adonis*, 132
Bohème, La (Puccini), 62
Boindin, Nicolas: *Lettres historiques*, 42
Bologna, Teatro Comunale, 42
Bottrigari, Ercole: *Il Desidero*, 43, *55*
Bourgeois, Loys, on rhythm, (*255*)
Bow (*see also* Bow technique), 44, **79–83**
Bow technique, **87–93**; articulation, 81, 83, 284, 286; for authenticity, 52; Babitz on, 88, 92; Boyden on, 88, 91; of cello, 38; chords, **92–3**; crescendo-diminuendo stroke, 88; *détaché*, 90; dynamics, 290, 294–5; *enflé*, 290; Farina on, 92; fingerboard, 91; of gamba, 38; Ganassi on, 92; Geminiani on, *89*; markings for, 34; *martelé* stroke, 91; Monteverdi on, *92*; Mozart, L., on, *88–9*, 90; pizzicato, 92; *poussé*, 290; Rameau on, *93*; 'Ricochets', 90; Rousseau on, 90, *93*; spiccato, 90; *sprung détaché*, 90; Tartini on, *88*, 91; *tiré*, 290
Boyden, David: *History of Violin Playing* . . ., 302; on bow technique, 80, 88, 91
Brandenburg Concertos (J. S. Bach), 95, 98
Brass (*see also under names of instruments*), 51, **100–2**
Breath control, 67–8, 98, 284
Breefe Introduction to . . . Musick (Playford), *see* Playford, J.
Breslau, Bishop's Chapel choir at, 76
Breve regola per imparar' . . . (Bianciardi), *157*
Briefe Introduction to . . . Song (Bathe), *114*
British Institute of Recorded Sound, 65
Broschi, Carlo, *see* Farinelli

309

INDEX

Brossard, Sébastien de: *Dictionaire de musique*: on recitative, *228*, *231*; on rhythm, *257*; on tempo, 243, 248 (*bis*)
Brown, Alan (ed.): *Tisdale's Virginal Book*, (154)
Buelow, George J.: *Thorough-Bass . . .*, 192, 302
Buff (*harpsichord lute stop*), 105
Burney, Charles: on accompaniment, *228*, *229*; on bel canto, *57*; *A General History of Music*, 141, *164*, *228*; on John Blow, *141*; on ornamentation, *164*, *170*; *Present State of Music in Germany*, *57*, *229*; in Rees' *Cyclopedia*, *170*
Butler, Charles, *19*, (148), *287*
Byrt, John, on rhythm, 257

Caccini, Giulio: *Le Nuove Musiche*, 163; 'Ardi, con mio', 161, (162); on dynamics, *292*; ornamentation in, *161*, (162); on rhythm, (263); on slide, 193
Cadences, 23, 49; delayed, 196, 237; double, (206); feminine, 187–90; masculine, 187–90; rallentandos and, 253; trill in, 195–6, (196), (206); turn and trill, (206)
Cadenzas, 23, 166, 167, 168–9
Cadmus et Hermione (Lully), (211)
Caffarelli (Gaetano Majorano), castrato singer, 69
Cantata (*see also* Bel canto, Choral singers *and* Voice production), 45
Cantates françoises (Morin), *228*
Cantilena, 59–60, 61, 63, 67–8
Caper Quartet, 87
Cappella Sistina (Vatican), 74
Capriccio basque (Sarasate), 87
Carelli, Emma (*soprano*), 62
Carestini, Giovanni (*male soprano*), 56
Carissimi, Giacomo (*see also* Carissimi, G., accidentals in): 'Amor mio', (153), (296); 'Apritevi, inferni', (129), (137); bel canto technique, 53, 69; 'Bel tempo per me se n'andò', 148, (149); 'Deh, memoria', (122), (144), 158, (159); hemiola in, (296); 'In un mar di pensieri', (119), 134, (135), (156); 'Nella più verde . . .', (144), (269); rhythm in, (269); underlay in, 287
Carissimi, G., accidentals in: in figured bass, 134, (135); flattening at peak of phrase, (153); harmonic indications, (144); new phrase influence, (122); Picardy Third, 158, (159); prospective influence, (119); retrospective influence, (129); sharpening leading note, 148, (149); tritones, (156)
Carleton, Nicholas: 'Gloria Tibi Trinitas', accidentals in, 142, (143)
Cartier, Jean-Baptiste, on tempo, 243
Caruso, Enrico (*tenor*), 62
Castanets, 103
Castiglione, Baldasar: *Il libro del Cortegiano*: on bel canto, *54*; on feeling, *19*
Castor et Pollux (Rameau), (152) (*bis*)
Castrato voice, 53, 56–7, **71–4**
Caswell, A. B.: *Commentary upon . . . Singing*, 302
Cavalieri, Emilio de: *Rappresentatione . . .*, on bel canto, 69

Cavalli, Pietro F., 69, 279
Cello (*see also* Bow, Bow technique, *and* String instruments): accompaniment, 228, 229, 230; continuo, 43; end-pin, 79; and gamba compared, 45, 94–5; orchestral use of, 38, 41; stringing, 78; technique, 38–9; virtuoso music, 50
Cenerentola, La (Rossini), 59
Cento concerti ecclesistici (Viadana), (126)
Cesti, Antonio: *Il Pomo d'Oro*: tremolo in, 194–5; underlay in, (288–9)
Chaconne, 250–1
Chambonnières, Jacques C. de: *Pièces de clavecin*, on slide, (193), 194
Chapman, R. E. (trs.): *Harmonie Universelle*, on vibrato, 85
Chest register (*petto*), 57, 58, 65–6, 71
Chitarrone (arch-lute), 227, 234
Choir, *see* Choral singers
Choral singers (*see also* Opera *and* Voice production), 37, 40–1; Bach, J. S., on, 75; bel canto technique, **74–6**; Boindin on, 42; chorus, size of, 75–6; conducting, 43–4; Marpurg on, 42, 75–6
Church music, *21–2*, 41, 230, 235–6
Cimento dell' Armonia . . . (Vivaldi), (140)
Clappers, 103
Clarinets, 41, 99–100, 230
Clavichord, **108**
Clavier-Buchlein . . . (J. S. Bach), (204)
Close shake (*vibrato*), 86
Code de Musique Pratique (Rameau), *56–7*
'Coffee Cantata' (J. S. Bach), (120)
Collectanea historiae musicae, 235–6
Collected Correspondence . . . of Joseph Haydn (Landon), *239*
Collins, Michael, 278, 280, 281, 302
Columbia (*recordings*), 61
Combattimento (Monteverdi), *92*
Comédie Française, 252
Comparison between . . . French and Italian Musick (Raguenet), *21, 99*
Compendio musico (Banner), 276
Compendium (Simpson), *115*
Componimenti musicali (Muffat), 194, 196
Concert Spirituels (Paris), 76
Concerto Grossi (Handel), 230
Conducting, **43–4**, 70–1, 231
Continuo instruments, *42–3*; accompaniment, 44, 210–11, 218–19, 228; bassoon, 99; cello, 43; double-bass, 43; guitar, 96; harpsichord, 42–3, 44, 91, 106, 210–211; in opera, 43; piano, 45
Coperario, Giovanni, accidentals in, (142)
Coranto, 248
Corelli, Arcangelo, 48; rhythm of, (277); his Rome orchestra, 84; Sonata, Op. 5, *258*; Trio Sonata, Op. 11, (212); Violin Sonatas, (167–8)
Cornetto (*little horn*), 100
Corrette, Michel: *Methode pour . . . la flute traversiere*, *258*; *Methode . . . pour . . . le violoncelle*, *258*; on rhythm, 257, *258*
Couler (slur), 262
Countertenor (*male alto*), **71**, 72
Coup de glotte, 59, 62, 63 (*bis*), 67
Couperin, François, 15; on accompaniment, *228*, 236; *L'Apothéose de Corelli*, (275); on appoggiatura, *181–2*, (183); *L'Art de toucher le Clavecin*, (q.v.); on

310

INDEX

311

INDEX

INDEX

314

INDEX

rhythm, *271*; *Volkommene Capellmeister*, *188*, *253*

Maugars, André, on conducting, *43*

Mazzocchi, Domenico: *Partitura de' madrigali* . . .: on accidentals, *117–18*, (118); on dynamics, *290*

Melba, Nellie (*soprano*), 63

Melchior, Lauritz (*Heldentenor*), 64

Melothesia (Locke), *148*

Mendel, Arthur: on pitch, 44; on recitative, 236

Mental conception in performance, **50–1**

Mercure galant, on baroque orchestra, *42*

Merope (Giacomelli), 164, (165)

Mersenne, Marin: *Harmonie universelle*: use of drums, 103; on feeling, *20*; on vibrato, 85

Messiah, The (Handel), 24

Methode . . . pour . . . le violoncelle (Corrette), *258*

Methode pour . . . la flute traversiere (Corrette), *258*

Metronome markings, 244

Meyerbeer, Giacomo: *Les Huguenots*, 63

Minuet, 248

Mischiati, Oscar, on accompaniment, 235–236

'Miss Mary Burwell's . . . Book for the Lute' (anon.), *256*, (*264*)

Mizler, Lorenz, on accompaniment, *227*

Modern Musick-Master (Prelleur), *236*

Mondonville, Jean-J., accidentals in, (120)

Montéclair, Michel de, on rhythm, *257*

Monteverdi, Claudio, 15, 53, 66, 69; accidentals in, (130), 141, 156; on *bel canto*, 55; castrato roles in, 72; *Combattimento*, 92; use of cornetto, 100; *Madrigali a cinque voci*, (130); *Orfeo*, (*q.v.*); on ornamentation, *161*; on pizzicato, 92; *Poppea*, 72; *Scherzi Musicali*, *161*

Moore, Jerrold (Yale University), 61, 301

Mordents, 181, **203–4**

Moreschi, Alessandro (*castrato singer*), 73–74, 74–5

Morin, Jean-B., on accompaniment, *228*

Morley, Thomas: *Plaine and Easie Introduction* . . .: on accidentals, *114*, *147–8*; on *bel canto*, 74; on tempo, 244, *246*; on underlay, *287*

Morte d'Orfeo, La (Landi), (128)

Mozart, Leopold: . . . *Violinschule*, 304; on appoggiatura, *186*; on bow technique, *88–9*, *90*; on dynamics, *295*; on rhythm, *272*; on string fingering, *84*, *85*; on string vibrato, *86*; on tempo, 243, *249*; on trill, 196

Mozart, Wolfgang Amadeus, 17, 30; *Ave Verum*, 74–5; castrato roles, 72; *Figaro*, 60; *Magic Flute*, 72

'Mr Hardel' (*harpsichord piece*), (*264*)

Muffat, Georg: *Apparatus Musico-organisticus*, 194; on feeling, *21*, 196; *Florilegium*, *21*, *256*; on rhythm, *256*; on slide, 194; on trill, 196

Muffat, Gottlieb: *Componimenti Musicali*: on slide, 194; on trill, 196

Museo Civico (Turin), 42

Music and Letters, Collins in, *280*, 281

Music Review, 301

Musica, 69

Musica Britannica, on accidentals, 142, (143)

Musica ficta (feigned music), 113

Musica Instrumentalis Deudsch (Agricola), 85

Musica Practica (Herbst), *200*

Musical Offering (J. S. Bach), (121), 245

Musical Quarterly: Donington on inequality, 303; Galliard on feeling, *21*; Hansell on recitative, 238; Mendel on pitch, 44; Mendel on recitative, 236; Newcomb on *bel canto*, *54–5*; Raguenet on dynamics, *292*; Raguenet on oboe, 99

Musical Times: Babitz on fingering, 92; Mackerras on Mozart's operas, 304

Musicalische Bibliothek (Mizler), 227

Musicalisches Lexicon (Walther), *248*

Musiche varie a una voce (Puliaschi), *256*

Musick's Monument (Mace), *see under* Mace, Thomas

Musikalische Handleitung (Niedt), *157*

Musurgia (Kircher), *244*

Mylius, Wolfgang: *Rudimenta Musices*, on dynamics, *292*

Nardini, Pietro: *La barchetta*, 61

Natalicia Musicologica Knud Jeppesen, 238

Navarini, Francesco (*bass*), 60, 64

Neapolitan Sixth, 156

Nerone (Rubinstein), 60

Neue Bach Ausgabe, 107

Neumann, Frederick: *Baroque . . . Ornamentation*, 304; on dotted rhythm, 281, 306

New Cyclopedia (Rees), *170*

New World of Words (ed. Phillips and others), *247*

New York Public Library, 65

Newcomb, Anthony, on *bel canto*, *54–5*

Niedt, Friedrich, on accidentals, *157*

Norma (Bellini), 59

North, Roger: on accompaniment, 28–29; *Autobiography*, *292*; on conducting, *43*; on dynamics, *292*; on feeling, *22*; on ornamentation, *170*; on rhythm, *256*, (*264*); *Roger North on Music* (*q.v.*)

Nouveau traité . . . (Saint Lambert), see *Traité de l'accompagnement*

Nozze di Figaro (Mozart), 60

Nuove Musiche (Caccini), *161*, (*162*), 193, (*263*)

Nouvelle methode . . . (Montéclair), *257*

Oboe, **98–9**, 230; Béthizy on, *99*; choice and use of, 37, 41; Raguenet on, *99*; in Vivaldi, 230

Observations on the Florid Song (Galliard), *see under* Galliard, J.

Odeon (*recordings*), Lilli Lehmann, 63

Opera (see also Bel canto, Choral singers *and* Voice production): Bayreuth, 62; continuo instruments, 43, 229–30; French, *see* French opera; instrumental ornamentation in, 166; orchestra, size of, 42; Paris, 42, 43; Venetian, 42; *verismo*, 61–3, 64–5, 73

Opinioni de' cantori . . . (Tosi), *see under* Tosi, P.

Orchestra (*see also* Instruments): Boindin on, 42; conducting, 43–4; continuo

INDEX